Beyond the Mother Tongue

Beyond the Mother Tongue

THE POSTMONOLINGUAL CONDITION

Yasemin Yildiz

FORDHAM UNIVERSITY PRESS *New York* 2012

THIS BOOK IS MADE POSSIBLE BY A COLLABORATIVE GRANT
FROM THE ANDREW W. MELLON FOUNDATION.

Fordham University Press has no responsibility for the
persistence or accuracy of URLs for external or third-
party Internet websites referred to in this publication
and does not guarantee that any content on such
websites is, or will remain, accurate or appropriate.

Fordham University Press also publishes its books
in a variety of electronic formats. Some content that
appears in print may not be available in electronic
books.

Library of Congress Cataloging-in-Publication Data

Yildiz, Yasemin.
  Beyond the mother tongue : the postmonolingual
condition / Yasemin Yildiz. — 1st ed.
    p. cm.
  Includes bibliographical references and index.
  ISBN 978-0-8232-4130-9 (cloth : alk. paper)
    1. German literature—20th century—History
and criticism—Theory, etc. 2. Multilingualism and
literature—Germany. I. Title.
PT405.Y55 2012
830.9'34—dc23

                                        2011028583

Printed in the United States of America

14 13 12   5 4 3 2 1

First edition

For Michael

CONTENTS

Acknowledgments ix

Introduction: Beyond the Mother Tongue?
Multilingual Practices and the Monolingual Paradigm 1

1. The Uncanny Mother Tongue: Monolingualism
   and Jewishness in Franz Kafka 30

2. The Foreign in the Mother Tongue: Words of Foreign
   Derivation and Utopia in Theodor W. Adorno 67

3. Detaching from the Mother Tongue: Bilingualism
   and Liberation in Yoko Tawada 109

4. Surviving the Mother Tongue: Literal Translation
   and Trauma in Emine Sevgi Özdamar 143

5. Inventing a Motherless Tongue: Mixed Language
   and Masculinity in Feridun Zaimoğlu 169

Conclusion: Toward a Multilingual Paradigm?
The Disaggregated Mother Tongue 203

Notes 213
Works Cited 259
Index 285

ACKNOWLEDGMENTS

I am delighted to acknowledge the many people who have supported this project in different ways over the years. I have been extremely lucky to have Leslie A. Adelson as a mentor. Thoughtful and generous, she is a scholar of the highest standards and has been an ideal interlocutor in the evolution of this project. I am grateful to her for challenging me to become a better scholar in so many ways. Both Peter Uwe Hohendahl and Biddy Martin enriched this project with their expertise and their clear-sighted questions. Nancy K. Miller's continued interest in my projects has meant a lot to me over the years.

At Illinois, a wonderful group of friends and colleagues made the work on this book deeply enjoyable. Lilya Kaganovsky and Rob Rushing, in particular, provided support and nourishment of many kinds and have made Urbana truly a home, while being equally excellent travel companions. They and the incomparable Dara Goldman were insightful readers of earlier versions of this argument and willing sounding boards for new ideas. With their detailed and encouraging feedback, as well as their own inspiring work, the members of my writing group—Ericka Beckman, Ellen Moodie, and Anna Stenport—have been an indispensable part of the process. I treasure especially the additional, invaluable meetings with Ericka. For excellent questions, conversations, and leads, I am grateful to Matti Bunzl, Jon and Meredith Ebel, Jed Esty, Jim Hansen, Matt Hart, Brett Kaplan, Harriet Murav, Bruce Rosenstock, Manuel Rota, Nora Stoppino, and Renée Trilling.

My colleagues in the Department of Germanic Languages and Literatures at the University of Illinois warmly welcomed me. As department heads, Mara Wade and Harriet Murav freed me from commitments that allowed me to complete this book under ideal circumstances. I thank especially Laurie Johnson, Carl Niekerk, and Anke Pinkert for stimulating conversations and responses to my work. For research assistance, I thank Renata Fuchs, Regine Kroh, Molly Markin, and Dustin Smith. Their assistance and a much-needed research leave in the form of Humanities Released Time were made possible by the Campus Research Board of the University of Illinois.

Earlier versions of three of the chapters in this book appeared in the journal *Gegenwartsliteratur* and in the collections *Globalization and the Future of German* and *Yoko Tawada: Voices from Everywhere*. I thank the editors of these publications for their support and feedback: Paul Michael Lützeler, Bernd Hüppauf and Andreas Gardt, and Doug Slaymaker.

At Fordham University Press, Helen Tartar and Thomas Lay have been fantastic to work with. I want to especially acknowledge Helen's role in establishing the Modern Language Initiative, which supports first-time book authors in non-Anglophone literatures with generous support by the Mellon Foundation. This book appears under the auspices of the initiative. Tom's combination of enthusiasm and practical skills has made the entire process a great experience. I was especially gratified by the positive responses of Amir Eshel and B. Venkat Mani as well as by their insightful suggestions, which helped shape the final draft of the manuscript.

Elsewhere, Beth Drenning and Neil Levi contributed much to this project as friends and keen intellectual thinkers. Beth brought *Wordsearch* to my attention and shared her copy of the catalogue with me. Neil provided helpful feedback on the Adorno chapter. Ute Bitzer, Jörg Bitzer, Bettina Brandt, Russ Castronovo, Rita Chin, Carola Hähnel-Mesnard, Dirk Moses, Anna Parkinson, Brad Prager, Kader Konuk, Matthew Lore, Barbara Mennel, Grit Schorch, Jennifer Uleman, and Karen Winkler supported this process with much-appreciated practical advice and their open ears at important moments. Yoko Tawada has been an inspiration; I have benefited from both her works and her conversation.

The quatrolingualism of Andrés Nader, Agnès Benoît, Naima Nader, and Elias Nader have inspired this work immensely and filled it with multilingual pleasures. Esra Özyürek has been a much-valued interlocutor on things Turkish and German. I am glad that the dialogue with Necla Açık-Toprak and Umut Erel continues in our double migrations and triple languages, even if only intermittently.

Und dann sind da die Cadıs, allen voran Şahinaz Akalın, Filiz Topal, Perihan Göktan, und Hamide Scheer. Ihr kritischer Blick, ihre Intelligenz, ihre Schlagfertigkeit und ihr unwiderstehlicher Stil werden für mich immer ein Maßstab bleiben. Lange Gespräche bei ausgiebigen Gelagen, in Cafés in der Schanze oder bei Wein an der Elbe (ja, Filiz!), am Frühstückstisch oder bei Baklava und Tee in Altona regen mich seit Jahren—mehrsprachig—an. Hem güzel, hem akıllı . . . Ihr wisst, was Ihr mir bedeutet.

Annem Zeynep ve babam Mehmet Fuat Yıldız çocukluğumdan beri eğitimimi ellerinden geldikce desteklediler. Başarılı olabileceğimden hiç bir zaman kuşkulu olmadıkları ve benim yeteneklerime her zaman inandıkları için onlara minetarım. Özellikle kendilerine haksızca verilmeyen imkanları çocuklarına verdikleri, ve bunu fedakârlıklar yaparak gerçekleştirdikleri için onları takdir etmek isterim. Teşekkür ederim, anneciğim, sıpas dıkım, babacığım.

Kardeşim Murat, eşi Berrin ve yeğenlerim Melissa-Şevin ve Cem-Devran ile dillerimizi mischen yaparak paylaştığımız için mutluyum. As my other niece, Shuli Jones, who takes after my wonderful mother-in-law, Sandy, might say, "That's awesome sauce."

I do not have enough words in any language to thank Michael Rothberg for his support through many, many years. His enthusiasm, intellectual curiosity, patience, and kindness are unmatched. I look forward to many more years together in the multiple languages we share. Aujourd'hui et demain, indeed.

Beyond the Mother Tongue?

Multilingual Practices and the
Monolingual Paradigm

RETHINKING MONOLINGUALISM

On September 29, 2002, the Sunday issue of the *New York Times* included a sixty-eight-page paid insert previewing a conceptual artwork called *Wordsearch: A Translinguistic Sculpture* conceived by German artist Karin Sander and sponsored by the Deutsche Bank, the world's biggest corporate art collector.[1] In response to the sponsor's request to offer a global perspective in a metropolitan location, Sander's project set out to document as many of the languages spoken in New York City as possible. It did so by finding one native speaker for each of 250 languages and asking each speaker to contribute one personally meaningful word in his or her "mother tongue" to a list. This list of unduplicated words was then translated into all the other languages. The resulting 62,500 words were arranged into columns resembling stock market tables and published as the actual "translinguistic sculpture" in another paid, eight-page insert in the business section of the *New York Times* on October 4, 2002. This commissioned artwork, *Wordsearch*, thus sought to render the novelty of globalized life at the turn of the millennium through attention to the proximate coexistence of many languages in the same space.

To *Wordsearch* and many other cultural texts, the phenomenon of multilingualism appears as a remarkable new development of the globalized age.[2] Yet as linguists have come to agree, and as scholars in other fields increasingly document, multilingualism is and has been far more common worldwide than had been previously acknowledged.[3] Indeed, it is monolingualism, not multilingualism, that is the result of a relatively recent, albeit highly successful, development.[4] But a monolingual paradigm, which first emerged in late-eighteenth century Europe, has functioned to obscure from view the widespread nature of multilingualism, both in the present and in the past. While scholars across different fields have noted the "monolingual bias" or the "monolingual habitus" in particular areas, no study to date has spelled out the far-reaching implications of this insight.[5] Recognizing the workings of the monolingual paradigm, I suggest, requires a fundamental reconceptualization of European and European-inflected thinking about language, identity, and modernity. For monolingualism is much more than a simple quantitative term designating the presence of just one language. Instead, it constitutes a key structuring principle that organizes the entire range of modern social life, from the construction of individuals and their proper subjectivities to the formation of disciplines and institutions, as well as of imagined collectives such as cultures and nations. According to this paradigm, individuals and social formations are imagined to possess one "true" language only, their "mother tongue," and through this possession to be organically linked to an exclusive, clearly demarcated ethnicity, culture, and nation. Indeed, as we will see, even an apparently multilingual artwork such as *Wordsearch* still functions according to the central precepts of the monolingual paradigm.

The pressures of this monolingual paradigm have not just obscured multilingual practices across history; they have also led to active processes of monolingualization, which have produced more monolingual subjects, more monolingual communities, and more monolingual institutions, without, however, fully eliminating multilingualism. Schooling has been one of the primary means of such a social engineering of monolingual populations.[6] The diverse linguistic landscape of eighteenth-century France, where large parts of the population did not speak French, for instance, was reengineered over time to produce a more monolingual population of French speakers.[7] This last point also underscores the significance of the modern nation-state for the monolingual paradigm, or rather, of the monolingual paradigm for the modern nation-state, with which it emerged at the same time.[8]

There are signs, however, that the tide is turning against such strict monolingualization. For a supranational entity such as the European Union, for instance, the challenge has become to manage multilingualism, not to discard it.[9] Increased migration and mobility, the advance of communication technologies, and the spread of media have also contributed to the sense that multiple languages coexist and interact in new constellations, a sense that an artwork such as *Wordsearch* reflects and contributes to. Even English-dominated domains such as the global entertainment industry see new linguistic diversity. Hollywood movies such as *Babel* and *Inglorious Basterds* or globally consumed American TV shows such as *Lost* and *Heroes* have begun to feature more languages accompanied by subtitles, while popular musical forms mixing languages have tempted audiences with "livin' la vida loca."[10] An increasing number of language memoirs thematize life in multiple languages as a significant experience.[11] Literary and cultural studies scholars, meanwhile, have begun to make both older and newer forms of multilingualism visible.[12] Yet this new *visibility* of multilingualism is not simply due to its more frequent practice, since forms of multilingualism have existed all along. Rather, globalization and the ensuing renegotiation of the place of the nation-state have begun to loosen the monolingualizing pressure and have thereby enabled the contestatory visibility of these practices in the first place, albeit still in circumscribed fashion.[13] Multilingualism, then, has not been absent in the last couple of centuries, but it has been and continues to be refracted through the monolingual paradigm. This persistence of a monolingual framework, I argue, is the backdrop against which we need to see today's seeming increase in multilingualism.

To capture this ongoing dominance of the monolingual as well as the incipient moves to overcome it, I introduce the term "postmonolingual." This "post" has, in the first place, a temporal dimension: it signifies the period *since* the emergence of monolingualism as dominant paradigm, which first occurred in late eighteenth-century Europe. Such a historicized understanding underscores the radical difference between multilingualism before and after the monolingual paradigm, a difference that previous studies have neglected.[14] This historicization is necessary, I argue, because the appearance of the monolingual paradigm substantially changes the meaning and resonance of multilingual practices.[15] But since the monolingual paradigm has spread only gradually and unevenly across different contexts and not at all to others, "postmonolingual" constitutes by necessity a situated and flexible periodization, inflected by contextual differences.[16] This flexibility of the term also means that it is not limited to one geographic area—in this case, Europe—but may extend to other contexts as well, whenever monolingualism becomes a dominant form.[17] It is in this sense that the present book should be understood as a study of the workings of the monolingual paradigm and multilingual attempts to overcome it, rather than as a study of multilingualism per se. Viewed through this—flexible—temporal lens, "postmonolingual" refers to the unfolding of the effects of the monolingual and not to its successful overcoming or transcendence. But besides the temporal dimension, the prefix "post" also has a critical function, where it refers to the opposition to the term that it qualifies and to a potential break with it, as in some notions of postmodernism. In this second sense, "postmonolingual" highlights the struggle *against* the monolingual paradigm. As Marianne Hirsch notes with regard to the "post" in her own term "postmemory," the prefix "reflects an uneasy oscillation between continuity and rupture" ("The Generation of Postmemory" 106).

Taking these dimensions together, "postmonolingual" in this study refers to a field of tension in which the monolingual paradigm continues to assert itself and multilingual practices persist or reemerge. This term therefore can bring into sharper focus the back-and-forth movement between these two tendencies that characterizes contemporary linguistic constellations. Focusing on the tension rather than on one or the other pole helps to account for many phenomena that initially appear to be contradictory. Early twentieth-century Prague, where Kafka lived, for instance, becomes graspable as both a multilingual space in which multiple languages coexisted and as a place rapidly transitioning to a monolingual structure with individuals increasingly embracing only one, ethnically predetermined language. As Emily Apter demonstrates in her book *The Translation Zone,* the complex entanglements of language(s) with culture and politics demand such a focus on tensions, struggles, and "language wars." This definition of the postmonolingual condition indicates also that in the primarily European context on which this study focuses, the opposite of the monolingual paradigm—that is, a multilingual paradigm that would restructure perceptions and social formations along new lines *after* monolingualism—does not yet truly exist. Yet imaginative works in literature and other fields suggest the possible contours of such a multilingual paradigm and contribute variously to just such a restructuring, as I demonstrate throughout this book.

Because the German tradition has played an important role in establishing the monolingual paradigm, *Beyond the Mother Tongue* focuses on German-language writers who are uncomfortably positioned within the paradigm and have thus had to grapple with it to a significant degree. This group includes pre- and post-Holocaust German-Jewish figures, such as Franz Kafka and Theodor W. Adorno, and contemporary writers from new immigrant communities, such as Turkish-Germans Emine Sevgi Özdamar and Feridun Zaimoğlu, as well as the unique case of bilingual Japanese-German author Yoko Tawada.[18] Using a range of multilingual forms to bring German into contact with a series of other languages, from Yiddish, French, Latin, and English, to Japanese, Afrikaans, Arabic, and Turkish, these authors provide a privileged position from which to explore the strictures of the monolingual paradigm and evaluate the means of reimagining the identitarian force of language. As this list of languages begins to indicate, even though "German" is the common denominator for all the writers considered, their multilingual connections open up paths to other languages and histories across the globe and resituate German itself in the process. To recognize the possibilities and pitfalls of multilingualism, however, requires the postmonolingual mode of reading that this book offers—a mode of reading attuned both to the existence of multilingual practices and to the continued force of the monolingual paradigm.

EMERGENCE OF A PARADIGM

Emerging only in the course of the eighteenth century at the confluence of radical political, philosophical, and cultural changes in Europe, the notion of monolingualism rapidly displaced previously unquestioned practices of living and writing in multiple languages.[19] "Exclusive first language allegiance [. . .] was not the most desired of linguistic identities or imagined communities in the late medieval period," Mary Davidson notes with regard to Chaucer and his contemporaries (*Medievalism* 137). This attitude extended to the political realm where it was of little concern to premodern rulers whether and how their subjects spoke one or more languages. They themselves did not necessarily privilege the local language either. As late as the 1780s, King Friedrich II of Prussia famously preferred to speak and write in French, while harshly dismissing German. With the gendered and affectively charged kinship concept of the unique "mother tongue" at its center, however, monolingualism established the idea that having one language was the natural norm, and that multiple languages constituted a threat to the cohesion of individuals and societies. Even as they supported the study of other languages, late eighteenth-century German thinkers such as Johann Gottfried

Herder, Wilhelm von Humboldt, and Friedrich Schleiermacher spearheaded the view that one could properly think, feel, and express oneself only in one's "mother tongue." This notion of the mother tongue has been in turn a vital element in the imagination and production of the homogenous nation-state.

Philosophically, a new conception of language prepared the way for this conjunction of language and nation. As linguistic anthropologist Susan Gal argues, it was only in the Enlightenment era and the subsequent Romantic reaction to it that language came to be considered as an object with particular attributes ("Migration" 14). In this conception, which largely persists to this day, "a language" is a clearly demarcated entity that has a name, is countable, and is the property of the group that speaks it, while also revealing that group's idiosyncrasies.[20] This reified conception of language enabled the distinction between mono- and multilingualism. It also relegated linguistic practices without proper names to the status of deviation, hodgepodge, or simply invisibility, rather than recognizing them as "language."[21]

With German thinkers at the forefront, the eighteenth century also witnessed the highly consequential political linkage of language and nation. Herder was one of the key figures to pave the way for this view. He celebrated the distinctness of each language, which he saw as emanating from the genius of a particular nation (*Volk*).[22] On the one hand, this perspective led to a greater recognition and appreciation of the multiplicity of languages. On the other hand, Herder insisted on the need to maintain the distinctness of these national languages lest they lose their authenticity and rootedness in their respective nations. He thus conceived of both languages and their speakers as more separate and different from each other than had previously been the case. Herder did therefore not abandon multilingualism in so far as it meant appreciation of many languages, but rather reworked it in relation to the new vision of language, subject, and nation. The multiplication of languages is not an issue for this Herderian view as long as each language is conceived as distinct and separate and as belonging to just one equally distinct and separate people. What this position cannot abide is the notion of blurred boundaries, crossed loyalties, and unrooted languages.[23]

This changing attitude towards language(s) finds a clear articulation in the field of translation.[24] While previously a "universalist" conception of languages prevailed, now a "relativist" perspective began to take hold.[25] The universalist conception, dominant until the eighteenth century, deemed languages to be essentially equivalent and their specific forms only an irrelevant surface feature compared to the more important aspect of the content of any text. The relativist perspective, on the other hand, saw languages as radically different from each other in their specificities and their makeup. In this new vision, translation no longer merely transported content from one form into an equivalent form without damage, but rather necessarily transformed the content in the process. Wilhelm von Humboldt's suggestion that languages were not a neutral media but rather inflected the thoughts they expressed was influential in this regard.[26] With this greater attention to form came also a greater sense of the difference of languages and their distance from each other. At the extreme end of this relativist view, languages were essentially seen as untranslatable and closed off from each other.

This new perspective not only drew attention to each language's specificity, but also to the individual's relationship to his or her—presumably singular—primary language. That relationship was now seen as more internal and innate, and also more circumscribed by inheritance and nationality. In his influential 1813 lecture on translation, Schleiermacher provides the image for this new model, while contrasting it to an older one:

> For whoever acknowledges the creative power of language, as it is one with the character of the nation [*Eigenthümlichkeit des Volkes*], must also concede that [. . .] no one adheres to his language only mechanically, as if it were something externally attached to him like a strap and as if one could as easily harness another language for one's thought as one would exchange a team of horses [*Gespann*]; rather, every writer can produce original work only in his mother

tongue [*Muttersprache*], and therefore the question cannot even be raised how he would have written his works
in another language. ("Über die verschiedenen Methoden
des Übersetzens" 85; "*From* On the Different Methods of
Translating" 50, trans. modified)

Schleiermacher introduces the image of interchangeable straps
and harnessed horses to reject the view of languages as external, indiscriminate means for transporting individuals from one
place to another. In a metaphoric move that is characteristic for
the period and indicates changing philosophical paradigms, he
replaces this mechanistic image of speakers' relation to language
with an organic one.[27] The counterimage to the mechanistic view
is encapsulated in the reference to the "mother tongue." Schleiermacher does not elaborate on this image in the same manner in
which he provides an extended metaphor for the rejected view.
The "mother tongue" functions as a shorthand that barely needs
explication. In this shorthand, the weight of the argument falls
on the element of "mother" in *Muttersprache*. It stands for a
unique, irreplaceable, unchangeable biological origin that situates the individual automatically in a kinship network and by extension in the nation.[28] In contrast to the mobility implied by the
harnessed horses, the "mother"—a markedly gendered kinship
concept—stresses a static mode of belonging to the national collective. Schleiermacher does not need to elaborate that one cannot willfully change one's mother like one can a team of horses;
this point appears self-evident and underscores the effectiveness
of the chosen metaphor.

The uniqueness and organic nature of language imagined as
"mother tongue" lends its authority to an aesthetics of originality and authenticity. In this view, a writer can become the origin
of creative works only with an origin in a mother tongue, itself
imagined to originate in a mother. The result is a disavowal of
the possibility of writing in nonnative languages or in multiple
languages at the same time.[29] By the mid-nineteenth century, this
position has become a truism, as borne out by composer Richard
Wagner's assertion that "to make poetry in a foreign tongue has

hitherto been impossible, even to geniuses of highest rank" (*Das Judentum in der Musik* 150; tr. *Judaism in Music* 85).[30] Such a "retrospective monolingualization of the West European literary system, based on the Romantic stress on the mother tongue as the primary material for literary creation," as decried by translation scholar André Lefevere ("Translated Literature" 76), effects a historical amnesia about all earlier multilingual configurations while it seeks to deter future turns to any language other than the solely sanctioned "mother tongue."

THE MOTHER TONGUE: A LINGUISTIC FAMILY ROMANCE

The "mother tongue" is the affective knot at the center of the monolingual paradigm and therefore a knot worth unraveling. This knot relies heavily on the invocation of the maternal, without however necessarily referencing actual mothers.[31] As the discussion of Schleiermacher begins to illustrate, the "mother" in "mother tongue" stands in for the allegedly organic nature of this structure by supplying it with notions of maternal origin, affective and corporeal intimacy, and natural kinship. Yet the emotional and ideological connotations of "mother tongue" on which Schleiermacher draws and with which we are still familiar today are themselves historical artifacts and not transhistorical constants. Originally a Latin term, *lingua materna* was used in the Middle Ages and the Early Modern period to refer to lay people's vernaculars in contrast to learned Latin.[32] *Muttersprache* first began to be an emotionalized term in the late eighteenth century, when it was newly linked to a notion of linguistic socialization—that is, at the same time as the monolingual paradigm took shape. This change itself occurred in the context of larger social and political transformations that produced new and interrelated conceptions of family, kinship, motherhood, nation, and state. The family, for instance, only then began to be thought of as consisting solely of biological kin and excluding other members of the household such as servants. This rethinking corresponded to the reorganization of labor and the household that resulted in a stricter separation of the private and public realms. The new context defined (bourgeois) motherhood increasingly as the site of affective care rather than simply physical care.[33] It was this image of the bourgeois mother that entered into the modern "mother tongue" discourse.

That the ensuing constellation of "mother" and "language" continues to be a complicated one is demonstrated by the diverse perspectives on it among contemporary feminists. Some feminist critics celebrate the "mother tongue" as bearing residues or traces of the maternal body. Feminists who view the mother tongue in this manner valorize it as the expression of the repressed and dominated maternal and set it against male authority.[34] Yet, other feminists, working within a psychoanalytic framework, stress the divergence between the maternal and the linguistic. For instance, some readings align the maternal with the pre-Oedipal and preverbal. Developed in particular by Julia Kristeva, this vision sees the maternal as preceding language. Kristeva's proposed structure thus locates language and the law of the father as separate from the mother, who is "pure bodily closeness" (Johnson, *Mother Tongues* 66). A third strand, which guides my approach here, rejects both of these utopian figurations of the mother. As feminist philosopher Rosi Braidotti puts it, "Lacanian psychoanalysis shows us that there is no such [. . .] thing as a mother tongue, that all tongues carry the name of the father and are stamped by its register" (*Nomadic Subjects* 11). For Braidotti, "mother" does not stand for something outside the law of the father but rather resides squarely within it. Nevertheless, the mother's body and all that it suggests about affection, proximity, and presence continues to function implicitly in the still-active concept of the mother tongue.

The complex imbrication of the mother's body with language and male authority is underscored by media theorist Friedrich Kittler's historical account of the turn to phonetics in literacy education.[35] Around 1800, the bourgeois mother began to be incorporated into the role of teaching her children to read. Kit-

tler demonstrates in great detail how the mother's mouth became the central conduit in the production of proper sounds in
the mother tongue.[36] The child was supposed to see and hear the
mother's mouth produce sound at the same time that she pointed
to the corresponding written letter. Thereby, a connection would
emerge between the mother's mouth, the sound, and the letter.
The mother, however, was first instructed in textbooks by male
experts in how to produce the sounds properly. Her body was
meant to function as a medium for those male experts in their
attempt to control the proper (re)production of language. As
this scenario strikingly demonstrates, the "mother tongue" coming out of a women's mouth was not just any language that a
mother spoke, but rather the result of male ventriloquism. While
this technique supported the ongoing standardization of the language, it also relied on the child's associating the written letter
with the proximity and intimacy of the maternal body.

As this historical account illustrates, the manufactured proximity between "mother" and "language" stages the fantasy behind the modern notion of the mother tongue—namely, that
the mother tongue emanates from the mother's body. This notion indicates that, within the monolingual paradigm, "mother
tongue" is more than a metaphor. Instead, it constitutes a condensed *narrative* about origin and identity. Freud describes origin fantasies that take the shape of narratives in order to give rise
to new subjects as "family romances." In these family romances,
children reimagine parents in a grandiose manner in order to deflect their growing sense of the parents' ordinariness.[37] Using this
basic structure, I propose to read the modern notion of "mother
tongue" as a linguistic family romance. The linguistic family
romance helps to fantasize a bodily as well as familial grounding in language that does not exist, say, in Schleiermacher's image of language as changeable horses strapped to a carriage. At
the same time, this model offers a blueprint for tracing the emergence of possible alternative family romances that produce different conceptions of the relationship between languages and subjects and the origins of their affective ties. As we will see, the

key elements of this linguistic family romance—namely, affect, gender, and kinship, tied to a story of origin and identity—reappear in numerous texts, albeit in altered form. Yoko Tawada, for instance, interpellates a German typewriter as her new "Sprachmutter" (language mother), in an ironic reversal of the organicist notions of "Muttersprache" (mother language). Time and again, going beyond the mother tongue towards a potential multilingual paradigm entails rewriting this linguistic family romance.

The notion of the unique "mother" insists on one predetermined and socially sanctioned language as the single locus of affect and attachment and thus attempts to obscure the possibility that languages other than the first or even primary one can take on emotional meaning. However, despite these strictures, different languages can and do elicit heterogeneous affective investments and emotional reactions. In fact, as psychoanalyst Jacqueline Amati-Mehler and her colleagues note, new languages can open up "new intellectual and affective pathways."[38] Such a notion differs from presumptions that the mother tongue is always the language of emotion and subsequent languages are merely languages of distance and detachment.[39] In the case of Kafka, for instance, French serves to negotiate a much-needed opening between German and Yiddish, as I demonstrate in chapter 1. For Özdamar, on the other hand, German is the language in which she successfully works through trauma that took place in Turkish, her erstwhile "mother tongue" (see chapter 4).

The fact that "mother tongue" is a highly ideological, charged, and misleading term is in some ways easy to recognize. Yet simply avoiding this term and substituting it with a more neutral one, such as "first language," does not in itself resolve the issues tied up in it. The conception of language, origin, and identity that "mother tongue" marks is very much in effect today, even when the term itself is not explicitly invoked.[40] It is therefore useful to think with this term rather than to ignore it. In fact, I argue that it is the affectively charged dimension of the "mother tongue" that accounts for the persistence of the monolingual paradigm and its homologous logic. We thus need to *work through* the mother tongue and not simply sidestep its force. Viewed from this vantage point, writing "beyond the mother tongue" does not simply mean writing in a nonnative language or in multiple languages. Rather, it means writing beyond the *concept* of the mother tongue.

SITUATING *BEYOND THE MOTHER TONGUE*

The postmonolingual perspective helps to throw a new light on the simultaneous presence and absence of multilingual dimensions across many disciplines. As Doris Sommer demonstrates in her important contribution to a "bilingual aesthetics," multiple languages appear in the margins or even at the center of many twentieth-century texts from philosophy, linguistics, psychology, literary and cultural criticism, and political theory, but remain unexplored. She points, for example, to Ludwig Wittgenstein's philosophy of language, and draws attention to the fact that he seems to explore every possible language game, but does not ever consider "bilingual games," although he himself lived in multiple languages.[41] Yet, Wittgenstein's insistence on publishing the German original of his text in the English edition of his work leads to the bilingualism of his *Philosophical Investigations*, in which German and English face each other on opposite pages. Such a "language game" goes "unremarked while monolanguage games get tireless attention from Wittgenstein," Sommer comments (*Bilingual Aesthetics* 159). With the lens of the present study, Wittgenstein's practice becomes legible as caught up in the postmonolingual condition. In contrast to scholars such as Sommer, who emphasize multilingual experimentation alone, this book keeps its focus on the tension between experimental practices and the dominant paradigm in order to explore why and how the monolingual persists even in the face of multilingual forays.

This focus on the postmonolingual tension is enabled by the interdisciplinary scholarship of the last two decades that has brought out the significance of multilingualism, albeit not that of monolingualism. Since the 1990s, literary and cultural studies have begun in earnest to note multilingualism both in the present and in the past. Because of the amnesia about multilingualism, the first step has been to reestablish its existence as a widespread phenomenon. Building on the pioneering but long ignored work of Leonard Forster, contemporary literary scholars have expanded on his initial archive of multilingualism in literature.[42] This has meant collecting diverse forms of multilingualism—from authors writing in two or more languages (such as Samuel Beckett, Yoko Tawada), writing in a so-called nonnative language (such as Joseph Conrad, Edwige Danticat), to mixing different languages in one text (such as James Joyce, Gloria Anzaldúa), to simply being multilingual, while writing in one language (such as Anita Desai).[43] Considering the twentieth century alone, these archives help to reveal the significance of multilingualism for modernism on the one hand and for postcolonial and transnational writing on the other. The makeup of *Beyond the Mother Tongue* pays heed to both of these realms of multilingual writing, and combines two chapters exploring a modernist framework (Kafka, Adorno) with three chapters exploring the globalizing present (Tawada, Özdamar, Zaimoğlu).

However, as this grouping of authors reveals, my archive differs from that of most scholars working in literary multilingualism. Most significantly, much scholarship on multilingualism focuses on constellations that involve English. Evelyn Ch'ien even goes so far as to claim that "weird English constitutes the new language of literature" (*Weird English* 4). Yet "weird German"—a version of which I will discuss via Zaimoğlu's book *Kanak Sprak* (Kanak Speak) in chapter 5—and many other multilingualized languages surely are also producing new literary effects.[44] It is also important to understand that the global circulation of English may even have limiting effects for multilingual experimentation. Tawada's German and Japanese writing, for instance, frequently builds on the presumption that her audiences do not understand one of the two languages she uses and therefore listen to its sounds or consider its forms more closely, a situation that would be radically different if she wrote in English and Japanese. To be sure, English figures as an important element of multilingualism in other places in this book, such as in its role in defining the place and racialized masculinity of young male migrants in Germany (chapter 5). However, considering constellations that involve languages other than English also opens up a view of different historical legacies. While the postcolonial legacy of German continues to be investigated, German has figured more prominently as a post-Holocaust language.[45] Embracing such a "tainted" language and bringing it into contact with others thus has different connotations, both for Jewish and non-Jewish writers of German, as chapter 2 demonstrates with regard to the crucial function of the "foreign-derived word" for Adorno's attachment to the language after Auschwitz. *Beyond the Mother Tongue* thus aims to contribute to the decentering of the study of multilingualism as a phenomenon limited to English.

This book's interest in monolingualism is partially inspired by Jacques Derrida and his reflections on the topic. In his autobiographically informed book, *Monolingualism of the Other, or, the Prosthesis of Origin*, which I discuss at greater length in chapter 1, Derrida suggests the exclusionary institutional force of this concept as well as the inherent fissures that could help unravel it. In his focus on monolingualism, even if it is the "monolingualism of the Other," he tends to overlook multilingualism too completely, however.[46] His discussion of German-Jewish political theorist Hannah Arendt's famous 1964 TV interview "Was bleibt? Es bleibt die Muttersprache" (What Remains? The Mother Tongue Remains), for instance, demonstrates this tendency. In that interview with a West German TV station, Arendt insists on the singularity of the German "mother tongue" and the place it occupies for her. Just as she attempts to articulate this position, however, she is suddenly at a loss for words and briefly switches into English.[47] This momentary code-switching constitutes a multilingual practice that slips into the very assertion of the unalterable monolingual core of the subject, and yet it has until now gone uncommented upon. Derrida beautifully unravels the notion of the singularity of the mother tongue that Arendt articulates, yet he does not register the multilingual practice, and thus postmonolingual tension, that occur at the very moment of articulation.

The institutional nature of monolingualism is a significant aspect of the postmonolingual condition that other scholars are also beginning to stress. In an important contribution, Brian Lennon draws attention specifically to the role of the Anglophone trade publishing industry and the ways in which its conventions stifle the actual expression of "plurilingualism," his term for the presence of untranslated words, phrases, and passages from other languages in a text (*In Babel's Shadow*). To put it in the terms suggested in the present book, Lennon demonstrates the workings of the monolingual paradigm in the very publishing of multilingual texts and the ways that industry actively limits the types of multilingualism that circulate widely in the public sphere. While Lennon's case study of publishing is a timely intervention, his exclusive focus on plurilingualism as a multilingual form cannot account for other writing strategies and the particularity of their challenges to the monolingual paradigm. *Beyond the Mother Tongue*, in contrast, insists on the necessity of analyzing a range of forms that multilingual writing can take and of seeing these in their context.[48]

With its focus on "German" writing, this book not only contributes to the ongoing discussion of multilingualism in Anglophone literary and cultural studies, but also seeks to recast the German language both inside and outside German studies as detached from German ethnicity. Instead of viewing German either as a dominant, oppressive language that is the property of socially sanctioned, ethnically German subjects or, inversely, as a minor language threatened by global English, *Beyond the Mother Tongue* makes visible contradictory, changing, and surprising meanings that can accrue to the multilingualized language, especially when delinked from ethnicity.[49] Even post-Holocaust German can then become an antitraumatic, healing language in new ways and for different subjects, as chapter 4 shows.

Because of the long history of Jewish engagements with the German language and the rich tradition of thinking about Jewish multilingualism, (German-) Jewish studies informs the book throughout.[50] As chronicled in chapter 1, neither Jewish multilingualism nor Jewish monolingualism ever fit easily into the monolingual paradigm. Contemporary reemergent multilingualism can draw productively on the history of Jewish encounters with the monolingual paradigm, which now appears as a privileged vantage point. In this regard, "Kafka," specifically, constitutes both a particular case of the postmonolingual condition *and* a shorthand for a linguistic position outside the monolingual paradigm usefully employed in contemporary contexts. The postmonolingual lens this book offers may also productively be used to approach other German-Jewish writers than the ones discussed here. Paul Celan, for instance, famously dismissed the notion of bilingualism in no uncertain terms and insisted on the singularity of the "mother tongue" for his poetry ("Antwort"). Yet the configuration of this mother tongue differed significantly from the monolingual ideal: although German was the language he learned from and spoke with his beloved mother, it was not sanctioned by ethnic, religious, or national categories. In the end, it was also the language of his mother's murderers. At the same time, Celan was thoroughly multilingual in many ways: from his multilingual upbringing in Czernowitz and the fact that he never wrote in a purely monolingually German environment to his specific multilingual poetic practices. Charting the tension between his monolingual assertion and his multilingual contexts and practices may illuminate his work in new ways. In his case, voicing adherence to the monolingual paradigm may even be a case of resistance precisely because he is not supposed to fit into it.

While notions of Jewish "assimilation into" and "enrichment of" German culture through the use of the German language had long prevailed in German-Jewish studies, alternative conceptualizations have been emerging more recently.[51] Stephan Braese's study of German as a Jewish language is an important step in the reimagination of German beyond its status as the allegedly exclusive property of fully sanctioned, ethnic, Christian German speakers (*Eine europäische Sprache*). Braese's account shows

Jewish speakers of German as active and important agents vis-à-vis the language rather than as passive assimilators to a ready-made product. He thus contributes to a scholarly decentering of the purely national definition of the German "mother tongue" and provides evidence for the long-standing function of German as a nonethnic lingua franca.

As the final three chapters of this book argue, this decentering of German is not limited to the German-Jewish context but extends to contemporary "migratory settings" as well (Aydemir and Rotas). Expanding Braese's use of the phrase, German may even be a "Turkish" language, or a "Kurdish" one, just as migrations may have turned Turkish into a "German" language, as I elaborate in the concluding chapter. The parallels and differences between German-Jewish experiences with the monolingual paradigm and those of young Turkish-Germans that chapter 5 in particular draws out also situate the longer Jewish history with German in greater proximity to new globalized developments in contexts that might at first appear rather distant. Like a number of scholars, I believe that these two fields are not entirely separate but that cross-connections exist. Following the lead of Leslie Adelson, this study takes up multilingualism as a site of "touching tales"—that is, as a site where "things Jewish" and "things Turkish" touch without being equated or translated into each other (*The Turkish Turn 85*).[52]

With two chapters on prominent Turkish-German writers, this book also participates in the field of Turkish-German studies. Like many other literatures born from migration, Turkish-German literature does not fit the monolingual paradigm. The majority of Turkish-German authors speak both languages, albeit with varying fluency. While most do not write in both languages, this multilingual context is ever-present in the reception of their works, if not their production.[53] Scholars have long been preoccupied with the question of how to classify this literature, using differing labels over the years.[54] If this question continues to be unresolved today, it is not due to a lack of scholarly agreement, I contend, but rather to the challenge that this literature poses to conceptions

dominated by the monolingual paradigm.[55] Existing categorizations are inadequate for literatures where the language(s) of the
author, his or her ethnicity and residence as well as the content
and the language(s) of their texts no longer fit the monolingual
equation of language, ethnicity, and culture. Because of this pronounced yet varied multilingual dimension, Turkish-German literature offers a fruitful site to investigate the tension between
monolingual paradigm and multilingual practice.

Situating Turkish-German literature in relationship to the
postmonolingual condition, in turn, adds a new analytic framework to the study of this writing, which complements and broad-
ens existing approaches.[56] By shifting the focus to the monolingual paradigm, unexpected constellations and potential literary
affiliations that had heretofore remained obscure can become visible, such as the ways in which Zaimoğlu's *Kanak Sprak* relates to
Kafka's linguistic situation, on the one hand, and to James Joyce's
literary experiments, on the other. I consider this broadening as
contributing to the project of undoing the "presumption," critically diagnosed by Adelson, "that Turks figure a cultural difference and a social reality that are a priori known and knowable
only in predetermined ways" (*The Turkish Turn* 17).

Among scholars investigating the multilingual dimension of
Turkish-German literature, Azade Seyhan has been most forceful. In *Writing outside the Nation*, she specifically focuses on
diasporic, exilic, and transnational literatures that are also multilingual in some form, adding a welcome comparative perspective through the inclusion of U.S. minority literatures alongside
Turkish-German ones. Because of the particular nature of these
texts, which frequently thematize loss and displacement, Seyhan stresses the recuperative power of literature, where cultural
memories of a lost land can be safeguarded and reconfigured.
This approach yields valuable insights into some forms of multilingualism. However, it also risks limiting the understanding
of other potential literary effects. While multilingualism can indeed be used to restore and recuperate loss and memory, it can
also function to liberate from and challenge the mother tongue,

as this study emphasizes. More importantly, while "bi- and multilingualism" are important reference points for Seyhan throughout her study, her actual analyses do not necessarily highlight multiple linguistic perspectives. In her readings of Özdamar, to which I return in chapter 4, for instance, Seyhan offers insightful readings of the Turkish linguistic dimension inherent in Özdamar's literary texts. Yet the impact of the German dimension of this writing remains absent from her discussion. This book, in contrast, proposes to think multilingualism in open-ended ways and from multiple vantage points simultaneously.

But how does a postmonolingual mode of reading—that is, a mode of reading that is attentive to both multilingual practices and the monolingual paradigm—proceed, and what does it reveal? A return to the artwork that I introduced at the outset demonstrates the productivity of this approach.

WORDSEARCH: A POSTMONOLINGUAL READING

The difficulty of moving into a new multilingual paradigm is exemplified by the artwork *Wordsearch*. A closer look at Sander's piece demonstrates that even forms that appear to be highly multilingual may ultimately follow a monolingual paradigm and thus do not automatically carry an innovative potential. Most strikingly, *Wordsearch*'s focus on the image of societal multilingualism in a global city, in fact, rests on a conception of the monolingualism of individuals. The magazine insert, which functions as the catalogue to the final art piece, features numerous full-page color photographs of individuals in the midst of their busy workdays as they take a moment to write down their particular words on pieces of paper. In these pictures, the catalogue highlights the individuals constituting the multilingual global city as speakers of distinct mother tongues who are effectively associated with that language only. Although the magazine insert mentions the multilingual competencies of the pictured individuals (Deutsche Bank Art 28; "Julia [. . .] speaks Tajiki, Russian, and English"), it identifies them solely with one language, their osten-

sible mother tongue: Julia is introduced under the heading "Tajiki" and is asked to contribute a word from this one language
only. While the artwork does render the social space as marked
by the presence of multiple disparate languages, it also continues
to cast the individual according to a monolingual model where all
languages but the singular mother tongue are treated as secondary and irrelevant.

The claim to the exclusivity of the mother tongue, however,
rests on the continued disavowal of multilingualism. Like Julia, many of the participating individuals actually speak multiple languages, as the brief notes on the speakers in the catalogue and the accompanying website reveal. Gambian immigrant
Sanna Kanuteh, who contributes a word in the West African language Soninke, for instance, also speaks "nine languages," with
Soninke just "one of his mother tongues."[57] By denying what it
also acknowledges on the margins, the artwork effects a form of
disavowal: "I know very well that these are speakers of multiple
languages but nevertheless I will present them as possessing a
single language only." This "I know very well, but nevertheless"
structure is, of course, the signature of fetishism. Fetishism, we
recall, preserves the wholeness of the mother in order to disavow
castration and lack.[58] In the case of the monolingual paradigm,
it is the mother tongue whose wholeness and exclusivity needs to
be preserved.

What is at stake in this staging of *individuals* as primarily
monolingual, as defined by their mother tongue, when at the
same time they are posited as the building blocks of a larger multilingual whole? Throughout the catalogue text, printed in both
English and German, the predominantly German commentators
equate language with culture. Sander, for instance, states about
the prospective reader of her translinguistic sculpture: "through
the use of his language [. . .] the reader finds his own culture of
origin represented" ("Wordsearch, 2002" 17).[59] The reference to
"origin" suggests that the term "culture" is in fact used in the
anthropological sense of ethnicity. The prevalence of embassies
and consulates as sources for native speakers for the project ex-

tends and further underscores the assumed homology between language, culture, ethnicity, and nationality that underwrites the project.[60] The insistence on identifying the individual with one language only—namely, the presumed mother tongue—then amounts to the insistence on the continued validity of a Herderian conception of language. The individual, in other words, becomes the site (or scale) at which the Herderian conception can be preserved even in the face of globalization.

To understand more fully the stakes behind reestablishing the distinctness of cultures and ethnicities, it is necessary to turn to another issue that *Wordsearch* raises but does not explicitly address. The project is the brainchild of a German artist who realizes it for a nominally German, but in fact transnational financial institution. To explore the coexistence of multiple languages, she turns to New York rather than considering a German site. Frankfurt am Main, the bank's headquarters, would have been a viable alternative as it is one of the country's most diverse, multiethnic, and multilingual cities.[61] Instead, it serves only as a place of reception, where the entire *New York Times* issue with the *Wordsearch* insert was printed by special arrangement and distributed to pedestrians on the same day. As so often since the nineteenth century, the United States—and New York in particular—serves as a site for German fantasies about cultural heterogeneity that are implicitly contrasted with an imagined German homogeneity.[62] *Wordsearch* displaces multilingualism outside Germany, into a space whose globalized and transnational nature is more readily recognized and acceptable than that of Germany. The displaced form of the project's multilingualism offers a safe distance for savoring difference and internal heterogeneity without having to acknowledge it at home. Ultimately, the assertion of the distinctness and separateness of cultures and ethnicities attempts to assuage the often-voiced German fears of being leveled by globalization. Rather than reconfiguring and altering languages, cultures, and ethnicities, the *Wordsearch* catalogue presents globalization as preserving and accommodating them harmoniously. The configuration of languages in this artwork thus carefully *manages* difference by producing it along preserved homogeneous, ethno-cultural lines and by situating it outside Germany. Multilingualism, in other words, does not simply constitute a straightforward expression of multiplicity, but rather a *malleable form* that can be put to different, and contradictory uses.

Wordsearch itself demonstrates this possibility in its dual form. The catalogue to *Wordsearch* is after all only one side of this artwork. The final piece itself lays out an entirely different logic. In contrast to the emphasis on particularity, cultural origin, and identity in the colorful catalogue, and to its stress on hand-written, and thus authenticated, words, the final "translinguistic sculpture" itself celebrates abstraction, universality, and equivalency. The arrangement of the words in stock market tables suggests that language is a commodity to be traded like any other, while translation becomes the means of producing equivalency and surplus value. As in a financial dream, the collected words begin to multiply; through translation, the starting capital of 250 words generates a massive 62,500.

This proliferation differs from heteroglossia by its very orderliness.[63] While multilingual environments generally lead to language contact and thus to new linguistic forms via borrowing and code-mixing, the words in these stock market columns stay separate and untouched by each other. They too, thus, reproduce globalization as a process that preserves distinctness. In this case, the unchanged nature of the words obscures the results of the global financial activity to which the arrangement of the words refers—namely, the deep-seated transformations such financial activity causes, the destabilization it brings, and the uneven distribution of wealth to which it leads.

Between the pictures of individuals in the catalogue and the endless columns of words in the verbal sculpture, *Wordsearch* performs multilingualism as a fantasy of preserved particularities and individuality, on the one hand, and as a fantasy of complete equivalency, anonymity, and unencumbered universality of the financial markets, on the other. Given this perfect self-image of neoliberal globalization, it may be symptomatic that an art critic refers to *Wordsearch* as an "artwork" and "exhibition" by Sander (Gregory Volk), while a business news report calls it a Deutsche Bank "integrated advertising campaign" (Businesswire). Through its form, *Wordsearch* enacts the tension between reemergent multilingualism and persistent monolingualism that defines the postmonolingual condition, but it does so in a way that recasts the monolingual paradigm for a new age and thus retains it.

OUTLINE OF THE BOOK

As the example of *Wordsearch* begins to indicate, the configuration of languages in aesthetic works shapes *how* social formations are imagined. That is, the particular *form* of multilingualism in a given cultural text encodes visions of social formations, individuals, and modes of belonging. As a result, the fact that an artwork—or any other cultural production—features multiple languages does not automatically mean that it stands for pluralism or multiplicity. Not the fact of multiple languages, but the form in which they are brought together and related to entities such as the social, the individual, and the affective plane matters. The work of multilingualism in the cultural sphere can thus only be understood if the particular form it takes is analyzed. Therefore, each of the subsequent chapters focuses on specific formal strategies of breaking with the premises of monolingualism and evaluates the promises and shortcomings of those strategies. While these strategies of literary multilingualism are in the forefront, my analysis also takes into account multilingualism in everyday practices. In many cases, the texts I examine take everyday practices (such as code-switching) as a starting point, yet they rework them in different ways. In other words, literary multilingualism may relate to quotidian, sociolinguistic practices but does not simply reflect them. In contrast to *Wordsearch*, the literary and essayistic texts to which I turn in the remainder of the book configure languages in ways that imagine new formations, subjects, and modes of belonging and, most crucially, offer a more critical way of dealing with the monolingual paradigm. Though the texts that I consider grapple with the ongoing force of the "mother tongue," they do so in ways that seek to disrupt the homology between language and ethno-cultural identity that the paradigm installs. In the process, they create a wide variety of multilingual aesthetics.

While monolingualism is a quintessentially modern structure, it is modernism that most clearly begins to unsettle it and that attempts to find ways out of it, even if the language crisis that animates modernism is generally articulated around "language" in the singular. The first two chapters of *Beyond the Mother Tongue* therefore consider authors working within a modernist framework. Because the book is interested in the force of the monolingual paradigm, however, it focuses on authors who seem to be indebted to it to some degree. Chapter 1 turns to Franz Kafka, who wrote in one language only, yet nevertheless did not fit easily into the monolingual paradigm because he did not have a socially sanctioned "mother tongue." As a Jewish speaker of German in the increasingly polarized multilingual environment of early twentieth-century Prague, Kafka had to contend with what Derrida calls the "monolingualism of the Other." I focus on Kafka's 1911 encounter with the Yiddish theater, which not only prepared the artistic breakthrough to his mature style, as has been well documented, but also, I argue, confronted him with a language through which Jews could potentially inhabit the monolingual paradigm. Although Kafka never considered writing in Yiddish, this chapter reveals that his writings *about* that language productively altered his relationship to the German language and allowed him to express the uncanniness of his "mother tongue."

Chapter 2 takes up a form of multilingualism frequently overlooked in contemporary scholarship in the field—namely, the presence within a given language of other languages via words of foreign derivation. Their presence constitutes a form of "internal multilingualism," as I call it, that inheres in all languages but that takes on different meanings in different contexts. Foreign-derived words have long been the objects of charged attacks by language purists, who have treated them as intruders to be repelled and excised from a "mother tongue" held to be pure. With his privileging of the German language, German-Jewish philosopher Theodor W. Adorno would not seem to be an obvious choice for thinking about multilingualism. Yet essays such as "Words from Abroad" (1959) offer important insights into *Fremdwörter* (words of foreign derivation) as indicative of the tensions of the postmonolingual condition. Adorno, who grew up at the historical height of chauvinistic anti-*Fremdwort* sentiment in the early twentieth century, explicitly comments on this category at significant moments in the development of his thought. In *Minima Moralia*, he memorably calls *Fremdwörter* "the Jews of language," thus suggestively linking linguistic conditions and historical experiences (200; tr. 110). In reading both his explicit commentary on these "words from abroad" and his own writing practice in drawing on them, this chapter shows how Adorno held on to German even after Auschwitz: he redefines the presence of the unassimilated *Fremdwort* as the core characteristic of the German language that retains the memory of enforced foreignness and fundamental alienation. As my chapter demonstrates, moreover, Adorno consistently relies on the interplay between "native" and "foreign-derived" words as part of his dialectical mode of writing, a strategy that turns his writing into a critically postmonolingual form.

The next three chapters move from the post–World War II period to the post–Cold War present and to prominent contemporary writers who embrace a much more visible multilingualism than Kafka or Adorno. Chapter 3 discusses a writer who draws on earlier avant-garde and modernist forms of writing, yet transforms these in new, globalized ways. It focuses specifically on "bilingual writing," defined here as writing and publishing in two (or more) languages.[64] Since the late 1980s, Yoko Tawada has produced two minimally overlapping oeuvres in Japanese and in German, for which she has been recognized separately in both countries. In contrast to her most famous twentieth-century predecessors in bilingual writing, Beckett and Nabokov, however, she does not go through periods of only writing in one of her languages, but rather uses the defamiliarizing effect of constantly switching between them. As this chapter demonstrates, Tawada's particular multilingual strategies serve to illuminate and alter a condition not often recognized as problematic—namely, *inclusion* into the monolingual paradigm. With Tawada we can see the cost of this inclusion, in addition to the forms of exclusion illuminated by the other writers.

While Tawada can be described as an expatriate writer in Germany, the last two chapters turn to multilingual effects coming out of different modalities of movement in the late twentieth-century: exile and mass migration. As a result of postwar labor recruitment, Germany has become home to a large resident Turkish community. The last two writers considered both hail from this group, although they belong to different generations and are differently situated in relationship to the monolingual paradigm. The striking dimension of Emine Sevgi Özdamar's texts has long been recognized as her strategy of literally translating Turkish expressions into German, thereby creating a jarring and poetic effect. This multilingual form, which I refer to as "literal translation" and which has analogues among postcolonial writers such as Gabriel Okara, has been primarily read as an expression of migration. My reading of Özdamar's key text "Mutterzunge" (Mother Tongue, 1990), however, reveals a different underlying issue that this form addresses, which is the traumatic experience of state violence prior to migration. Özdamar's literal translations both recall and forget that violence in German and in the process become a means of working through the original trauma, underscoring the affective possibilities opened up by going beyond the mother tongue.

In contrast to Özdamar and Tawada, who both arrived in Germany as adults and learned (one of) their literary language(s) belatedly, Feridun Zaimoğlu grew up with two languages from the start, so that German was never a foreign language to him. Yet it has been difficult for him, as it has for many nonethnic Germans, to be accepted as a legitimate user of the language by his ethnically German compatriots, confirming how the monolingual paradigm reproduces ethnically based exclusions. According to this logic, a "Turk" could only ever have Turkish as his mother tongue never German, and certainly not both. In his best-seller *Kanak Sprak* (1995), Zaimoğlu responds to this situation by creating a stylized language inspired by the code-switching creativity of socially marginalized young Turkish-German men. In a virtuoso performance mixing different codes drawn from such diverse sources as biblical German, hip-hop English, and Germanized Yiddish to render a provocative, dense, and highly original language, Zaimoğlu aims to unsettle the exclusionary logic of the monolingual paradigm by laying claim to a broad linguistic home. His book thus allows a consideration of the particular multilingual form of "mixed writing"—that is, of featuring multiple languages within one literary text. The surprising absence of Turkish from this mix, however—an absence motivated by fear of "feminization"—indicates that even innovative and critical projects of multilingualism remain haunted by aspects of the paradigm.

The concluding chapter reflects on the political significance of introducing a postmonolingual analysis today. It takes stock of contradictory developments in contemporary Germany and suggests a highly "selective" embrace of multilingualism at work. Asking how a critical multilingual paradigm might look based on the readings developed throughout this book, it finally offers an alternative conceptualization of the mother tongue that disaggregates linguistic origins, communal belongings, and affective investments.

Multilingual forms are most productive and promising when they help to change the conceptual frameworks through which we perceive languages and the arenas in which they circulate. A critical multilingualism can help open "new affective paths" via linguistic practices not tied to kinship and ethnic identity. As this book argues throughout, the postmonolingual condition holds this promise, but without guarantees.

CHAPTER ONE

The Uncanny Mother Tongue

Monolingualism and Jewishness
in Franz Kafka

PRODUCING MONOLINGUALISM
IN A MULTILINGUAL CONTEXT

With the current revalorization of multilingualism, the Austro-Hungarian empire has gained importance as a reference point.[1] In contrast to the German *Kaiserreich*, which was conceived as a monolingual nation-state, the Habsburg empire acknowledged its broad multilingual makeup in its political structure. Yet the multilingualism of the empire does not offer a positive model to be emulated in the present. In fact it cautions us against facile celebration of what appears to be a state of multilingualism without closer scrutiny of its configuration of—and its underlying premises regarding—language, culture, and ethnicity. For the multilingualism of the empire increasingly shifted from being constituted by subjects with diverse multilingual competences to a multilingualism constituted by the side-by-side existence of a series of monolingual communities. Through educational and cultural policies, such as the opening of separate schools, the multilingual empire increasingly produced monolingual subjects and participated in what Hanna Burger calls the "expulsion of multilingualism" ("Vertreibung der Mehrsprachigkeit"). Thus, what looks like a multilingual context can indeed be governed by a monolingual paradigm.[2]

This insight puts a prominent "multilingual" site such as early twentieth-century Prague in a new light. A city in which German and Czech were historically anchored and widely spoken, Prague became one of the frontlines in the language wars of the Austro-Hungarian empire.[3] By the turn of the twentieth century, a primarily Czech-speaking majority with national aspirations was fighting against the dominance of a small, primarily German-speaking middle and upper class whose power was gradually eroding. Because nationalist movements—be they Czech or German—treated a person's native language as a solid indicator of his or her nationality, they were invested in asserting that the people they represented had only one language. In this manner, an increasingly combative nationalism propelled the turn to monolingualism and sought to discourage existing practices and attitudes that crisscrossed between languages.[4] The city's linguistic situation was thus "multilingual" insofar as multiple languages were spoken, but increasingly "monolingual" in the manner in which individuals were forced to conceive of themselves as members of one language community only.

Early twentieth-century Prague was then not just a site of tensions between specific languages and language communities who fought for hegemony, as has been so well documented already. Rather, as my framework suggests, it was also a site of tensions between different linguistic paradigms: a multilingual paradigm, in which linguistic practices did not necessarily follow exclusive identitarian logics, and an emergent monolingual one, for which the connection between language and identity was paramount. Even as multilingual practices persisted to differing degrees, however, it was the monolingual paradigm's conception of subjects, communities, and modes of belonging that carried the day. In this conception, the "mother tongue" was the medium through which one was tied organically to one's nation as well as the only basis of access to proper subjectivity and legitimacy.

This ascendant monolingual paradigm, in which mother tongue putatively equaled nationality, persisted even in the face of its own inconsistency, as nineteenth- and early twentieth-century German-speaking Jews experienced firsthand. In Prague, as in many parts of the Austro-Hungarian empire, the Jewish minority had predominantly embraced German as their language by the nineteenth century. In fact, more than half of German-speakers in the city were Jewish (Spector 4). This attachment arose from the particular emancipatory promise of German-language culture in the late eighteenth century and was encouraged by leading Jewish thinkers such as Moses Mendelssohn. Austrian emperor Joseph II's 1782 Edict of Toleration, which allowed Central European Jews entry into the gentile world for the first time, seemed to manifest this promise in political terms, while the writings of Lessing, Schiller, and Goethe offered a cultural vision of belonging to which their Jewish readers responded strongly. Yet most Christian Germans did not accept German-speaking Jews as part of their community or view them as fellow Germans, just as most Christian Czechs did not accept Czech-speaking Jews as Czechs. As the assimilated Jewish communities experienced, the link between mother tongue and identity, solid and unbreachable according to the monolingual paradigm, was in fact highly tenuous.

How does one relate to languages and write in such a context? This complex political and cultural conjunction proved fertile ground for literature.[5] Prague was home to a large number of significant German-language writers, many of them Jewish.[6] Yet while writers such as Franz Werfel, Max Brod, Egon Erwin Kisch, and Hugo Bergmann shared a linguistic predicament, their aesthetic production sharply differed from each other and from that of their most famous peer, Franz Kafka, whose writing constitutes the focus of this chapter.[7] More so than his fellow writers, Kafka explored from within the impossibility of the linguistic situation in which he found himself, a situation brought about by the monolingual paradigm.

The combination of Kafka's distinct writing style and his complex linguistic situation has given rise to numerous claims about

the status of his language. To this day, Kafka's language continues to be a controversial site at which competing models of linguistic affiliation are formulated. Already in the 1960s, critics de-
bated whether the peculiarity of Kafka's literary language could
be related to a linguistic entity other than standard High German—namely, the distinct Prague dialect.[8] This debate occurred
at a time when Prague German was almost extinct as a spoken
community language due to the Holocaust and large-scale population movements after the war. When scholars considered Kafka's language as Prague German at that point, it appeared as a
dead language belonging to a specific time and place. Given that
many German speakers in Prague were Jewish, this reference also
gestured to what some critics implicitly presumed to be a specifically Jewish form of local German.

More recently, scholars have attempted to relate Kafka's writing explicitly to languages considered Jewish. On the one hand,
David Suchoff, citing Yoram Ben-David, speaks of Kafka's writings as "exercises in 'how to write Hebrew in German words'"
(255). Pascale Casanova, in a short section of her book *The World
Republic of Letters*, on the other hand, situates Kafka with other
"translated men," primarily Anglophone and Francophone postcolonial writers, and asserts that Kafka's work "can be considered as entirely translated from a language that he could not
write, Yiddish" (269). These scholarly evaluations move in different directions. Suchoff attempts to bring out a more Jewish
Kafka. In his account, the assertion of a positive Jewish identification rests on a linguistic claim of proximity to Hebrew. For Casanova, in contrast, Kafka's Jewishness is secondary to the fact
of his "translated" nature, which gives him a more recognizable,
even "contemporary" place in world literature.

Even when scholars highlight Kafka's relation to the German
language, their view of this relationship varies. As Gilles Deleuze
and Felix Guattari argue in their influential study, *Kafka: Toward a Minor Literature*, Kafka's writing amounts to an inten-
sification and subversion of the German language from within.
They do not relate Kafka's literary language back either to a di-

alect, or to other languages, but rather to an aesthetic form in which he is said to bring out the "polylingualism" of language in general. On this basis, they define "minor" literature as a form of writing in a major, well-established language, such as German, in a way that destabilizes it.[9] Against such attempts to account for Kafka's literary language through recourse to other languages, local dialects, or even anticanonical aesthetics, other critics, such as the eminent Kafka scholar Stanley Corngold, emphasize Kafka's affinity to canonical German literary traditions and his indebtedness to Goethe.

These contradictory assessments arise, I suggest, because Kafka's writing itself explores the modern problem of a putative homology between native language and ethno-cultural identity—that is, the monolingual paradigm—in a concentrated manner as part of his very aesthetics. Although raised in an environment in which multiple languages were spoken, and personally fluent in a number of languages, Kafka wrote his literary texts indeed entirely in German.[10] Neither the context, in which he confronted social challenges to his claim on his primary language, nor his own multilingual competence led him to consider writing in another language, or even to incorporate other languages in any immediately visible way into his texts.[11] He thus fashioned himself as a monolingual writer. Yet the context necessarily left a mark on his writing as it continuously forced him to reflect on his relationship to language. Ultimately, Kafka embraced a paradigm that fundamentally excluded him and from this impossible situation developed his characteristic high modernist aesthetics of negativity.

What Kafka helps to reveal, then, is the force of the monolingual paradigm even for those excluded from it. The postmonolingual condition cannot be understood without a proper grasp of this force as well as its disjunctures. This chapter illuminates the postmonolingual condition by pursuing the tensions inherent in the monolingual paradigm and the mother tongue. Because the paradigm structures much of modern life and the subject's intelligibility within it, it cannot simply be disregarded or willfully changed, but must be *worked through*. Kafka undertakes such a working-through from within the paradigm itself.

Kafka explores the tension within the monolingual paradigm and his position towards it most incisively in his writings on Yiddish. That language entered his life in a transformative manner through a Yiddish theater group in 1911, when he was 28 years old.[12] It was thus not a native or familiar language for him. Yet as a language defined as distinctly Jewish, it offered a glimpse of what it might mean to be within the homology posited by the monolingual paradigm *as a Jew*, a glimpse of an alleged sense of continuity between language and identity. While Kafka's engagement with Yiddish did not result in his using or explicitly thematizing the language in any of his fictional texts, he reflected on Yiddish extensively in other sites of his writing, particularly in his diaries, letters, and, most publicly, in a speech he delivered in February 1912. Neither the speech nor his diaries and letters can easily be separated from his more explicitly fictional writings, however. As many scholars agree, Kafka's diaries and letters are not simply sites of biographical information, but rather form an important part of his textual production.[13]

Writing *on* Yiddish but *in* German in these varied genres, Kafka addresses the problem of having a mother tongue that is socially unsanctioned within a larger structure increasingly governed by the monolingual paradigm. In the process, he rearticulates the mother tongue itself as inescapably uncanny (*unheimlich*) rather than familiar, as the paradigm would have it. At the same time, the fact that writing on another language is key to (re)articulating his relationship to this mother tongue underscores that a much more "multilingual" practice is at work than appears at first sight. Kafka's inquiry into and repositioning of the monolingual paradigm as an uncanny one takes place in relation to other languages that are decidedly not "native." As the following discussion will show, nonnative languages such as Yiddish and French play a crucial identity- and affect-producing role, even if they never enter the texts themselves. Thus, what looks like a monolingual text may, in fact, suggest the contours of a multilingual paradigm.

MONOLINGUALISM AND JEWISHNESS

In order to grasp the specificity of Kafka's relationship to the monolingual paradigm, it is necessary to understand the broader discourses on Jewishness and language that he was inevitably forced to confront, as well as to consider contemporary scholarly attempts to redescribe those discourses. The notion that Jews could not possibly be legitimate speakers of German or any other European language, even if they spoke it flawlessly, was most infamously and influentially advanced by composer Richard Wagner. In his essay "Judaism in Music" (1850, revised and expanded 1869), Wagner not only denies Jews' aesthetic sense and musical creativity, but goes further to claim that Jews are inherently unable to master any so-called non-Jewish languages:

> The Jew speaks the language of the nation in whose midst he dwells from generation to generation, but he speaks it always as an alien. [. . .] In the first place, then, the general circumstance that the Jew talks the modern European languages merely as learnt, and not as mother tongues, must necessarily debar him from all capability of therein expressing himself idiomatically, independently, and conformably to his nature. A language, with its expression and its evolution, is not the work of scattered units, but of an historical community: only he who has unconsciously grown up within the bond of this community, takes also any share in its creations. [. . .] Now, to make poetry in a foreign tongue has hitherto been impossible, even to geniuses of highest rank. Our whole European art and civilisation, however, have remained to the Jew a foreign tongue; for, just as he has taken no part in the evolution of the one, so has he taken none in that of the other; but at most the homeless wight has been a cold, nay more, a hostile looker-on. In this Speech, this Art, the Jew can only after-speak and after-patch—not truly make a poem of his words, an artwork of his doings. (149–50; trans. 84–85)[14]

While Wagner's central point is the denial of aesthetic creativity to Jews—the immediate occasion for the essay is a polemical

attack against the success of the German-Jewish composer Gia-
como Meyerbeer—he extends this denial to language.[15] He ob-
sessively repeats the assertion that Jews, or rather his figure of
"the Jew," cannot possibly be native speakers of German or other
European languages. His denial, of course, is necessitated by the
very existence of such native speakers. By the mid-nineteenth century, the vast majority of German Jews had been native speakers
of German for at least two generations, and poets such as Heinrich Heine had been leaving their mark on German literature.
Based on the notion that the mother tongue ties the individual organically to a community, Wagner would thus need to acknowledge German Jews as fellow Germans. By denying that German
could ever be a mother tongue to Jewish speakers, Wagner not
only excludes Jews but also attempts to maintain the fantasy of
the natural link between mother tongue and identity.

Wagner links aesthetics and language in his discourse because
he sees both of them as depending on authenticity and grounded-
ness. True creativity and the ability to express oneself, in his view,
are only possible with a deep, innate connection to the mother
tongue. With that, Wagner builds and expands on the Romantic notion of the link between mother tongue and creativity. As
discussed in this book's introduction, Friedrich Schleiermacher
had already stated in 1813 that "every writer can produce original work only in his mother tongue, and therefore the question
cannot even be raised how he would have written his works in
another language" ("*From* On the Different Methods of Translating" 50). The composer offers a specifically antisemitic reading of this premise by denying the possibility that Jews could be
native speakers of European languages and therefore creative and
original in them.[16]

Wagner participates in what Sander Gilman has identified as
the key element of German discourses on Jewishness and language: the trope of the "hidden language of Jews." Gilman argues
for the existence of a discourse ranging from the Middle Ages to
the twentieth century in which linguistic difference is ascribed
to Jews, though the content of that projected difference changes

over time. According to this trope, Jews are set apart from their Christian neighbors through their language, be it because they are said to speak another language (Hebrew, Yiddish) or to speak German with a "Jewish" accent. As Gilman elaborates, the (real or supposed) presence of this other language is read by majority culture as a sign of duplicity and deception. Linguistic difference is taken to attest to an essential, unalterable difference that by the late nineteenth century is couched in biological and racial terms. By then, the keyword for this linguistic difference becomes "mauscheln." This word, derived from the name "Moishe," refers to the idea of a Jewish-inflected German, marked by "altered syntax and bits of Hebrew vocabulary and a specific pattern of gestures [. . .]. What is stressed is the specifically 'Jewish' intonation, the mode of articulation, as well as the semantic context" (*Jewish Self-Hatred* 139). In the increased emphasis on intonation, gestures, and discursive practices of argumentation, the notion of linguistic difference becomes fully disconnected from criteria of grammatical correctness and moves to an even more subjective, in fact, phantasmatic level. The effects of this discourse of denying German and other languages as proper "mother tongues" to Jews reverberated strongly among German Jews of the late nineteenth and early twentieth century and posed a problem for German-Jewish writers especially. They were confronted with a theory of subjectivity, collectivity, and belonging, as well as with a theory of aesthetic creativity, that required possessing a "mother tongue," yet they were denied access to it—"debar[red]," as Wagner puts it—at the same time.

While the obvious antisemitic dimensions of this discourse are naturally repudiated today, one of its central premises still recurs in different guises, which is the notion that a language is the property of a particular social group. For instance, it is still common to define Yiddish and Hebrew as "Jewish" languages, in contrast to German and other European languages, which are viewed as "non-Jewish" languages.[17] Although this widespread perspective on language as a group's property certainly does not by itself lead to or signify the antisemitic attitude that the likes of Wagner display, the latter's reliance on it reveals the potential problems inherent in this premise. This proprietary perspective on language has long determined the approach to German-Jewish studies. Literary scholar Dieter Lamping, for instance, writes:

> A Jewish writer, [. . .] who had decided for German, generally moved away from Jewish culture. German was for Jews first of all the language of Lessing, Kant, Schiller, and Goethe that they associated with a certain rationalistic-humanistic non-Jewish tradition. [. . .] German—like English—hence was the language of assimilation. (255)

This view presumes a demarcation of Jewish culture and German culture in which individual writers may move from one distinct side to another by switching languages but in which the understanding of these sides themselves—"their" languages and "their" cultures—does not change as a result.[18]

Yet German may also be considered a site of Jewish identity. Indeed, some scholars in German and Jewish studies have begun to argue in recent years for an understanding of German as a *Jewish* language. Andreas Gotzmann, a scholar of religion, documents how nineteenth-century German Jews increasingly came to see German as the only appropriate language for Jewish religious practice, while considering Hebrew an outdated and foreign language. Rather than serving assimilation or an abandonment of Jewishness, German was adopted as a language for Jewish religious practice. Gotzmann demonstrates how the changing attitude to German and Hebrew was closely connected to a changing notion of Jewish religion in the nineteenth century in Germany. The shift away from a religious practice based on fulfilling ritual duties and towards a practice emphasizing inward feeling seemed to require the concomitant shift from a primarily ritualistic language to one comprehensible to the believer. In accordance with the dominant monolingual paradigm, only a native language, in this case, German, was seen as allowing the experience of inner feeling. In a different vein, in *Eine europäische Sprache*, literary scholar Stephan Braese argues for German as a Jewish language because German was adopted as a *Kultursprache* in Central and Eastern Europe predominantly by Jews. The spread of the language thus does not necessarily signal assimilation into German culture, but rather an appropriation of the language and its integration into a Central and Eastern European Jewish culture. In both cases, the emphasis on German as a Jewish language is an important corrective to views that situate Jewishness as external to German language and culture. Both scholars accomplish this correction by abandoning the still-dominant paradigm of uniform assimilation to describe the linguistic and cultural changes that Jewish communities and individuals underwent in the modern period.[19] Instead of assimilation, these scholars turn to a model of appropriation, a model that foregrounds the appropriation of a majority language for a minority's own purposes.

Although the model of *language appropriation* redefines which identities are produced and mediated through a given language and thereby undermines the notion of a simple homology between one language and one identity, it continues to rest on a fundamental assumption of language as property. This means that it imagines language as an object that one can acquire, possess, and lose rather than a structure of signification or a practice. The second model to question a homologous monolingualism, *language depropriation*, emerges from the scrutiny of this very assumption. While the proponents of language appropriation aim to counter a framework of linguistic exclusion—in this case, the discursive exclusion of Jewish subjects from German—a focus on language depropriation explores the very condition of possibility of this exclusion: the assumption that language is a form of property.

Jacques Derrida's short book *Monolingualism of the Other or The Prosthesis of Origin* offers one of the most productive explorations along these lines. Drawing on his own experience as a monolingual, French-speaking Algerian Jew whose claim to his only language became unsettled at an early age, Derrida reflects on what it means to "have" a language. He recounts how the withdrawal of French citizenship from Algerian Jews during the

Vichy regime did not just leave his community stateless for several years, but also shook the sense of legitimate linguistic grounding and direct, inalienable connection to its only language, French. What he describes, in other words, is the painful revelation that a subject's relationship to his or her language is institutionally mediated and can be ruptured. "Having" a language, even if it is one's only language, does not ensure the recognition of one's claims on it. This "other" monolingualism lacks the attributes ascribed to the mother tongue: the sense of an almost organic, intimate link to a language that results in socially sanctioned and reproduced identitarian claims.

Probing further, Derrida relates this form of language dispossession, which is politically engineered and historically specific, to the impossibility of language possession in general. Even those in the position of "master," as he puts it, are subject to a universal condition—namely, that language as such is not and cannot be possessed. Yet some subjects can enforce the notion that they possess *a* language and have sole mastery over it, while others do not. In fact, the master's claim seems to arise out of the felt lack of such control, in fits of "appropriative madness" (24), a formulation that brings Wagner's feverish rhetoric to mind. The master's attempts at control, meanwhile, proceed through "politico-phantasmatic constructions" (that is, through the realm of belief and ideology), facilitated by concrete institutions such as schools and armies (23). According to Derrida, only a strategy that does not reestablish language as a property through its own ideological and institutional constructions—even in the form of minoritarian appropriation—can hope to overcome the historical structures that enabled linguistic power relations in the first place. To this end, he identifies the impossibility of "assimilating" or "owning" language as the common ground that all speaking subjects share. He writes: "Anyone should be able to declare under oath: I have only one language and it is not mine; my 'own' language is, for me, a language that cannot be assimilated" (25). Whereas the language appropriation model rejects the assimilation paradigm for minoritarian subjects and cultural practices,

Derrida's call for depropriation insists that language itself is not assimilable by anyone.

While both critical models respond to monolingualism's premise that a language is the property of a particular group (with the mother tongue as the access point for the individual), they focus on different elements of this premise. The model of language appropriation takes issue with the number of groups that can be proprietors and suggests that a language can be an identitarian site for multiple communities at the same time. The model of language depropriation, in contrast, focuses on the aspect of property and offers an ethical injunction to transcend proprietary thinking vis-à-vis language(s). Both of these conceptualizations offer valuable perspectives and useful distinctions—between acts of appropriation, the experience of historically imposed dispossession, and unavoidable structural depropriation—for an analysis of the postmonolingual condition. Indeed, only when taken together do they describe the tensions inherent in the monolingual paradigm and the steps necessary towards a nonhomologous multilingual practice. A look at the early twentieth-century Prague context and Kafka's writing within it begins to indicate the overlap between these tendencies.

Although the dispossession of the mother tongue concerned all German-Jewish writers, they did not all respond to this predicament in the same way. Reactions to this lack of authorization in the mother tongue led to a range of responses and attempts to grapple with the condition.[20] Some turned to other "authorized" languages, such as Hugo Bergmann, who embraced Hebrew. Others, such as Max Brod, attempted to compensate in German by appropriating the language for an explicitly Jewish discourse. What makes Kafka stand out and what has inspired much commentary is the fact that he does not seek to claim such authorization, but writes in a manner that is cognizant of that lack of authorization. This writing style is part of his negative aesthetics of sobriety, of a hunger art, rather than an art of plenitude and multiplicity. In the following section, I demonstrate how Kafka's underlying depropriated relationship to German actually is enabled by traversing the possibility of language appropriation in the encounter with Yiddish.

KAFKA IN THE YIDDISH THEATER: FINDING A FOREIGN MOTHER

In the fall of 1911, Kafka and his friend Max Brod went to see a wandering Yiddish theater troupe in a rather run-down café on a makeshift stage and then returned with great enthusiasm to the plays and the actors for the next few months.[21] The majority of their friends and family did not share this enthusiasm and instead held a skeptical, if not hostile, attitude towards both the language and the Eastern Jewish culture that the Yiddish theater (re)presented. In the assimilatory attempts of the Prague Jewish middle-class, a clear distinction between so-called Eastern and Western Jewish life and, concomitantly, between Yiddish and German, was paramount. Many in the older generation of Western Jews thus considered the slowly growing interest of the younger generation in Yiddish and Eastern Jewish culture as a threat.[22]

For Kafka, meanwhile, this encounter proved deeply transformative. As an immediate effect, it led to a sudden and intense interest in Jewish history and Eastern European Jewish life, as his diaries demonstrate.[23] More importantly, it had a long-term effect on his literary development. Evelyn Torton Beck's detailed study documents how Kafka drew on the Yiddish plays he saw during this period in much of his subsequent writing. Beck identifies specific plot elements, scenes, and characters in the Yiddish plays that reappear throughout Kafka's literary writing, albeit in a transformed manner. Besides this manner of incorporating Yiddish literary forms in his writing, some of Kafka's texts are also read as commentaries on his experience with the Yiddish theater. The singing and dancing dogs that the narrator of "Forschungen eines Hundes" (Investigations of a Dog) encounters in his youth and that leave a life-long impression, for instance, have frequently been read as references to the Yiddish troupe.

What does not enter Kafka's writing, however, is the language itself. From the first encounter, Kafka is excited by the Yiddish language and the Eastern European Jewish culture he sees expressed in it, and he quickly begins learning the language from the lead actor Yitzhak Löwy. Yet, he does not attempt to use it as his own literary language or even to mix a few Yiddish expressions directly into his writing. Instead of appropriating Yiddish, Kafka's interest in that language leads to a depropriation of German. His diaries record this process as it unfolds.

Yiddish, as staged in the theater, provides Kafka with the first experience of what it might mean to inhabit the homologous structure of language and identity, posited by the monolingual paradigm as essential, *as a Jew.* His very first diary entry on the theater already expresses this sentiment. Written over a period of a few days, the lengthy entry provides a detailed portrayal of the actress Frau Klug, a description of some people in the audience, an account of the impression the entire performance made, and a plot summary of the play. As Kafka repeatedly acknowledges, he does not fully understand the play or the characters—that is, he neither understands the language nor the cultural context fully (48; tr. 79). After describing in detail Frau Klug, who performs both solo and with the ensemble, Kafka writes:

> Some songs, the pronunciation "jüdische Kinderloch," the sight of this woman, who, on the stage, because she is a Jewess, draws us listeners to her because we are Jews, without any longing for or curiosity about Christians, made my cheeks tremble. (*Tagebücher* 1:49, Oktober 6, 1911; *Diaries* 80–81, trans. modified)[24]

The Yiddish theater creates a space for a communal experience of Jewishness. In Kafka's depiction, this communal experience outweighs any artistic one. The identitarian aspect of this experience is articulated in the way that the actress is not directly identified as a performer but rather as "this woman" and "a Jewess." Her performance does not consist solely of her songs, but also her pronunciation, her looks, and most importantly her Jewishness.

As the title of Vivian Liska's illuminating study suggests, it is always noteworthy *When Kafka Says We*. In this case, the performance of Jewishness that the actress provides on stage prompts such a communal configuration, as it leads him to write "because *we* are Jews" (weil *wir* Juden sind; emphasis added). Part of this configuration is the concomitant marginalization of Christians, which Kafka also notes with some astonishment regarding the play's disinterest in its gentile characters. This unabashed marginalization of Christians and the unquestioned centrality of Jewish figures further add to the experience of an unfamiliar social and representational order. The notion of a language native to Jews and functioning as the basis for asserting a positive Jewish identity offers Kafka the glimpse of a Jewish existence within the structures of homology. It allows for an affective space in which a non-marginalized, explicitly Jewish, communal identity is possible.

Despite the promise of a collective identity, however, this scene is not free of an unsettling quality. The sense of community recorded in the identification as "wir Juden" quickly gives way to an individual subject's physical experience of the situation. As a first-person narrator, Kafka writes of this physical sensation, the shiver that travels across his cheeks. Through attention to this sensation, he both marks his bodily affectedness by the situation as well as his continued separate existence, even in a state of being interpellated as part of a community. This disjuncture further underscores that while Kafka glimpses the possibility of a Jewish existence within the homologous structure of language and identity asserted by the monolingual paradigm, he himself is not located within it.

This experience, both collective and set apart, is prompted by a specifically gendered performance of Jewishness in Yiddish. Kafka stresses Yiddish as produced by a Jewish woman, while the only line that he records of that performance is the actress's pronunciation of the phrase "jüdische Kinderloch" (little Jewish children). These gender and language coordinates make her into a Jewish mother, who is calling on Jewish children in her Yiddish pronunciation. The actress draws the audience into an embrace ("an sich ziehen") that is thus coded as maternal.[25] For a moment, Kafka becomes interpellated as one of those Jewish children and seems to respond to this interpellation. Briefly, the fantasy of an alternative—Yiddish-speaking—mother, affirming a positively lived Jewish origin and belonging, takes shape.

The elements of this fantasy—language, mother, affective power, and identity—help to identify it as a linguistic family romance. As detailed in the introduction to this book, a linguistic family romance is a particular fantasy encapsulated in a condensed narrative about linguistic origin giving rise to an ensuing "true" identity. Seen in this light, the notion of a "mother tongue" itself constitutes a linguistic family romance as it produces a fantasy about the natural, bodily origin of one's native language and its inalienable familiarity that is said to establish kinship and belonging. At the same time, it is this imagined familial link that seemingly justifies proprietary claims on one's "own" language.

The fantasized Yiddish "mother" does not lead Kafka to a new Yiddish "mother tongue," however, but rather to a recalibration of the link both to the "mother" and the "mother tongue" in German. "Mutter" (mother) becomes the pivot through which the experience of Yiddish leads to the questioning of German. In a famous passage in his diary, composed just over two weeks after the earlier entry about Frau Klug, Kafka writes:

> Yesterday it occurred to me that I did not always love
> mother as she deserved and as I could, only because the
> German language prevented it. The Jewish mother is no
> "mother" [*Mutter*], the designation as mother makes her a
> little comic (not itself, because we are in Germany), we give
> a Jewish woman the name of a German mother, but for-
> get the contradiction that sinks into the emotions so much
> the more heavily, "mother" is peculiarly German for the
> Jew, it unconsciously contains, together with the Christian
> splendor Christian coldness also, the Jewish woman who is
> referred to as mother therefore becomes not only comic but
> strange [*fremd*]. Mama would be a better name if only one

didn't imagine "mother" behind it. I believe that it is only the memories of the ghetto that still preserve the Jewish family, for the word father too is far from meaning the Jewish father. (*Tagebücher* 1:84, October 24, 1911; *Diaries* 111, trans. modified)

In contrast to the maternal embrace that Yiddish promises, Kafka casts the German language as profoundly alienating. From the beginning of this passage, he does not speak of *his* mother, but calls her "die Mutter" ("the mother") thereby stressing the generic and impersonal aspect of this word. After a series of reformulations (e.g., "Jewish mother," "designation as mother," "Jewish woman"), "the mother" becomes "the Jewish woman who is referred to as mother." In this gradual elaboration, "Mutter" becomes a mere signifier that is not attached to this specific signified, since the signified in question (the German-Jewish woman as mother) is always already alien to it.

In Kafka's depiction, the German language produces an alienated Jewish subject without grounding because there does not seem to be continuity between his language and his identity. This perspective owes much, of course, to the notion that a language is the property of a particular ethno-cultural group and that this property can only be shared through biological inheritance but not through appropriation. Far from challenging it, Kafka takes this central premise of the monolingual paradigm for granted and thinks his own position from within it.

Yet Kafka's depiction of German also constitutes a fantasy. Where "mother tongue" stands for an authentic, bodily origin from which language is supposed to emanate and thus guarantee a deep natural link, Kafka's fantasy is of the "mother tongue" as a barrier. However alienating, this fantasy of the German language as an insurmountable barrier between him and his mother, between German-Jewish sons and German-Jewish mothers, also has a positive effect: it is a means of liberation from guilt for the lack of emotional closeness to the mother. Both mother and son are equally guiltless in this scenario: "I did not always love mother as she deserved and as I could, *only* because the German

language prevented it." The son can assert his capability for fil-
ial love, while also allowing himself to describe the mother as
"comic" and "strange." It is thus that the passage carries a sense
of relief rather than guilt. Taken together, the ability to name the
strangeness of the mother (tongue) and the mother tongue's inability to provide grounding are unsettling and liberating at the
same time.

By unearthing the defamiliarizing potential of German, Yiddish—unfamiliar as a language and as a configuration of language and identity—helps to open up a new affective path in the
familiar tongue. This new affective path leads to the production
of *more* German, not less. Kafka cannot find another name for
"Mutter," but instead adds and supplements the term to emphasize its Jewishness—with more German descriptions. This finding, in other words, propels his writing forward rather than ar-
resting it. Kafka can now express the strangeness within the
family, within his own mother tongue *in German*, because he has
become aware of it in his encounter with Yiddish. He thus continues to be a "monolingual" writer in German, yet in contrast to
the claims of the monolingual paradigm about the exclusive link
between mother tongue and identity, mother tongue and affect,
mother tongue and creative expression, it is the detour through
another, nonnative language that is enabling and productive in
this context.

"JARGON" AND THE UNCANNINESS OF GERMAN

In February 1912, four months after first encountering the Yiddish theater group, Kafka organized an evening of Yiddish poetry and song performances in the Prague Jewish town hall. He
introduced the event with a short speech.[26] Long overlooked, this
speech has drawn a great deal of critical attention in recent years
and is now considered as a poetic text in its own right.[27] Written
after months of exposure to the Yiddish theater and its actors,
and after Kafka had immersed himself in much reading on the
language, literature, and general Jewish history, the speech con-

stitutes the culmination of Kafka's engagement with and reflections on Yiddish. At the same time, this culmination also marks the endpoint of this intensive phase, as Kafka soon loses interest in Yiddish. Although he later refers back to this intensive phase and fondly tells Felice Bauer in his letters about this encounter, he never engages with Yiddish in the same manner again. Instead, several years later, he begins to learn Hebrew and continues to do so for seven years until his death.[28]

The speech introduces an evening with recitations of poems by well-known contemporary Yiddish writers Morris Rosenfeld, Simon Samuel Frug, and David Frischmann that Kafka himself had chosen and arranged to be performed by his friend Yitzhak Löwy.[29] Kafka, in fact, single-handedly organized the entire event in order to help the struggling actor. According to scholar Giuliano Baioni, this event, and in particular his speech, was the most important cultural contribution Kafka made to the *public* life of his hometown during his lifetime (*Kafka* 50). Besides the concrete goal of raising money for the impoverished Löwy, the evening was also meant to raise interest in Yiddish performance and in Eastern European Jewish culture among the German-speaking middle-class Jewish population of Prague, to which Kafka himself belonged.

Given this ostensible objective of introducing a low-status language, along with its literature and culture, and gaining sympathy for it, the actual direction of the speech is surprising. Instead of making it more respectable and attractive, as Martin Buber attempted to do, Kafka insists on the ways in which the language is a site of disturbance and unsettles the "order of things" in Western Jewish life (149). Preoccupied on the one hand with the characteristics of the language, and on the other hand with the audience's presumed relationship to it and to itself, the speech invokes a number of key terms of Kafka's writing such as anxiety, law, punishment, and the difficulty of belonging. These terms appear as part of a public speech act that stages the uncanny nature of the mother tongue for German-speaking Jews via a confrontation with Yiddish. The speech thus seeks to reenact for the audience

Kafka's own experience of being productively unsettled by Yiddish—yet in German. In this German-language speech on Yiddish Kafka brings language anxieties to the fore that result from the pressures of the monolingual paradigm.

Kafka's first significant rhetorical move towards this end is to speak to his audience not about Yiddish, but about "Jargon."[30] Although Max Brod published Kafka's remarks for the first time in 1953 under the title "Rede über die jiddische Sprache" (Speech on the Yiddish Language), the critical edition's title, "Einleitungsvortrag über Jargon" (Introductory Lecture on Jargon), follows Kafka's own terminology more closely.[31] This difference in nomenclature has wide-ranging implications due to the history of these labels and their respective affective charges.

The word "Jargon" carries with it an entire complex social history. As the term is used today in German, *Jargon* refers to the overly specialized, inaccessible language of a social or professional group. The word entered German as a French loan word in this sense in the eighteenth century and even then had a pejorative connotation. Yet in another strand, this word is closely connected to discourses of the Jewish enlightenment (*Haskalah*) and assimilation. Language played a central role for the adherents of the *Haskalah* and their views of Jewish life in the diaspora. They viewed the colloquial language spoken by most Jews in German lands in the eighteenth century, the so-called *Judendeutsch* or *taytsch*, as a flawed, incorrect German into which other languages and especially Hebrew were mixed. Considering this idiom as indicative of a degraded and degrading status, and moreover as incapable of providing the means for articulating complex—enlightened—ideas, they rejected it and instead propagated a turn to what they considered to be pure German. Moses Mendelssohn and his fellow *Maskilim* underscored this rejection by calling the idiom a *Jargon*.[32] Mendelssohn's linguistic purism quickly took hold among Jews in German-speaking lands and led to their massive turn to High German by the early nineteenth century.[33] At the same time, the negative view of *Jargon* grew and became dominant. By the end of the nineteenth century, the influential German-Jewish historian Heinrich Graetz, for example, contemptuously called it a "lallendes Kauderwelsch" (mumbling gibberish) in his 1888–89 work, *Volkstümliche Geschichte der Juden* (cit. in Natzmer Cooper 47), a text Kafka read with great interest after discovering the Yiddish theater.[34] In such formulations, *Jargon* is constituted not as a language, but rather as a hodgepodge of incoherent sounds produced without rational control and self-discipline; *lallen* (to slur one's speech; to babble), after all, refers to the way one speaks in an intoxicated state in which one has no control over one's tongue, or as an infant before mastering language.

In contrast to the German-Jewish rejection of *Jargon*, Eastern European Jews continued to speak their "Jewish language," or *mame-loshn* (mother language), and at times even referred to it as *zhargon*, though treating the latter as a neutral term. However, the pejorative connotation of *zhargon* became an issue in the early twentieth-century debate over which language should be the national one for the Jewish people. This question became urgent with the founding of the Zionist movement and pitted advocates of Hebrew against those of Yiddish.[35] In order to give their language a more positive connotation, adherents abandoned the term *Jargon* in favor of *Jiddisch* (Yiddish).[36] In German usage, *Jargon* also was displaced around the years of World War I (Weinreich 322).[37] This shift from *Jargon* to *Jiddisch* was an important indicator of the changed prestige of the language in the German-speaking *Kulturbereich*, according to historian Israel Bartal.

Around 1912, the time of Kafka's speech, *Jargon* was thus a negatively connoted word that was being challenged by the alternative, more positively connoted term *Jiddisch*, though the former was still widely used by German-speaking Jews at that time. Through his readings, Kafka was aware of the origin and the negative connotation of *Jargon* and of the existence of the alternative word Yiddish.[38] Yet, he nevertheless uses the word in his speech. Even if we assume that he is using the term with which his audience would have been most familiar, his actual rhetoric suggests that his terminology is not accidental.

Kafka draws out precisely the dimensions of "Jargon" that seem to make it different and unsettling to a bourgeois Western Jewish audience. Rather than reducing the language's otherness, he in fact goes to the other extreme of romanticizing and exoticizing its difference. He asserts, for instance, that "Jargon" consists only of dialects and is made up of words from many languages:

> It consists only of foreign-derived words (*Fremdwörtern*). Yet these do not rest in it, but retain the hurry and liveliness with which they were taken. Great migrations move through Jargon, from one end to the other. All this German, Hebrew, French, English, Slavic, Dutch, Romanian, and even Latin is seized with curiosity and frivolity once it is within Jargon. ("Jargon" 150; tr. 264)

Instead of being a proper language with clear boundaries and its own designated vocabulary, Kafka casts "Jargon" as a realm of ceaseless activity, driven by "curiosity and frivolity," in which foreign words are appropriated without hesitation. At a time of acute antipathy against *Fremdwörter* and all signs of language mixture, this characterization amounts to a provocative assertion of all that is disdainful to the reigning norms of authenticity, purity, and respectability.[39] Kafka further plays up this difference by asserting that "Jargon" cannot be contained within a grammar: "Devotees attempt to write grammars but Jargon is ceaselessly spoken; it does not come to rest. The people (*Volk*) will not leave it to the grammarians" (149; tr. 264). This vision invokes the notion of a people so close to its language that it does not allow any mediating institutions and a language so dynamic that it cannot be reified. Ultimately, "Jargon" is different because it is both less *and* more of a "proper" language than other languages. By speaking of "Jargon" rather than *Jiddisch*, Kafka continuously reminds the audience of this difference and injects a provocative affective charge into his speech.

This charge continues in other aspects of the speech. Throughout the speech, the audience figures as an affective site, while the affect that Kafka foregrounds time and again is anxiety (*Angst*). Already at the outset he announces:

> I would like [the effect of the verses of the Eastern Jewish poets] to be released, if it deserves it. Yet this cannot occur so long as many of you are so afraid of Jargon that one can almost see it in your faces. Of those who take an arrogant attitude to Jargon I do not even speak. But fear [*Angst*] of Jargon, fear [*Angst*] with a certain aversion at bottom, is, after all, understandable, if one will. (149; tr. 263)

Since this opening is part of the text that he composed prior to the event, Kafka's reference to the faces of the audience is not based on what he sees in front of him, but what he seeks to produce rhetorically as part of his presentation.[40] This peculiar address to the audience and its figuration in the speech itself constitutes Kafka's second major rhetorical move. In what sounds like a warning rather than an invitation, Kafka promises those who allow themselves the experience of the language: "Then you will get to feel the true unity of Jargon, so strongly, that you will be frightened, but no longer of Jargon, but rather of yourself" (153; tr. 266). He closes with a statement that is more threatening than reassuring in light of what he has just said: "Enjoy yourself as best as you can! [. . .] Because we do not mean to punish you" (153; tr. 266).

Kafka seeks to bring out an anxiety that negates the safe, regulated distance between the audience and "Jargon."[41] He states that the audience's anxiety is so powerful that it "almost" manifests itself physically. In this description, he implicitly locates anxiety just beneath the surface. Although it remains in the interior, anxiety still threatens to come out and become both visible and legible. The form of anxiety at play here is the uncanny.[42] Freud defines the uncanny as a special case of anxiety—namely, one in which the familiar and unfamiliar slide disturbingly into each other and disable the comforting distinction between them. This form of disquiet emerges when something heretofore familiar becomes strange, thus revealing that that which was assumed to be familiar might have been strange all along and vice versa. It is not any object in itself, but the process of revelation that gives rise to the uncanny: "Uncanny is everything that was a secret and meant to remain hidden but has stepped forth" ("Das Unheimliche" 236; tr. "Uncanny" 375, trans. modified), writes Freud, paraphrasing a definition derived from Schelling.

The uncanny, however, has also a distinctly linguistic side, situating it between mother tongue and foreign language. Freud approaches the uncanny first and at great length through a reading of dictionary entries in numerous languages in what appears to be a multilingual move. He turns to the archives of other languages in order to consider if they add something to the understanding of the social/psychic/aesthetic phenomenon of the uncanny. This engagement with other languages leads him to conclude that as *Fremdsprachige* (nonnative speakers), we cannot discern the uncanny in other languages (232; tr. 370, trans. modified). What this means is that the *Unheimliche* is not specific to German, as it might at first appear, but rather accessible only to a speaker intimately familiar with a given language. Otherwise, the distance is too large and the effect is lost. In this manner, not a "foreign" language but a "familiar" one becomes a potential site of the uncanny. The ability to arouse a feeling of uncanniness then attests to a high degree of familiarity with that which provokes such feeling. While "Jargon" appears as the source of anxiety in Kafka's rhetoric in the speech, it is German, I contend, that becomes truly uncanny.[43]

Of all the languages "Jargon" relates to, Kafka highlights its relationship to German and through this emphasis begins a simultaneous discourse on the German language in the speech. This discourse presents German through the lens of "Jargon"—that is, from an unfamiliar, defamiliarizing angle. Kafka characterizes the linguistic relationship between "Jargon" and German as simultaneously close and separate: "Jargon stems for example in its beginnings from the time when Middle High German crossed over into New High German. At that moment, there existed formal options, Middle High German took one, Jargon the other" (150; tr. 264). He characterizes New High German and "Jargon" as equally legitimate forms coming from the same root, rather than "Jargon" being a symptom of decay, as much discourse of his own time would have it, or relating it primarily to Hebrew, as the language's characteristics could also warrant. In fact, Kafka even claims that "Jargon" developed Middle High German words "more logically than even New High German [. . .] and more naturally" (150; tr. 264). He thereby links the language on the one hand to a higher rationality ("more logically"), and on the other to a more organic development ("more naturally"), somewhat in contrast to the earlier characterization of "Jargon" as filled with "curiosity and frivolity." Significantly, the example he gives of the common root and divergent development of the languages is the phrase "we are." He proclaims: "Jargon's 'mir seien' (New High German 'wir sind') is developed from Middle High German 'sîn' more naturally than the New High German 'wir sind' [we are]" (150; tr. 264).[44] The claim that "Jargon" provides a more naturally developed form of communal being (in the form "we are") suggests a critique of modern German forms of such community.[45] In this instance, linguistic evidence is suggestively cast as corresponding to social organization.

This differential proximity affects both "Jargon" and German in Kafka's further elaboration. Because "the external comprehensibility of Jargon" is constituted by German, every speaker of that language is able to understand "Jargon," he asserts. This situation sets German apart from all other languages: "this is a privilege over all languages of the world" (152; tr. 265). Yet while German enjoys this privilege, it is also set apart from other languages through a unique lack:

> As a matter of fairness, it also has a disadvantage over all other languages. The fact is, Jargon cannot be translated into the German language. The links between Jargon and German are too delicate and significant not to be immediately torn if Jargon is led back to German, that is, it is no longer Jargon which is led back, but rather something without essence. If it is translated into French, for example, Jargon can be conveyed to the French, if it is translated into German it is annihilated. *Toit,* for instance, is simply not *tot* [dead] and *Blüt* is by no means *Blut* [blood]. (152; 266)

German is distinct because of the impossibility of translation into it from "Jargon." In an essay focusing on Kafka's speech, Bernhard Siegert argues that this untranslatability is due to the "incompatibility of two different structures of signification. [. . .] German is *a priori* not going to offer a synonymous sign. [. . .] Geography cannot be translated into history" (228). In Siegert's reading, Yiddish, equated with "Geography," is not just the Other of German but emerges as "the Other of all languages that have made history" (225–26). In the above-cited passage from the speech there is indeed incompatibility between modes of signification. However, in Kafka's construction, this incompatibility is specifically between "Jargon" and German, whose relations are both "delicate and significant." Untranslatability is not a property of "Jargon" as such, since it can be translated into French. While Kafka represents French as functioning unhampered in a system of translational exchanges, the unique relationship between German and "Jargon" identifies something unique to German.

As evidenced by the morbid vocabulary of the passage (annihilated, dead, blood), Kafka implies that there is something like a dead zone within German. To be sure, it is "Jargon" that suffers in this special relationship, since its words are in danger of being *vernichtet* (annihilated) by German. For it, translation into German is deadly. At the same time, this deadliness throws an unsettling light on German. *Tot* and *Blut* are not simply proper, flawless German words, but also the inessential remains, the lifeless corpses of the "Jargon" expressions *toit* and *Blüt*. We can no longer be sure if we are dealing with a "German" word at all or with the related remains of another language and a related structure of signification. In this uncertainty, German becomes uncanny, as its boundaries, coherence, and identity are put into question from within. This uncanniness does not rely on any change of German words, but precisely on their seeming self-sameness. Kafka's speech on "Jargon," ostensibly a rehabilitation of that much-despised idiom, is in fact a text that explores German from within. It does so not by turning to "Jargon" as an alternative language. Rather, this exploration of German, which emerges in the course of writing about another language, is a doubling from within in which German ceases to be a unified language with impermeable boundaries. The uncanny thus paradoxically creates the space within German in which to articulate a German-Jewish existence in early twentieth-century Prague. The monolingual paradigm can only be inhabited as an uncanny space.

FRENCH DETOURS, NEW AFFECTS

If Yiddish provides Kafka the sense of what it might mean to live within the homologous structure of language and identity, the further context of his engagement with the language suggests that, in actuality, it developed along an even more nonhomologous affective-linguistic path than that. While Yiddish still might be seen as part of a possible identitarian monolingual paradigm, it is French, another nonnative language, that creates a new affective path, a fact whose significance has been overlooked by scholarship until now.

Kafka's main source on the Yiddish language and literature is a French text: namely, Meyer Isser Pinès's *Histoire de la littérature judéo-allemande* (1911).[46] In fact, various parts of the speech draw closely on the arguments of this book, albeit without ever simply reproducing them.[47] In his diary, Kafka remarks on the extraordinary joy he felt while reading, if not devouring, the French book. After finishing Pinès's book in January 1912, he writes that he read "500 pages, with such thoroughness, haste, and joy as I have never yet shown in the case of similar books" (*Tagebücher* 2:22; tr. *Diaries* 223).[48] The intensity of this reading experience is also evidenced in the detailed excerpts he makes in his diary (*Tagebücher* 2:23–28; tr. *Diaries* 224–27).

Kafka's intense reaction is provoked by a text that is largely in French and not in Yiddish. Pinès's book is meant to introduce a largely unfamiliar literature to a non-Yiddish speaking audience. As part of his mission, he provides numerous long citations of poetry and prose. Yet these citations are for the most part French translations of the originals. Only intermittently are the translations accompanied by passages in Yiddish. Where Pinès quotes directly in Yiddish, he transcribes it in Latin letters rather than rendering it in its customary Hebrew script. Kafka follows a similar pattern. In his excerpts, he at times quotes Pinès in French, and at times translates the French or Yiddish text into German. The only full Yiddish passage that he cites from Pinès is a defiant declaration of Jewishness: "Wos mir seinen, seinen mir / Ober jueden seinen mir" (*Tagebücher* 2:24; tr. *Diaries* 224; Pinès 72; What we are, we are / But Jews we are). This assertion of a collective Jewish identity stands apart, untranslated, in his diary. It recalls the earlier passage on the Yiddish theater in which he recorded a temporary experience of Jewishness, following a Yiddish interpellation: "weil wir Juden sind" (because we are Jews). Now Kafka notes an expression in which a Jewish language and identity seem to correspond to each other affirmatively, yet the expression remains disconnected from and uncommented in his own writing.

This Yiddish quote is an exception. More often Kafka writes down his own German renditions of Pinès's French translations from Yiddish. Hence, when Pinès cites a popular song about the plight of Jewish conscripts in the Russian army: "On nous coupe la barbe et les pattes / Et on nous empêche d'observer les samedis et les jours de fête" (Pinès 69), Kafka notes in his diary: "Man schneidet uns Bart und Schläfenlocken / Und man verbietet uns den Samstag und die Festtage zu feiern" (*Tagebücher* 2:24; tr. *Diaries* 224; They cut off our beard and earlocks / and they forbid us to keep the Saturday and the holy days; trans. modified). In other places, Kafka summarizes in his own translation entire poems and stories.[49] As it turns out, then, Kafka's study of Yiddish literature is a translational interaction primarily between French and High German in which Yiddish appears largely absent as a language.

What language is Kafka engaging with when he reads in French about Yiddish? Is the joy he expresses about reading Pinès directed at Yiddish literature or at the French book? Kafka's reading of this book barely involves Yiddish, insofar as the words he is reading are for the most part in French. Yet the French account is *about* Yiddish and does render the literature of that language in translation. What this means is that the new affective path forged in Kafka's reading is significantly mediated through French, another entirely "nonnative" language to Kafka. Though in his speech Kafka portrays the French translations as a means of conveying the nature of "Jargon" to "the French," thus equating a language and a nationality, his own triangulated reading experience of "Jargon," which he understands on the basis of German, but reads about in French, does not obey such national and identitarian affiliations. In fact, in his own practice, language, identity and identification, affective engagement and emotional transformation, do not line up and do not reestablish proprietary claims. This multilingual configuration belies the claims of the monolingual paradigm and its structuring power.

LANGUAGE AND LEGITIMACY: ON UNGERMAN MOTHERS AND STOLEN CHILDREN

The speech on "Jargon," as I noted earlier, is the culmination of Kafka's interest in Yiddish. Following it, references to the language almost entirely disappear from his writings. What remains is Kafka's altered relationship to German. Yet the uncanny space within a self-same German that Kafka explores in early 1912 and that marks his mature style is not an easy space to inhabit. Just think of the burrow in which the animal-narrator of the story "Der Bau" (The Burrow) relentlessly moves from one spot to another in his labyrinthine home, yet can only imagine being at ease in the place where he is not. Like the animal he conjures up and whose ceaseless expression of unease at home allows the story to keep moving—and thus allows Kafka's writing to continue—Kafka has to push his depropriation further and further in order to have any space at all. Yet he is always haunted by the specter of illegitimacy and struggles to keep the purity of his monolingualism of the Other from falling into a mode of linguistic appropriation. This struggle emerges time and again in crucial passages in his letters to Max Brod in which he faces the ambivalence of German-Jewish language affiliations.

Several years after his speech on "Jargon," Kafka encounters the very problem of translation from Yiddish into German that he described in his speech. He is once again attempting to help his actor-friend Löwy, this time to publish an autobiographical sketch in Martin Buber's journal *Der Jude*. In a letter to Max Brod in September 1917, Kafka writes about the draft that he had just received from Löwy:

> I consider the piece very usable but naturally it needs to be polished up grammatically ever so slightly and this would take an impossibly delicate hand. [. . .] An example of the difficulties: [Löwy] comments on the Polish theater's audience, as opposed to the audience for the Jewish theater: tuxedoed men and ballgowned ladies. Excellently put, but the German language balks. And there is a great deal like that; his mistakes are the more striking since his language veers between Yiddish and German, inclining more toward the German. If only I had your powers of translation! (*Briefe* 173; *Letters* 148, trans. modified)

Kafka recognizes Löwy's expressions "tuxedoed men and ballgowned ladies" ("frackierte Herren und negligierte Damen" for the grammatically correct "Herren im Frack und Damen im Neglige" [men in tuxedos and ladies in ball gowns]) for their stylistic appropriateness and enjoys them, yet he believes that they do not sufficiently conform to the rules of German language. From the point of view of normative German grammar, *frackiert* (tuxedoed) is incorrect insofar as it treats a noun (*Frack* [tuxedo]) as a verb (in this case, the nonexistent *frackieren* [to tuxedo]) and then turns it into an adjective (*frackiert* [tuxedoed]) but the form itself follows the grammatically correct logic of transforming verbs into adjectives. That is, the morphology is correct, but not the word to which it is applied. From a "German" perspective, the word thus indeed mixes *Willkür und Gesetz* (whim and law), a characteristic Kafka ascribed to "Jargon" in his earlier speech. What is so "excellent" about Löwy's formulation is the way it performs the dislocation that the scene describes at the very level of language. Just as Löwy felt himself an interloper into the cultural sphere of properly dressed bourgeois theatergoers in the central site of turn-of-the-century high culture, his expressions diverge from the rules of High German. In Kafka's depiction, the German language appears as a subject able to refuse this offer of stylistic innovation ("but the German language balks"). It cannot refuse the construction of such expressions, but according to Kafka it refuses to acknowledge their legitimacy. Kafka does not see himself as the censor, but as the hapless mediator who might not have the necessary "impossibly delicate hand." The relations between German and "Jargon," we recall from the earlier speech, are highly "delicate."

Though Kafka in his comment on Löwy's writing identifies the German language as the law, he himself is the one who repeatedly guards its boundaries. Commenting on Max Brod's translation of a Czech opera libretto into German, Kafka remarks: "'You see, then one is supposed to love you?' Is that not German that we still have in our ears from our ungerman mothers?" (*Briefe* 178; "Siehst Du, dann soll man Dich lieben?" Ist das nicht Deutsch, das wir von unseren undeutschen Müttern noch im Ohre haben?). Once again, "mother" and "language" appear jointly with the problematic of German-Jewish mothers and sons, as a site of rupture rather than conjunction. The occasion for this commentary—namely, a translation from Czech—indicates the "multilingual" world of Kafka and his peers and their engagement with the majority language around them. Yet Kafka holds on to a linguistic purism and a concept of proper linguistic descent based on the monolingual paradigm. In the present case he is telling Brod that their German sounds too Jewish. He recognizes their "mother tongue," but not its legitimacy. In contrast to Pascale Casanova's assertion that Kafka has to be seen in the vicinity of translated authors, these comments indicate that Kafka aims to shed any "translated" quality whenever it threatens to become visible, betraying an anxiety similar to the one he ascribed to the "Jargon" speech audience.

A full decade after his encounter with Yiddish, in a well-known letter to Max Brod from June 1921 that deals extensively with the problematic of German-Jewish literature, Kafka echoes the sense of illegitimacy about using the German language that was propagated by Wagner and his likes in reference to Jews:

> in this German-Jewish world hardly anyone can do anything else [but *mauscheln*]. This *mauscheln*—taken in a wider sense, and that is the only way it should be taken—consists in a bumptious, tacit, or self-pitying *appropriation of some-one else's property, something not earned, but stolen by means of a relatively casual gesture. Yet it remains some-one else's property, even though there is no evidence of a single-most [einzigste] solecism.* That does not matter, for in this realm, the whispering voice of conscience confesses the whole crime in a penitent hour. (*Briefe* 336; *Letters* 288; trans. modified, emphasis added)

Here, Kafka speaks of German as a foreign property.[50] The guid-ing premise that remained implicit in his take on *Mutter* in his 1911 diary, becomes explicit and more sharply worded in the later letter. He asserts that the German language as an historical entity belongs to Germans and cannot ever be "acquired" (*erwor-ben*) by German Jews, even if they master it perfectly.[51] The only form of appropriation is theft, in contrast to a legitimate acquisi-tion or inheritance.[52]

But in contrast to Wagner's denial of creativity to Jews on this basis, Kafka describes the torn loyalties of young German-Jewish writers "who began to write German" as their main source of inspiration: "the ensuing despair became their inspiration" (337; tr. 289). Not wholeness and seamless integration into a commu-nity is the source of creativity, as a Romanticist conception would have it, but, in a characteristic modernist turn, alienation and a liminal position. Yet in another twist, Kafka does not celebrate this inspiration. In fact, he does not even consider the literature that arises out of this despair as the "German literature, though outwardly it seemed to be so" (337; tr. 289). The external appear-ance of this literature as German derives from the fact that it is written in German. But what is written in German words is not automatically German literature for Kafka, contrary to a model of appropriation. Instead, he sees German-Jewish literature as constituted by a series of impossibilities:

> The impossibility of not writing, the impossibility of writing in German, the impossibility of writing otherwise. One might also add a fourth impossibility, the impossibility of writing [. . .]. Thus what resulted was a literature impossible in all respects, a gypsy literature, which had stolen the German child out of its cradle and in great haste put it through some kind of training, for someone has to dance on the tightrope. (But it wasn't even a German child, it was nothing; people merely said that somebody was dancing) [BREAKS OFF] (*Briefe* 338; *Letters* 289; final brackets in original)

Neither writing in German nor writing "otherwise" (*anders*) is possible, Kafka asserts as he builds a series of antinomies. As he had expressed with regard to the German word "Mutter" years earlier, the German language is forbidding, yet also inescapable. These impossibilities are the very condition of possibility of German-Jewish literature. What results out of these impossibilities is an illegitimate, socially abject "gypsy literature."[53]

The image of "gypsy literature," building on the racist stereotype of gypsies stealing children—thus substituting the social abjection of mostly middle-class Jewish writers with that of the even more outcast Roma and Sinti—provides a new image of relation to the German language. Kafka figures German as an infant in a crib, thereby reversing the usual figuration of language as a "mother tongue." The "child" in Kafka's figuration is native to his or her own family, but not the source of further nativeness to those who "steal" it. The parents of this child, and therefore the rightful "owners," if we follow the logic of the passage, are gentile Germans. With this image of an infant stolen from the crib, the notion of language as someone's property slips over into a family romance. Language is both a child and a property that can be stolen. In either case, those outside the family can never gain a sanctioned and legitimate relationship to it. The child itself, like an object, remains mute: it is pure material. Even the reversal of figuration from language as "mother" to language as "infant" maintains the fantasy that this infant does have "natural" links to "Germans." Appropriation via "theft" does not fundamentally put this notion into question. Kafka's casting of German as an uncanny mother tongue or a kidnapped child still accepts the notion of the mother tongue as a natural property and source of kinship for non-Jewish Germans.

Yet before ending the letter abruptly—perhaps as a sign of having reached a point of impossibility for further writing—Kafka rewrites the scene once again. In the parenthetical remark following the image of the stolen child and the tightrope, he denies the scene itself: "(But it wasn't even a German child, it was nothing; people merely said that somebody was dancing)." In this denial, Kafka shifts from the image of a marginal art (*Zigeunerliteratur* and tightrope walking), which could be seen in a framework of appropriation that itself reestablishes the concept of language as property, to a hallucination. The materiality of the reference dissolves into a collective hallucination. It is here that Kafka abandons the fantasy of language as property or as source of kinship altogether, because "it was not even a German child." The "mother tongue" becomes a mere rumor. In this way, this letter shifts from portraying German-Jewish literature as an illegitimate appropriation of the German language to the writing of a more radical depropriation, "es war nichts" (there was nothing).

CONCLUSION

As I have suggested, early twentieth-century Prague was marked by tensions between different linguistic paradigms insofar as multilingual practices were increasingly subject to a process of monolingualization, itself driven by nationalism, that sought to remake both the communities and individuals within it in its own image. Monolingualism, in this context, did not so much mean speaking only one language, as being defined solely by one language—one's "mother tongue"—as a proper subject fully embedded in a national community. German-speaking Prague Jews were among those who most acutely experienced the effects of this monolingualizing process, because they were denied possession of a "mother tongue" that would assure their identity and even basic intelligibility as subjects. In this manner, they were barred from the central access point for partaking in the monolingual paradigm. At the same time, the paradigm influenced their conceptions of communities, subjects, and modes of belonging just as much as that of their fellow non-Jewish Germans or Czechs. Franz Kafka's reflections on Yiddish in his diaries, letters and his 1912 speech are a testament to this complex situation of being excluded by a paradigm, yet sharing many of its premises and therefore trying to operate from within it.

Even as Kafka is deeply wedded to the monolingual paradigm, however, the contours of a different configuration—if not decoupling—of language and identity, that is, of a multilingual paradigm for a postmonolingual age, emerge in his writing at various points. His 1921 letter to Max Brod seemingly accedes to the most anti-Semitic versions of mother tongue and monolingual paradigm for long stretches, then attempts a reversal of the mother tongue figuration via the image of language as a stolen child, before finally abandoning the figuration of language both in kinship and property terms altogether. Kafka goes beyond the premises of the mother tongue family romance and towards a yet-to-be-explored new realm of radical depropriation via negation and a negative aesthetics ("there was nothing"). The abrupt ending of the letter at this point underscores that this is neither an easy step to take nor a comfortable space to inhabit.

While this negative aesthetics recalls the uncanny nature of the mother tongue that Kafka brings to the fore in his speech on "Jargon," not all explorations of multilingual configurations need necessarily be connected to "negative" affects. This becomes apparent in the context of Kafka's French reading on Yiddish. The significance of French for his relationship to Yiddish, and through it to German, points to a linguistic configuration in which language, origin, identity, and affective investment do not line up. It is the "nonnative" language French that opens up a path through which *joy* runs unencumbered by identitarian or even appropriative modes imposed by the monolingual paradigm and held in place by the figure of the "mother" in its different guises. The "mother tongue" is indeed *unheimlich* (uncanny), but other languages beckon.

The word "Jargon," which helped Kafka to bring out this uncanny dimension of the mother tongue during his speech, belongs to a peculiar category of words with a long and charged history in the German tradition: it is a *Fremdwort*, a word derived from another language, whose foreign (*fremd*) provenance is said to be still perceptible to a German speaker. The next chapter turns to the functioning of this ambivalent category, which establishes the presence of other languages within a national language and thus makes visible how any language is always already internally multilingual. In other words, it puts into question the alleged "purity" and "nativeness" of the mother tongue for all its speakers, and not just those excluded from it. In the postmonolingual condition, the mobilization of this internal difference can be an illuminating path on the way to recoding the mother tongue, as Kafka's example begins to indicate and as Theodor W. Adorno's writings on *Fremdwörter*, to be considered next, will help elaborate.

CHAPTER TWO

The Foreign in the Mother Tongue

Words of Foreign Derivation and Utopia in Theodor W. Adorno

p 7. "For the monolingual paradigm, the mother tongue is the site of nativity and pure origin." (...)

— "all languages are sites of constant traffic, of constant transformative give-and-take within and between them"

— "associated categories such as nations and cultures"

INTERNAL MULTILINGUALISM

For the monolingual paradigm, the mother tongue is the site of nativity and pure origin. But what if this mother tongue itself is not really monolingual, homogenous, and fully familiar? After all, all languages are sites of constant traffic, of a constant transformative give-and-take between and within them. Yet when the strict separation of languages is central for maintaining the distinctness of other associated categories such as nations and cultures, this view of the mother tongue as internally multilingual can appear threatening.[1] Words of foreign derivation put this separateness into question more pointedly than any other linguistic phenomenon. They open up the possibility that the foreign is lodged right in the mother tongue. For this reason, words of foreign derivation have long been the objects of highly charged linguistic, political, and aesthetic discourses in Europe. Employing such words deliberately in a context that seeks to monolingualize a language thus amounts to a provocative assertion of multilingualism and constitutes one facet of the postmonolingual condition in the twentieth century.

In the German context, internal multilingualism has primarily come into view through the strictly delimited category of the *Fremdwort*. A *Fremdwort*, literally "foreign word," is a German word of non-German derivation whose foreign origin is still perceptible to most speakers. This category includes both unusual and everyday words, such as *Zäsur* (caesura), *restaurieren* (to restore, renovate), and *Handy* (cell phone). The *Fremdwort* is distinguished, on the one hand, from linguistically unintegrated foreign words and, on the other hand, from words whose foreign origin is no longer perceived. No average speaker would suspect that *Fenster* (window) and *Käse* (cheese) are Latin entries into the German language. In this distinction, the category of the *Fremdwort* is determined by the double criteria of the words' origin from another language and the visibility of this origin. Because a word is no longer considered a *Fremdwort* as soon as it is assimilated, this category, by definition, designates the segment of the lexicon that most visibly carries the trace of other languages. It is this visibility of otherness, gathered into a handy linguistic category, that has been taken as a provocation and met at times with an aggressive rejection.

Both the derivation of words from other languages and the call for language purism appear to be universal.[2] American English, for instance, also underwent such phases periodically, most recently at the beginning of the twentieth century when mass immigration brought new English speakers to the country (North, *Dialect of Modernism* 17–18). To this day, English orthography requires the italicization of many foreign words—a convention that I also follow here—thus visually setting them apart within any English-language text, and reproducing a form of linguistic distinction. What differs from language to language, instead, is the intensity, motivation, and specific form of language purism that is advocated (Thomas, *Linguistic Purism* 195). In this regard, the broad cultural saturation with a language consciousness regarding such words, as well as the well-organized attack on them that can be observed in German history, stand out in comparison to other languages.[3] The routine production and widespread use of *Fremdwörterbücher*, dictionaries that are solely dedicated to this category, support this language consciousness in institutionalized form.[4] Since the seventeenth century, foreign-derived words have repeatedly been the object of intense attacks that aimed to eradicate them from the German language. These attacks, as well as the defenses that rose up in response, took place in highly charged public discourses that were by no means limited to philologists and linguists. Because of the close ties between language and nation in Germany, where language was for a long time the only common denominator, the shape of the language and its constitution have been exceptionally critical matters. As such, they have not simply been objects of scholarly description, but rather of the way in which the language has been imagined. In this imagination, internal multilingualism, conceived of as the intrusion of elements of foreign origin that have remained unassimilated, has functioned as a site where belonging and non-belonging, Germanness and foreignness, have been negotiated. Though seemingly a linguistic category, the foreign-derived word has thus been more consequentially a site of the imagination of internal otherness in politically inflected German cultural discourses.

Considering the foreign-derived word as indicator of internal multilingualism helps to rethink writing practices that deliberately use *Fremdwörter* as critically postmonolingual projects. In this chapter, I propose that this is the case in the essays of German-Jewish philosopher Theodor W. Adorno. Writing in an elaborate style full of *Fremdwörter*, Adorno explicitly reflects on this category at crucial moments throughout his career. His best-known essay on the topic, "Wörter aus der Fremde" (Words from Abroad, 1959), is one of the most important contributions to this debate in the latter half of the twentieth century. There, as elsewhere, he defends foreign-derived words for their resistance to assimilation into the flow of the remaining language. What sets his defense apart from that of other leading intellectuals in the twentieth century, such as Karl Kraus, Leo Spitzer, and Hugo von Hofmannsthal, is this insistence on the words' foreignness. As he puts it in his earlier essay, "Über den Gebrauch von Fremdwörtern" (On the Use of Words of Foreign Derivation), his aim is "not to deny what is foreign in them but to use it" (640; tr. 286).[5] Adorno thus positions himself against a monolingual conception of a language, whether by those who would eject a part of the lexicon they deem foreign or by those who would retain that part of the lexicon by deeming it assimilated. *Fremdwörter* thus appear doubly to be sites of *nonidentity* that testify to the resistance of the particular to the universal, to use one of Adorno's central philosophical concepts (Buck-Morss, *Origin of Negative Dialectics*; Levin, "Nationalities of Language"). As I further elaborate in the following, moreover, Adorno's employment of such words is not just characteristic of his style and emblematic of his concepts but—along with his peculiar syntax—constitutes a crucial element of the dialectical form of his writing on the level of almost every sentence. In other words, a full account of Adorno's dialectical philosophy requires recognition of this postmonolingual dimension of his writing.

In the scholarship on Adorno, the philosopher's comments on foreign-derived words in his two main essays on the topic, "Über den Gebrauch von Fremdwörtern" and "Wörter aus der Fremde," as well as in an important aphorism in *Minima Moralia* centering on the linguistic category, are frequently referenced in passing, but they are rarely scrutinized in depth.[6] In the publications that focus on these essays more closely, confusion prevails at times about what a *Fremdwort* is. Some scholars, such as Thomas Levin and Sinkwan Cheng, mistake *Fremdwörter* for foreign words. This mistake is further propagated by the misleading translation of *Fremdwort* as "foreign word" in *Notes to Literature*.[7] In Levin's case, in an otherwise insightful essay, this inaccuracy leads him to interpret Adorno's comments on this category as applying to the numerous English expressions in Adorno's exile and postexile writing. He thus believes that Adorno identifies those foreign language elements as sites of nonidentity. As I demonstrate, however, Adorno makes a clear distinction between foreign words and foreign-derived words in his writerly practice and uses these categories, along with "native" Germanic words, as distinct elements in his linguistic configurations. In Cheng's less sympathetic reading, this confusion leads her to accuse Adorno of not having a concept of internal difference. Yet the foreign-derived word is nothing if not a prime example of internal difference. The discourse on *Fremdwörter* is precisely fueled by the internal presence of something deemed foreign, a presence that language purists continuously attempt to eject and keep out. Any contribution that takes part in the *Fremdwort* discourse thus inevitably also takes a stand on how to negotiate internal difference, how to define and treat foreignness within the German language and, by extension, within the German cultural sphere.

Although Adorno consistently defends and uses *Fremdwörter* in his writing, this defense takes on different connotations before and after his exile from Nazi Germany, as I show in the following detailed close reading of his writing. His first essay on the topic, "Über den Gebrauch von Fremdwörtern," written in the final years of the Weimar Republic, focuses primarily on the conception of language underlying the *Fremdwort* debate and criticizes its false organicism. "Wörter aus der Fremde" (1959), on the other hand, emerges from his interaction with a postwar German public after his return from long-term American exile and addresses more directly the German dimension of the discourse.[8] There he reads the status of foreign-derived words as conveying something about the—failed—historical development of Germany and not just about language in general. This shift, I suggest, can be read as part of Adorno's own reconceptualization of foreignness in Germany before and after the Holocaust. Ultimately, it is the *Fremdwort* that enables his continued attachment to the German language even after Auschwitz. In an unexpected way, then, this philosopher, who has been criticized for his privileging of German over other languages, reveals the different dimensions of that which is *fremd* (foreign, alien, strange) within the "mother tongue" and participates in a critically postmonolingual move beyond that linguistic family romance of maternal origin and purity. To understand both the place of the *Fremdwort* in relation to the monolingual paradigm and the innovative nature of Adorno's interventions, however, the outlines of this long-standing discourse first need to come into sharper relief.

FREMDWÖRTER AND THE MONOLINGUAL PARADIGM

Language purism predates the emergence of the monolingual paradigm, yet it provides crucial discursive resources to the latter, as a look into its history quickly demonstrates. The first significant discourse around foreign-derived words in German came with the Baroque *Sprachgesellschaften* (language societies), which aimed to establish and heighten the prestige of German vis-à-vis Latin, French, and other European languages at a time when the language was not yet standardized. These elite societies saw the elevation of German as necessitating the eradication of the traces of other languages within it and thus developed suggestions for replacing those words with Germanic ones.[9] Yet even as they pursued this agenda, many of the members of these language societies felt no compunction about using languages other than German to express themselves. Gottfried Wilhelm Leibniz, for instance, famously advocated the use of German, yet nevertheless published all of his philosophical and scientific work only in Latin and French. Philipp von Zesen, one of the most active and passionate "Germanizers," who continuously provided newly coined words for a purified German, also wrote poems in Dutch and French (Forster, *In the Poet's Tongues* 38). These cases indicate the complete absence of the mother tongue–centric monolingual paradigm in the seventeenth century when it came to writing practices, but they also suggest the beginnings of a desired monolingualization of particular languages and the erection of clear boundaries between them.

The process of monolingualization of a language took place under the guiding principle of purism. In the context of language, purity primarily has been understood to refer to the constitution of a language from elements deemed to be autochthonous. By conflating autochthony with purity and purity with clarity, and thereby rendering elements from other origins as impure, this discourse installed the opposition between "pure" and "foreign."[10] Through this conjunction, the linguistic category of the *Fremdwort* came to be situated at the intersection of aesthetic, moral, and political discourses.[11] If purity is considered a prime characteristic of the language that sets it apart from others and makes it superior, then the presence of foreign language elements is not simply a lamentable adulteration, but rather a threat to the very identity and definition of the language and its standing vis-à-vis others. The claim to greater purity also propels an intensified process of purification. Instead of "purifying" the language to a satisfying degree, this discourse reproduces itself and fosters its own dynamic, as the German case clearly demonstrates.

Although language purism did not require monolingual practices, as the beginning of the purism discourse indicates, its monolingualizing tendencies and the concomitant focus on purity and origin contributed to the shape of the emerging monolingual paradigm. The compound term *Fremdwort* itself dates to the 1810s, the period of early German nationalism following the Napoleonic period, as well as that of the rapid rise of the paradigm. This one word replaced the heretofore common range of expressions such as "fremdes/ausländisches/undeutsches Wort, Welschwort" (Polenz, *Sprachgeschichte* 3:265; foreign/alien/ungerman word, Latinate word). The earliest usage of *Fremdwort* is in fact documented in the writings of nationalist activist Friedrich Ludwig Jahn, who proclaims in 1816: "Foreign-derived words as such never go into the blood, even if they are called naturalized citizens a hundred thousand times. A foreign-derived word always remains a mere mongrel without generative power; or else it would have to change its essence and become an originary sound and an originary word. Without becoming an originary word it goes through language ostracized" (*Die Deutsche Turnkunst* LVIII). Jahn's rhetoric on *Fremdwörter* draws on biological images (blood) as well as political-legal terms (acquiring citizenship) in ways that develop into racist discourse in the latter half of the century.[12] He specifically juxtaposes biological models of belonging with civic models of membership, which he deems superficial and inconsequential. The reference to naturalization and citizenship constitutes a hinge that connects this discourse on language to politics. In the political arena, admission to civic membership at that time was an issue primarily concerning Jews, whose legal emancipation was occurring in fits and starts, accompanied by a simultaneous rapid cultural and linguistic assimilation. Jahn's description of foreign-derived words as biologically inassimilable outcasts could well be his description of the status of Jews in German lands as he saw it, a point to which I will return later.[13]

The biological and organicist imagery and the notion that only purity is generative connect this form of language purism to the rising mother tongue discourse of the time. Jahn indeed explicitly decries multilingualism in the same essay as the "cesspool of sin" (*Vielspracherei ist der Sündenpfuhl*) that leads to the tendency to accept words from other languages (*Die Deutsche Turnkunst* LVII). The multilingualism he attacks is specifically the then-common practice of the elites to raise their children in the prestige languages of the time, primarily French. German children are "cheated out of their mother tongue [*Muttersprache*] in their childhood," he complains, "as long as one robs them of the language-mother [*Sprachmutter*] and violently forces a foreign-language wetnurse [*fremde Sprachamme*] on them" (LVII). Monolingualism, here figured as the subject's exclusive nurture by the mother, thus appears as one means to facilitate language purism by avoiding alternative affiliations, sources of nourishment, and sites of intimacy.

In the later half of the nineteenth century, with monolingualism firmly established as the norm, purist attempts at monolingualizing the language become only more pronounced, rather than less. As rhetoric such as Jahn's foreshadowed, language increasingly became linked to racial purity in the new discourse of biological racism and antisemitism (Townson, *Mother-Tongue and Fatherland* 106–7). The chauvinist overtones towards other languages, whether directed against *Fremdwörter* or against other forms of multilingualism, marked purist agitation more generally after

1871, the founding of the *Deutsches Reich*. The most influential organization in the history of language purism, the *Allgemeiner Deutscher Sprachverein* (ADSV; General German Language Association), was founded in the context of this political development and participated actively in it (Thomas, *Linguistic Purism* 214). With groups such as the aggressive ADSV asserting their influence, the *Kaiserreich* saw a period of flourishing agitation against *Fremdwörter* (Polenz, "Fremdwort"). As a result, there was great vigilance regarding the appearance of foreign-derived words in all arenas of social life, whether on restaurant menus or in literary language. Theodor Fontane, for instance, was regularly attacked for his use of *Fremdwörter* and had to defend himself repeatedly (Khalil, *Das Fremdwort*). The primary agents of this repressive language policing were bourgeois men in the lower ranks of the civil service, such as teachers and bureaucrats. Yet they acted in the name of the *Muttersprache*—not coincidentally the name of the main ADSV publication—as the entity whose purity was at stake. Born in 1903, Adorno grew up in this public atmosphere and experienced the excessively charged quality of the use of foreign-derived words, a formative experience that sensitized him towards their peculiar status and to which he explicitly returns in "Wörter aus der Fremde."

It is noteworthy that during the same period, the attitude towards *Fremdwörter* was quite different in the officially multilingual Austro-Hungarian empire. Although language purists were also active in Austria, they never dominated public discourse in a way comparable to the German *Reich*. These divergent tendencies underscore the affinity of nineteenth- and early twentieth-century *Fremdwort* discourse with monolingualism and nation-state frameworks.[14] That language purism nevertheless did occur and become worrisome to some intellectuals is evident from the voices speaking out against it. Such prominent Austrian figures as Karl Kraus, Hugo von Hofmannsthal, and Leo Spitzer opposed it.[15] Hofmannsthal aimed to recode the *Fremdwort* by proposing the label "Borgwort" (borrowed word). He and Spitzer further based their arguments in favor of foreign-derived words on these words' place in a specifically *Austrian* German as a distinct German located within a multilingual network.

While national sentiment, language purism, and monolingualization appear to be closely intertwined around 1900, they develop in unexpected ways in the Third Reich. One of the most surprising aspects of National Socialist ideology at first sight is that the Nazis did not eradicate *Fremdwörter*, although there was an initial anti-*Fremdwort* rhetoric.[16] In the early years after the Nazi rise to power, language purists saw this change as an opportunity finally to realize their dream of a *Fremdwort*-free German language. In this period, some functionaries called for greater language purity by drawing on the racist ideology of the Nazis. Indeed, some foreign-derived terms were replaced by more "Germanic" ones in the official language, such as *Literatur* by *Schrifttum*, as in the name of the *Reichsschrifttumskammer*, the central institution that oversaw all writers and publications.[17] Yet, overall the Nazi leadership did not turn against foreign-derived words, as is most clearly evinced by the fact that their own designation, *Nationalsozialismus*, was coined from the Latinate *Fremdwörter* "national" and "Sozialismus." Instead, they utilized such words extensively in their policies. The language purists of the ADSV (later: *Deutscher Sprachverein* or DSV), who initially imagined that they shared the same struggle with the National Socialists, unwittingly revealed the function of the *Fremdwort* in the Nazi era. Calling for a Germanization of such words as *Konzentrationslager* (concentration camp), *Euthanasie* (euthanasia), *Sterilisation* (sterilization), or *arisieren* (aryanize, take over Jewish property), they were in effect asking for a blunt admission of what these activities and structures referred to. They were quickly rebuffed and ultimately forced to close down their organization in 1940 by a direct order from Hitler (see Polenz, "Fremdwort" 11–14). The revelation that anti-*Fremdwort* activist Eduard Engel, who was revered by the members of the *Sprachverein*, was Jewish was used as a pretext to disparage language purism. In an astonishing act of complete reversal, purism was now cast as a Jewish attack on the German language.[18] While

the radical nationalist purists drew on a language of racial purism in their attack on *Fremdwörter*, the ideology that ultimately
carried out racial purges did not pursue the linguistic angle in the
same manner.[19] This different attitude appears to derive from the
fact that the Nazis did not consider language a sufficient criterion
for racial ideology and antisemitic exclusion. Since anyone could
acquire the German language, and German Jews were of course
native speakers, language was too porous a category for their
purposes.[20] The fully racial ideology rejected the racial analogy
that was dominant in the language purist elements of even the
völkisch movement.[21] At the same time, these startling changes in
attitude towards words of foreign derivation underscore the malleable and political nature of the category most clearly.

What the seeming anomaly of the Nazi discourse about foreign-derived words indicates is this: the *Fremdwort* discourse
is closely connected to the function of language as the basis for
identity. The more important that language is for securing identity and drawing and guarding boundaries, the more charged its
form becomes. When other categories—such as race—replace it,
its significance can wane. As long as language is central, "purifying" it and removing visible traces of internal multilingualism—
that is, traces of constitutive contact with an other—appears paramount. That tradition predates the Nazis and lives on beyond
them, well into the postwar period.[22] It is that longer tradition in
which the place of foreignness vis-à-vis a language-based identity
is negotiated that Adorno engages with. Yet, he does so in a way
that ultimately also registers the impact of Nazism and the Holocaust in the German language.

FOREIGNNESS OR ALIENATION? ADORNO'S EARLY DISCOURSE ON THE *FREMDWORT*

That Adorno takes an active stance in the dominant *Fremdwort*
discourse of his time becomes apparent in almost every sentence
he has ever written. As one unsympathetic critic complains, even
beyond the general technical terminology that might be neces-

sary for articulating philosophical thought, Adorno often employs the most rarefied, uncommon foreign-derived words in his writing.[23] The appearance of these words tests the assumed familiarity of the mother tongue time and again and installs disruptive elements into the flow of language. Thus, Adorno, who insists on writing in German and privileges this language over all others, nevertheless actively resists its monolingualization. Yet while his basic attitude towards the foreign-derived word and his reliance on it in his writing practice do not change, his analyses of the stakes of *Fremdwort* discourse do. In his first essay on the topic, "Über den Gebrauch von Fremdwörtern," Adorno attacks the notion of language as an organic entity, the central premise of both *Fremdwort* discourse and monolingual paradigm, as a way of recoding the *fremd* in *Fremdwort* and thereby altering the discourse as a whole.

Despite clear indications that his essay engages with the category of the *Fremdwort* in the German language, that language remains curiously unnamed. Instead, Adorno speaks generically of "language" throughout the essay. In tone and attitude, this essay, which contains Adorno's most spirited defense of *Fremdwörter,* does convey a sense of urgency and of high stakes in the discourse on foreign-derived words. The young Adorno throws himself forcefully and sharply into the "fight against purism": "A determined defense of the use of foreign-derived words cannot have the task of summarizing familiar arguments or keeping alive the traditional debate through new evasions. It is valid only where it works towards a decision" (640; tr. 286, trans. modified). Using a remarkably military register, he locates himself on a discursive battlefield. As the unelaborated reference to "familiar arguments" and the "traditional debate" indicates, Adorno is all too aware of the long-standing history of the discourse on *Fremdwörter,* the current status of which he characterizes as a stalemate. He also gives specific German examples of foreign-derived words (*Symbol, Komplex, Initiative*) as well as of fully assimilated loan words (*Bank, Siegel, Acker*), indicating that he has the German language in mind (640; tr. 286–87). Yet he also exclaims that foreign-derived words' "stance towards language is an alien one" (644; tr. 289), as if these words were outside "language." This generic reference is not an oversight but rather the first significant move in his intervention.

Adorno explicitly identifies the issue underlying the debate on *Fremdwörter* to be the conception of language, and not the contours of a given language or a national discourse that avails itself of language in particular ways. The conception against which he argues is that of language as an organism, the "conception of a language closed and purposeful within itself, a language developing immanently, for which the metaphor would remain growth" (642; tr. 288). Such a view of language is shared by both linguistic purists and the defenders of foreign-derived words, he contends. Adorno attacks the latter for their argument that *Fremdwörter* should be tolerated because they will ultimately become unobtrusive loan words and cease to stand out in the language. The denial of the foreignness of the foreign-derived word and the unquestioned demand for assimilation into a homogenous mass of language is unacceptable to Adorno. If *Fremdwörter* have an alien stance to "language," then it is to language conceived as a coherent, self-contained organism.

From our contemporary perspective, one might expect that Adorno's rejection of language as an organism aligns him with linguistic conceptions of language as a signification system based on the arbitrary relationship between signifier and signified. Yet, as Peter Uwe Hohendahl demonstrates, Adorno does not accept such a Saussurean sign theory (*Prismatic Thought* 225).[24] That means that for Adorno, contra Saussure and modern linguistics, the semantic and semiotic aspects of language are not separate and arbitrary, but related. That view in turn seems to locate him closer to ontological conceptions of language as enabling direct access to existential questions through a contemplation of language. In this perspective, chiefly associated with Martin Heidegger, language is seen as directly grounded in meaning. However, as Hohendahl further argues, Adorno also rejects the ontological conception of language as a futile attempt to return to premodern linguistic conditions that are historically not available anymore, because "modern societies are characterized by a reified model that splits signs and referents" (*Prismatic Thought* 224). As Adorno puts it in his essay: "While their transpersonal life, as the law in accordance with which words come together to form truth, cannot be disputed, this life is not organic in the strict sense" ("Über den Gebrauch von Fremdwörtern" 642; tr. 288). He thus insists simultaneously that words partake of truth and therefore are not arbitrary signs, but also that they are nevertheless not organic. The concept that allows him to make such a claim is that of language as naming: "This is why the life of language is not lived with the teleological rhythm of creaturely life with birth, growth, and death, but rather with naming as the enigmatic ur-phenomenon in between grasping thought and manifested truth, with crystallization and disintegration" ("Über den Gebrauch von Fremdwörtern" 643; tr. 288). Through the focus on naming, Adorno conceptualizes language as both produced, rather than naturally unfolding, and meaningful, rather than arbitrary. For him, language is not organically born, but set in an instantaneous act that involves the interplay of thought (*ergreifendem Denken* [grasping thought] and truth (*erscheinender Wahrheit* [manifested truth]).[25] In this emphasis on naming as a constitutive act, Adorno underscores the nonorganic nature of all language.

Foreign-derived words have a special status in this conception since they display their man-made nature openly: "Each newly set foreign-derived word, however, profanely celebrates in the moment of its emergence the true ur-historical naming anew" (643).[26] While other, "native," words blend in seemingly naturally and thus give the impression of language as a coherent whole, the foreign-derived words serve as reminders of the origin of language in acts of naming. In this manner, not the "native" words, but these categorically strange words relate back to the moment of emergence of originary language. They are thus heightened forms of language. Whereas original acts of naming are located in a mythical framework, the *Fremdwort* as an act of naming is a profane reminder of a theologically informed origin. In their profanity, *Fremdwörter* are historical; they are "points at which cognizing consciousness irrupts." What enters through them is freedom, as they signify the "incursion of freedom" (643; tr. 289) outside determination by the quasi-natural logic of organicism.

The nonorganic, unassimilated existence of foreign-derived words testifies to a more general disjuncture in society, according to Adorno: "The more alienated human beings have become from their things in society, the more strange [*fremder*] will have to be the words that represent them if they are to reach them and to indicate allegorically that the things be brought home" (643; tr. 289, trans. modified). The distance between humans and their things is produced socially and cannot be closed by language, but it can be expressed in it, according to Adorno. Such an expression can occur "allegorically," when words signal their distance to the things they designate in a manner similar to the distance that separates humans from these things. The foreignness of words is thus a site at which social relations become legible. Because they are defined as words that jarringly display their foreignness, *Fremdwörter* can express the degree of strangeness or foreignness in these relations better than other words. In the sense of the foreignness that they convey, the *Fremdwörter* indicate a societal distance and alienation. In this allegory, Adorno translates linguistic foreignness into social alienation. He thereby transforms the terms of the *Fremdwort* debate into a social critique of alienation. What needs to be brought home (*heimgebracht*) are not the words in use, by replacing *Fremdwörter* with native words, but rather the things that surround humans in an alien fashion. This dimension of social critique that *Fremdwörter* can express leads Adorno to argue that their foreignness should not be denied, but rather used (640; tr. 286).

Instead of referring to nationalism and chauvinism, the central categories in early twentieth-century discourses on the *Fremdwort*, Adorno identifies alienation as the crucial phenomenon that affects the status of these words.[27] This alienation is brought about historically, by the entwined forces of instrumental reason and commodity fetishism: "The division of labor that led to the formation of the specific scientific terminologies that dismembered the Latin and Greek heritage gave foreign-derived words their reified character: that inhuman, fetishistic commodity character by which the purist is rightly offended" (644; tr. 289). Focusing on the case of scientific terminology, Adorno invokes the process of disciplinary specialization and segregation as a source of a violent dismemberment. If the words were already foreign to begin with, such processes render them "fully" reified. With his reference to the commodity character of the foreign-derived word, Adorno identifies capitalism as the framework in which to make sense of this linguistic category. It is not the fact that these words represent the traces of other languages within a given language that makes them so provocative, but rather the fact that they allegorically represent growing social alienation and reification. This dimension is the real reason that language purists take issue with these words, he contends.

Yet, while Adorno now seems to have located both language and *Fremdwörter* squarely in a historical space and connected them to the sphere of social relations, the essay does not end here, but transcends the historical dimension in favor of a utopian one. This move occurs when Adorno speaks of the use of *Fremdwörter* by writers—that is, in a turn to the literary realm.[28] He writes about authors' use of foreign-derived words as citations from other realms:

> But while the writer still thinks that he is quoting from his education and from special knowledge, he is actually quoting from a hidden language that is unknown in the positive sense, a language that overtakes, overshadows, and transfigures the existing one as though it were getting ready to be transformed into the language of the future. [. . .] The power of an unknown, genuine language that is not open to any calculus, a language that arises only in pieces and out of the disintegration of the existing one; this negative, dangerous, and yet assuredly promised power is the true justification of foreign-derived words. (645–46; tr. 291, trans. modified)

In this passage, "language" fully leaves behind the realm of actual natural languages and denotes language—in the singular—of a different sort. Foreign-derived words do not refer back to the foreign languages from where they came. They do not even allegorically express social alienation. Instead of a past genealogy or a present allegory, they indicate the possibility of a future affiliation. Their foreignness in this sense is due to an affiliation to a language that is not yet known. The words turn from belonging to actual languages to belonging to an invisible language that is reminiscent of Benjamin's "pure language." Adorno does not take up the *Fremdwort* as an element of a discourse on Germanness, but rather because it is a privileged site, a kind of hinge, where empirical language can evoke an invisible language. That language transcends existing languages as well as the social formations in which they exist and in which concepts such as national contours matter.

In his early discourse on words of foreign derivation, Adorno, then, reconfigures the foreignness of the *Fremdwort*, disconnecting it from identitarian categories such as German and non-German and linking it instead to social alienation. This strategy has both enabling and disabling effects. Most usefully, it brings into view the assumptions underlying the discourse, rather than merely repeating the discourse itself. The primary premise that it uncovers in this manner is that language is a self-contained organism. Revealing this premise is particularly effective as a critique of the "lax defense" brought forth by the apologists of the *Fremdwort*, who advocate the words under the condition that they too will assimilate into the organism. As Adorno argues, this defense reproduces the underlying premise of the organic, immanent nature of language that denies the foreign-derived words' legitimacy in the first place. Against this assimilationist argument, Adorno favors the emphasis on the alienness of the words as allegorical of rifts in the social realm.

What Adorno disavows in his focus on language as such rather than on German is the fact that nationalism and chauvinism do play such a significant role in the discourse. Thus, he ascribes to purists a perspective that rejects the "inhuman, fetishistic commodity character" of the *Fremdwort*, but he does not acknowledge that what most purists reject is the nonnative, "un-German" character of the words. While Adorno reads the *fremd* in *Fremdwort* as connected to *Entfremdung* (alienation), a condition afflicting all subjects in modernity, most early twentieth-century purists read it as connected to *Fremde* (foreigners), those who are ostensibly strictly different from the purists. Adorno might be right in his analysis that the unease with foreign-derived words stems from resentment against growing linguistic and social reification. Yet in this early essay he does not articulate how this implicit structure relates to the explicitly articulated "familiar arguments" that center on chauvinism. The question still remains: How are "alienation" and "foreignness," as two distinct analytics, mediated in the discourse on *Fremdwörter*?

"*FREMDWÖRTER* ARE THE JEWS OF LANGUAGE": RETHINKING GERMAN AFTER THE HOLOCAUST

More than a decade after his first extensive engagement with foreign-derived words, Adorno returns to them briefly but powerfully in a one-sentence aphorism in *Minima Moralia*. In the section "Zweite Lese" (Second Harvest), composed in 1945, he writes: "Fremdwörter sind die Juden der Sprache" (200; tr. 110; German words of foreign derivation are the Jews of language). Adorno relates the position of the linguistic category to the position of the most persecuted minority of the time, a minority to which he also belongs according to the racial classifications of the Nazi regime. Immediately following a one-sentence aphorism on antisemitism (200; tr. 110; "Anti-Semitism is the rumour about the Jews"), it is clear that the mention of "Jews" in the context of foreign-derived words suggests the racist discourse in which they were modeled into the primary other.[29] The conjunction of these disparate figures within a sentence illuminates the extraordinary overlap between the two discourses that the earlier passage from Jahn already suggested. For both foreign-derived words and Jews are continuously exposed to questions about the legitimacy of their belonging. Both had long been under attack as foreign intruders who could never assimilate and who would always display an unacceptable difference. By relating the foreign-derived word to Jews and to antisemitism in this manner, Adorno introduces into the *Fremdwort* discourse the element of racialization that he had neglected before.

This shift of focus from a predominantly Marxist analysis that brings out the capitalist structure to a recognition of the force of antisemitism as an element in need of its own analysis is characteristic for the development of thought in the Frankfurt School in general.[30] In a 1940 letter to Horkheimer, Adorno articulates this changing perspective: "Often it seems to me as if all that which we were used to see under the aspect of the proletariat has now been transferred to the Jews in a terribly concentrated form [*in furchtbarer Konzentration*]. I ask myself whether we should not [. . .] say the things which we really want to say in the context of the Jews who represent the counterpoint to the concentration of power" (cit. in Claussen 281–82). In a passage in which the foreign-derived word *Konzentration* is not arbitrarily chosen but rather evokes the Nazis' concentration camps, a new analytic orientation emerges. Class as a category gives way to a focus on a racialized minority.[31] Yet this shift does not mean that the economic analysis is abandoned, but rather supplemented. After all, it is the association of Jews with the commodity sphere that turns them into prime targets, according to Adorno and Horkheimer's eventual analysis in the antisemitism chapter of *Dialectic of Enlightenment*.

Through the invocation of "Jews," Adorno introduces into the discourse on foreign-derived words a rhetorical figure that complexly interweaves both alienation and foreignness, to return to the terms I juxtaposed earlier. Jews are deemed unchangeably and irredeemably foreign by antisemites. Yet, as Adorno and Horkheimer argue, Jews primarily function as a site of *projection* in antisemitic discourse. Through projection they are made into scapegoats for capitalism and modernity. An alienation suffered

by all is translated into the supposed foreignness of a singled-
out group.[32] It is through the concept of projection that the two
thinkers articulate the link between alienation and foreignness
that was absent in Adorno's earlier analysis on foreign-derived
words. Because of the complexity of the link, the invocation of
"Jews" in the context of the *Fremdwort* in *Minima Moralia* does
not stand for a full shift from a discourse on alienation to a discourse on foreignness. Rather, the figure of "Jews" is a point in
Adorno's discourse at which alienation and foreignness blur into
each other.[33]

This interrelationship between alienation and foreignness is itself located within a universal framework of language. In *Minima Moralia*, Adorno still does not name German as the reference point for *Fremdwort* discourse. This perspective changes in
Adorno's second extended reflection on words of foreign derivation. In contrast to the early essay as well as the apothegm
in *Minima Moralia*, "Wörter aus der Fremde" (1959), written
after the return from exile, not only mentions the German language, but also identifies the *Fremdwort* as specific to German.
This new specificity may be partially attributed to the context of
the essay. Adorno conceives "Wörter aus der Fremde" as a radio
lecture in response to complaints about his use of foreign-derived
words in a previous broadcast on Proust (published as "Kleine
Proust-Kommentare").[34] His goal in "Wörter aus der Fremde" is
thus to defend and legitimize his own use of these words. This
direct attack on his language provides a radically different point
of departure from the one in the early essay, where his own position vis-à-vis his language is not contested. As Hohendahl suggests, one could indeed read the essay "as an acknowledgement
of [Adorno's] own vulnerability in writing un-German Jewish
German" (*Prismatic Thought* 117)—that is, as potentially falling outside the monolingual paradigm vis-à-vis German in a way
similar to Kafka.

Yet despite the essay's emergence from an actual interaction
with a postwar, post-Holocaust German public, and its explicit
foregrounding of this interaction, it is not simply structured by

an opposition between the German-Jewish exile and returnee, on the one hand, and the non-Jewish German audience, on the other. For, almost at the outset of the essay, Adorno recalls how he was attacked once even in exile for his use of foreign-derived words in a speech from which he had specifically eliminated all of them.[35] What is important here is the parallel positioning of the anti-*Fremdwort* attitudes of German exiles and emigrants in the United States, on the one hand, and the German listeners in the Federal Republic, on the other. Through this parallel, Adorno underscores that the attitude towards the *Fremdwort* is not a dividing line between—mostly Jewish—exiles and those—non-Jewish—Germans in Germany. That is, it is not an identitarian divide. Although the essay is a response to West German listeners attacking his language use, Adorno maps a discursive space that encompasses them as well as the exiles.

Both exiled and nonexiled Germans are united, in Adorno's interpretation, by the rejection of complex ideas whose *Befremdende*[s] (unpleasantly estranging quality) they displace onto the foreign-derived word. Speaking about his Proust essay, he observes:

> The syntax may have sounded more foreign than the vocabulary. Attempts at formulation that swim against the stream of the usual linguistic splashing in order to capture the intended matter precisely, and that take pains to fit complex conceptual relationships into the framework of syntax, arouse rage because they require effort. The person who is naïve about language will ascribe the estranging quality [*Befremdendes*] of such writing to the foreign-derived words, which he holds responsible for everything he doesn't understand even when he is quite familiar with the words. (216; tr. 185, trans. modified)

While Adorno seeks to represent complex lines of thought through the syntax of his sentences, the reaction to this complexity, he asserts, is an uncomprehending displeasure at being forced to retrace this complexity, which ultimately leads to rage. Adorno's reference to the *Befremdende* (estranging quality) in this context adds a third term to the dimensions of *Fremde* (foreigners or foreignness) and *Entfremdung* (alienation) in his discourse on *Fremdwörter*. In contrast to both alienation and foreignness, however, estrangement is not an explanatory concept; it does not explain which structures underlie the negative resonance of the foreign-derived word, but rather registers this negative response itself. In the above passage, it is intricately linked to form and representation.[36]

Those individuals reacting negatively, the "linguistically naïve" who might encompass those who lived through exile as well as those in Germany, blame this sense of unsettling estrangement on foreign-derived words, whether they are actually present or not. Not the structure of the represented thought is recognized as estranging, but rather the estrangement is imagined to derive from the foreignness of words. That is, structurally produced estrangement is overlooked and not grasped in favor of a ready-made shorthand for linguistic estrangement, embodied in the form of foreignness on the level of individual words. The displacement of a perceived strangeness onto the imagined presence of foreign-derived words is one that strongly parallels Adorno and Horkheimer's earlier analysis of the function of Jews in antisemitism. As noted, a general alienation, initiated by capitalism and modernity, is displaced onto the figure of the "Jew" through the mechanism of projection. In the process, alienation is translated into foreignness and embodied in the "Jew." The fact that Adorno finds the same structure in the reaction of presumably Jewish exiles and emigrants and presumably non-Jewish West Germans indicates that the structure of displacement is not a non-Jewish German problem alone.

While Adorno describes the function of foreign-derived words in a way parallel to that of "Jews" in antisemitic discourse, and thereby confirms his own statement in *Minima Moralia*, the explicit reference to Jewishness disappears in "Wörter aus der Fremde." Katja Garloff, who makes this important observation, rightly sees this move as evidence of a larger shift on Adorno's part towards a more generalized notion of displacement in his postwar writings ("Essay, Exile, Efficacy" 82).[37] Yet this move from the presence of an identitarian marker to its absence is accompanied by a second, countertendency. The essay, in fact, features a double move, where the identitarian naming of the status of the *Fremdwort* (as metaphorically Jewish) is replaced with the identitarian naming of the language in question as *German* for the first time. This replacement indicates a shift from a focus on the status of the rejected *Fremdwort* to a more explicit engagement with the totality from which it is set apart—namely, the German language. "Wörter aus der Fremde" should thus be read as engaged in a diagnosis of the German language in the postwar years via an emphasis on the presence and function of the foreign-derived word, rather than simply being about that type of word.

Although Adorno is keenly aware of and articulates the caesura that the Holocaust constitutes in all arenas, he does not see the *German* language as such as implicated in those events. Contrary to intellectuals like George Steiner, who decries the post-Holocaust state of the German language as a "hollow miracle" ("Hollow Miracle"), Adorno does not lay blame on the German language. Although his most famous statement, "nach Auschwitz ein Gedicht zu schreiben, ist barbarisch" ("Kulturkritik" 31; "Cultural Criticism" 34; To write poetry after Auschwitz is barbaric) expresses the epochal mark of the event as reaching poetic language, this dictum is not directed against German poetry, but formulated as a universal affliction.[38] In the places where Adorno specifically links the foreign-derived word to German, this does not result in a reading of the *Fremdwort* in a discourse centered on nationalism or racialization, nor does it involve a negative evaluation of the language as exclusionary. Rather, for Adorno the foreign-derived word is indicative of German specificity both in its positive and negative aspects:

> The words of foreign derivation in the German language are reminders of that: the fact that no *pax romana* was concluded, that the untamed survived, and the fact that, when Humanism [*Humanismus*] took the reins, it was experi-

enced not as the substance of human beings [*Menschen*], as
intended, but as something unreconciled, something imposed upon them. To this extent German is both less and
more than the Western languages; it is less by virtue of the
brittle and unfinished quality that provides the individual
writer with so little that is firm, a quality that stands out
[. . .] in the relationship of foreign-derived words to their
context; and it is more because the language is not completely trapped within the net of socialization and communication. It can be used for expression because it does not
guarantee expression in advance. (219–20; tr. 188, trans.
modified)

Adorno reads the conspicuousness of the foreign-derived word
in German as the result of the unevenness of historical processes
of modernization. The absence of a form of pacification and integration imposed from above and outside, implied by the term
pax romana, results not just in a society whose development de-
viates from that of Western nations, but also in a language that
testifies to this unintegrated, unpacified process.[39] Though German, too, cannot escape the "net of socialization and communication" that modernization produces, it is not as fully captured
by it as the other languages, according to Adorno. The form of
alienation resulting from capitalism and modernization that he
already identified as a crucial dimension in *Fremdwort* discourse
in the early essay is again relevant here. Yet this time, the foreign-
derived word is a sign that the *German* language is not as fully
reified as "Western" languages—i.e., French and English—may
be. Because linguistic elements exist in it that testify to an ongoing social reification, it is capable of expressing that condition. As
a result of the unassimilated status of foreign-derived words, the
German language is marked by a tension unknown to the other
languages: "This tension, however, seems peculiar to German"
(218; tr. 187, trans. modified). Despite its downside, Adorno
deems this tension valuable. While he thus observes both the positive and negative effects of this condition on the language, the
final turn towards German as especially expressive indicates an

overall positive evaluation of the language, arrived at through the consideration of the conspicuousness of the foreign-derived word.

Adorno suggests that a writer can productively use this tension "between the foreign-derived word and the language by incorporating that tension into his own reflections and his own technique" (220; tr.189, trans. modified). His own writing presents the case for such a use of the inherent tension for expressive purposes. The phrase that most stands out in the above passage, for instance, is *pax romana*. Unassimilated into German morphology, the phrase is not a *Fremdwort*, but rather a foreign-language term. This unintegrated phrase itself underscores and expresses the unintegrated quality of the phenomenon it describes. *Pax romana* literally remains a foreign concept in German. *Humanismus*, on the other hand, is an example where "civilization as Latinization only partially succeeded" (218). An intellectual movement that became coterminous with the knowledge of Latin and Greek, *Humanismus* is partially integrated into German as a foreign-derived word. In its partial integration, however, it remains at a distance to the Germanic *Mensch* [human]. What Adorno expresses in this passage, he expresses in part through this configuration of foreign, foreign-derived, and native words. This writing practice recurs throughout Adorno's work. He never simply uses *Fremdwörter*; instead, they always appear as part of a configuration of linguistic levels provided by German.[40]

Adorno's take on the crucial role of the foreign-derived word for German provides a different angle on his infamous philosophical privileging of the language. In his 1965 essay "On the Question: 'What is German?'" he suggests that there appears to be an "elective affinity" between German and speculative philosophy (212), which developed most intensively in Germany, and he conjectures that this might have something to do with the German language. In this regard, his argument is surprisingly proximate to that of an otherwise radically different philosopher: namely, Heidegger.[41] Similar to Adorno, who claims a "metaphysical surplus" in the German language, Heidegger contends: "Along with German the Greek language is (in regard to its possibilities for thought) at once the most powerful and most spiritual of all languages" (*An Introduction to Metaphysics*, cit. in Levin, "Nationalities of Language" 113n4). This premise leads Heidegger to turn to the etymologies of German words and pursue them as sources of philosophical truth. In the process, he creates his own distinct vocabulary based on Germanic words. Yet Adorno famously dismisses Heidegger's Germanic neologisms as "Jargon" in his polemic *Jargon der Eigentlichkeit* (Jargon of Authenticity, 1964). He attacks the *Jargon* not just as the language of one philosopher but as the language that has taken over public discourse in postwar Germany and that undermines attempts at facing and working through the Nazi past.[42] The difference between Adorno's and Heidegger's privileging of the German language thus lies in their separate understandings of what constitutes German. For Heidegger, native German words are the core of the language and the proper sites for philosophical meditation. For Adorno, German is a language that is marked by an inherent tension, which is most clearly exemplified by *Fremdwörter*.

The simultaneous privileging of German and the insistence on the *Fremdwort* finally situate Adorno vis-à-vis the monolingual paradigm. In the same essay reflecting on the question "what is German"—the answer is: a language—Adorno shifts at one point from positing German as the site of privilege to viewing any "native language" as such as providing this philosophical privilege (213). His understanding of the qualities of a native language both do and do not conform to the monolingual paradigm. Drawing on his own experience of writing in English, Adorno reflects on the native language when considering the difficulty of writing in a foreign language.[43] What bothers him about writing in a foreign language is not his inability to communicate. Rather, it is what he sees as the preponderance of communication over expression:

> If one writes in a truly foreign language, then whether it is acknowledged or not, one falls under the captivating spell to communicate, to say it in such a way that others can understand. In one's own language, however, if one says the matter as exactly and uncompromisingly as possible, one may

hope through such unyielding efforts to become understandable as well. In the domain of one's own language, it is this very language that stands as a guarantee for one's fellow human being. ("Auf die Frage" 111; tr. 212–13)

In a foreign language, Adorno asserts, one cannot help but strive to communicate information, whereas in the native language one can even hope to be understood if one expresses oneself as precisely as possible and "without compromise." It is here that he appears to share the monolingual premise of being able to express oneself truly only in the native language and of the native language coming with promises of understanding that are lacking elsewhere. Foreign language and native language are divided along the lines of *Mitteilung* (communication) and *Ausdruck* (expression), two concepts that recur in much of his writing.[44] Communication for Adorno is the act of conveying information by using words for their immediate referential function. The right not to communicate, not to be limited to the referential function of language, is reserved for the native language. This kind of noncommunicative expression is not possible in the foreign language, according to Adorno.[45] The implication is that the articulation of otherness, of a remainder beyond the immediately functional, translatable, is possible only in the native language. Difference— or rather, nonidentity—is limited to the native. In this manner, native language in Adorno, in this postexile essay, is not simply the seat of authenticity as the monolingual paradigm would have it, but the site at which nonidentity is possible in the first place. Given the importance of the foreign-derived word, it is not the native in the native language, but its interplay with the foreign, unassimilated, opaque element that underwrites its expressive quality.[46] This partial adherence to the monolingual paradigm combined with a partial departure from it signals the manner in which Adorno's practice partakes of the tensions constitutive of the postmonolingual condition.

While Adorno shares the belief that one can only truly write in a native language and thus adheres to aspects of the monolingual paradigm, both his thinking about the *Fremdwort* and his use of it in his writing actively break with monolingualization. He does so throughout his work, but in different ways. In "Über den Gebrauch von Fremdwörtern," he identifies foreign-derived words as sites of the expression of alienation through their artificial, nonorganic, reified status. Through invocation of Jewishness in *Minima Moralia*, Adorno acknowledges that the discourse on foreign-derived words is one that is racialized in a manner mirroring the antisemitic discourse on Jews. Only after his return from exile does German come into view, in the essay "Wörter aus der Fremde." In contrast to the discourse of postwar Germany that Adorno attacks as *Jargon*—a language that aims to recover German through Germanic neologisms—Adorno considers the presence of foreign-derived words as essential to the German language. He refunctions the *Fremdwort* discourse, which had long been a discourse about the boundaries of native and foreign, into the very means of envisioning the German language as a site of nonidentity, an internally non-monolingual language. This refunctioning has strong affective dimensions that also constitute an implicit engagement with the figuration of the "mother tongue," as the next section demonstrates.

SEDUCTION AND SHOCK: *FREMDWÖRTER* AS AFFECTIVE PATHS OUT OF THE MOTHER TONGUE

In Adorno's writing, foreign-derived words consistently open up paths out of an enforced monolingualization of language. This aspect is especially pronounced in "Wörter aus der Fremde," which engages the post-Holocaust German language and, within that, the nature of a "mother tongue." From the beginning of his reflections on his personal encounter with *Fremdwörter*, Adorno undermines any notion of the language as belonging simply to the intimate family sphere. Remembering his initial encounter with foreign-derived words as an adolescent growing up at the height of language purism, he instead describes such words as "tiny cells of resistance against the nationalism of the First War" (218; tr. 186, trans. modified). This resistance immediately comes paired with pleasure: "Using *Ze-lotentum* [zealotry] or *Paränese* [paraenesis] was so pleasur-able because we sensed that some of the gentlemen to whom we were entrusted for our education during the First War were not quite sure what those words meant" (217; tr.186, trans. modi-fied).[47] In Adorno's reminiscence, the use of these relatively ex-travagant words yields pleasure that ultimately derives from the subversion of authority. Using words from this censured cate-gory functions as half-open rebellion against male authority fig-ures and the sanctioned language usage during the First World War.[48] In fact, this constellation of language, power, and sub-version provides the matrix for one dimension of Adorno's over-all perspective on *Fremdwörter*. For Adorno, foreign-derived words, especially if they are not immediately comprehensible, are not signs of oppression but rather a means of resistance and of the possibility of expression of nonconformist particularity. Even if Adorno downplays the openly political efficacy of for-eign-derived words (as in the reference to them as "*tiny* cells of resistance"), this matrix explains the tenor of his arguments about foreign-derived words and particularly his unwillingness to consider the problem of exclusion by incomprehension. How-ever much one may disagree with him on this point—and I do think that he disregards the problem of lack of access too com-pletely—for Adorno *Fremdwörter* are primarily a means to sub-vert authority, not to establish it. His own use of these words can thus also be read in this light, as "subversive" in intention rather than snobbish, even if subversiveness is not a category he would have necessarily endorsed. As Adorno's reference to the "gentlemen" indicates, the control over the domain of language is in male hands. Adorno aligns the enforcement of the Ger-manic elements of the language with male authority figures at school. The mother tongue, where it is reduced to words deemed autochthonous, is thus a male institutional domain. It is not a domain of intimacy with language, but rather of the enforce-ment of the law of the father, to gesture towards another theo-retical idiom.[49]

The *Fremdwörter* that are censored from and by this "mother tongue," on the other hand, give rise to intimate desires. Adorno describes his own and his best friend Erich's affinity for foreign-derived words as an attraction primarily colored in erotic terms:

> The fact that we happened upon foreign-derived words was hardly due to political considerations. Rather, since language is erotically charged in its words, at least for the kind of person who is capable of expression, love drives us to foreign-derived words. In reality, it is that love that sets off the indignation over their use. The early urge [*Drang*] for foreign-derived words is like the craving for foreign and if possible exotic girls; what lures us is a kind of exogamy of language [*Exogamie der Sprache*], which would like to escape from the sphere of what is always the same, the spell of what one is and knows anyway. At that time foreign-derived words made us blush, like saying the name of a secret love. [National communities] who want one-dish meals even in language find these stirrings hateful. It is from this stratum that the affective tension [*affektive Spannung*] that gives foreign-derived words their fecund and dangerous quality arises, the quality that their friends are seduced by and their enemies sense more readily than do people who are indifferent to them. (218; tr. 187, trans. modified)

Against simple political readings of language, Adorno emphasizes the affective investment in it as more consequential and fundamental. The "drive" towards foreign-derived words comes specifically from libidinal investment in language and results in an uncontrollable urge towards them: "love *drives*" (*treibt* die Liebe) "erotically *charged*" or "*cathected*" (erotisch *besetzt*) "*urge, craving*" (*Drang*). Through these formulations, he describes the dynamics underlying the attraction to foreign-derived words in psychoanalytic terms. The gamut of affective qualities and reactions to foreign-derived words that he lists—from erotic charge, love, indignation, craving, lure, blushing, hatred, danger, and seduction to indifference—indicates that this affective energy relating to foreign-derived words takes on different qualities as it circulates. While these affective qualities are foregrounded and described as prior to the political, they are also entwined with politics. Although the attraction to words of foreign derivation may not be politically motivated, the resentment against this attraction takes on political significance. In this schema, it is the language purist who introduces the political dimension. The purist politicizes the positive affect of the *Fremdwort* user (love, craving, seduction) while his own negative affect—here: indignation and hatred—leads to political action. This aversion is not directed merely at the fact that some speakers do not understand the words and therefore feel excluded. Rather, Adorno sees it as directed at the love of those using foreign-derived words for something outside the native. What he diagnoses is thus a case of *ressentiment,* to use another politically significant affective term of the twentieth century—and a *Fremdwort*!—that Adorno evokes in the same context (217; tr. 186).[50]

While *ressentiment* describes the affective and political structure of anti-*Fremdwort* sentiment, the image that stands out in this passage and underwrites the positive attraction to foreign-derived words is that of the "exotic girls." I noted earlier Garloff's observation that the explicit reference to Jewishness in connection with the foreign-derived word disappears in "Wörter aus der Fremde." Yet what does not disappear is the acknowledgement of the racialization of the *Fremdwort* discourse that the introduction of the figure of "Jews" in *Minima Moralia* also registered. In this case, however, it is not articulated in connection with "Jews," but rather transferred to the figure of the "exotic girls." In this suggestive simile, the racialized quality of foreign-derived words is retained in the "exoticism" of the girls. The contrast between "from another country" (*ausländisch*) and "possibly exotic" (*womöglich exotisch*) inscribes not just a heightened foreignness but an implicit racial difference, as "exotic" usually designates nonwhite and non-European.

The heightening of foreignness that the shift from *ausländisch* to *womöglich exotisch* indicates is achieved through a shift from a Germanic word to a foreign-derived one. The German word merely designates someone from another country. In a literal sense, *exotisch* means the same thing, as the original Greek word means "from another country." Yet both words have very different connotations and affective values. *Ausländisch* is at best a descriptive term, if not even a negative one; it belongs to a political and bureaucratic register. *Exotisch*, on the other hand, belongs to an anthropological register; it denotes an enticing foreignness. This quality, if we follow Adorno, derives from the fact that the word itself is of foreign provenance, stands out from the language surrounding it. It thus performs the foreignness it is meant to index, rather than merely referring to it.

In contrast to the mention of Jews directly in the context of antisemitism, this racialization is not tied to abjection. Here the gender and sexual dynamic of "exotic girls" comes into play. The feminine gendering of foreign-derived words, in combination with an underlying heterosexual matrix, in which the language subjects are male (Adorno and his friend Erich), while the foreign-derived words are female, sexualizes the relationship. In the combination of sexualization and racialization, the "exotic girls" are attractive outsiders, rather than foreign intruders.[51] Foreignness—and we are dealing with this sense of *fremd* rather than with alienation as the initial reference to *ausländisch* indicates— is in this case translated into exoticism. In the guise of the exotic, the foreign becomes desirable.

What is desired through the exotic girls is a "kind of exogamy of language." Since the Greek-derived term "exogamy" designates the practice of marrying outside one's kin, it introduces the dimension of kinship into Adorno's discourse on language, albeit as something to be transgressed. Both through the element of kinship that exogamy introduces and the gender, racial, and affective aspects of the figure of exotic girls, Adorno circles a term that is not mentioned explicitly in this passage or anywhere in the essay—namely, the mother tongue. Both the mother tongue and the exotic girls are defined by gender as female, their kinship status is highlighted (as maternal or as exogamous), and their affective value plays a central role—one is the object of a child's love while the other is the object of erotic love. While the gender aspect and the positive affective value thus stay the same, the kinship dimension is radically altered—towards exogamy—in connection with a different form of intimacy. The contrast between mother tongue and exotic girls that I am suggesting here is not a symmetrical one, since the former refers to the entire language, while the latter designates only an element of the language. The exotic girls are therefore not the opposite of the mother tongue; they do not take its place. Yet the desire for the exotic girls is a desire to step *outside* the mother tongue into another language.[52] The lure towards the other that the *Fremdwort* installs institutes an inherent tension in the language.

Exogamie as a foreign-derived word provides insight into what this inherent tension means in terms of representation. In contrast to *erotisch* and *exotisch*, the other Greek-derived words of the passage that stand out and that are connected to *Exogamie* through alliteration, the word itself is not already affectively charged in a titillating manner. Rather, it is an anthropological term that is almost technical in comparison. If the word is seductive for the speaker, it is so through a break in register. This kind of break that foreign-derived words can engender is the representational use to which Adorno puts them time and again. The foreign-derived words offer an inventory in the language that can be used to break the flow of the language, to make the reader stumble and reorient, to notice a difference within the language.[53] Not the foreign-derived words in isolation, but their configuration with "native" and at times foreign words create this break (as in "*affektive* Spannung," "*Exogamie* der Sprache" and other formulations combining *Fremdwort* and Germanic word). The foreign-derived words that Adorno prefers are often of a technical nature; they do not have emotional or lyrical meanings on the referential level or even in connotation.[54] The affective—not necessarily emotional—charge that they nevertheless generate as part of a configuration derives from the stoppage and disjuncture to which they give rise.

Such an affective charge and recoding of the "mother tongue" already marks the relationship to his language in exile. In the section "Zweite Lese" in *Minima Moralia*, the apothegm on *Fremdwörter* is immediately followed by a paragraph recalling the dialect of Adorno's hometown. In contrast to the preceding aphoristic statements, this paragraph suddenly shifts to the first person singular and with that to a highly emotional autobiographical act.[55] I cite the paragraph in full:

> One evening, in a mood of stunned sadness, I caught myself using a ridiculously wrong subjunctive form of a verb that was itself not entirely correct High German, being part of the dialect of my paternal hometown [*Vaterstadt*]. I had not heard, let alone used, the endearing misconstruction since my first years at school. Melancholy [*Schwermut*], drawing me irresistibly into the abyss of childhood, awakened this old, impotently yearning sound in its depths. Language sent back to me like an echo the humiliation which unhappiness had inflicted on me in forgetting what I am. (200–201; tr. 110–11, trans. modified)

In a situation of uprootedness and exile, it is the memory of the dialect of the paternal hometown that draws Adorno back into childhood. Not German as a mother tongue, not the standard High German in which he lived and wrote gives rise to this overwhelming sadness, but rather the sudden emergence of a fragment from a local dialect. This local dialect is characterized as belonging to the paternal site of origin (*Vaterstadt*), not the sphere of maternal language. By explicitly mentioning the paternal dimension of origin, rather than the maternal one, Adorno shifts the common gender of language kinship. This shift does not result in an attenuation of affect. On the contrary, Adorno's invocation of paternal affiliation retains all the emotional intensity usually associated with the mother tongue. In his specific case, this shift means an emphasis on his Jewish father rather than his Catholic mother, whose Italian maiden name he adopted in exile. It was his father who was directly persecuted by the Nazis and forced to leave his hometown.[56] The altered linguistic family romance, following the statement on *Fremdwörter* as the "Jews of language," thus gestures towards and registers this expulsion, rather than a form of belonging.

Yet the passage is not written in the dialectal form of the paternal hometown. In fact, neither is the word that brought about this sorrow named, nor are further memories elaborated that the word activated. Instead, the unnamed form that returns from the deepest recesses is described on the one hand as a dialectal expression (*Dialekt* [dialect]), and on the other as a linguistic mood (*Konjunktiv* [subjunctive]). The subjunctive describes the unreal case, the hypothetical condition, or the expression of a wish.[57] It is this form that takes Adorno back from the facts of the present moment into what could have been or could be wished for. As in other places in his writing, Adorno evokes childhood as a utopian realm. In the essay "Auf die Frage: Was ist deutsch?" for instance, he links language, childhood, home, and exile. Explaining what about Germany and German culture drew him to return from exile on a personal level, he states: "I simply wanted to go back to the place where I spent my childhood, where what is specifically mine [*mein Spezifisches*] was imparted [*vermittelt*] to the very core [*bis ins Innerste*]" (107; tr. 210). It is noteworthy, as Jamie Owen Daniel remarks, that this response does not in effect provide a glimpse of the national, but rather of the local (32). It is local attachment, located specifically in childhood, that draws him back. The local is also the site at which the *Fremdwort* (*Spezifisches*) and the Germanic word (*Innerste*), each designating aspects of particularity and subjectivity, appear as mediated (*vermittelt*); this observation brings us back to considering the place of words of foreign derivation in this context.

Interestingly, the passage in "Zweite Lese" features fewer foreign-derived words than can generally be found in Adorno's writing. Particularly noticeable is the use of the German term *Schwermut* rather than the foreign-derived *Melancholie*, which Adorno could have employed.[58] The concreteness of the German word and its emphasis on a mood that feels *schwer* (heavy, weighty) serves to underscore the downward pull, towards the *Abgrund* (abyss) and the *Grund* (depth, bottom) that the sentence further attests to. The Germanic term spatializes melancholia more explicitly than the foreign-derived word.[59] In contrast to such German-derived words, the paragraph features three technical *Fremdwörter* that stand out: namely, *Konjunktiv, Verb* and *Dialekt*.[60] All these words refer to classifications of language, either on the grammatical level (*Konjunktiv* and *Verb*), or that of language typology (*Dialekt*). Together, they describe the unnamed word with the greatest classificatory specificity, while other formulations such as *Mißform* (misconstruction) merely evoke the word in general terms.[61] This means that the dialectal expression itself is circled by the series of *Fremdwörter* and stands in a special relationship to them. Adorno chooses them to articulate the experience without naming the word itself. Instead of merely communicating the word to his readers, he thus expresses the distance from it through this recourse to the jarringly technical, classificatory, foreign-derived words. As in earlier examples (*affektiv, Exogamie, Paränese*), these words do not have an intimate emotional quality by themselves. Yet, together with the German-derived words of the passage (such as *fassungslose Traurigkeit* [stunned sadness], *zutraulich* [endearing], *Schwermut* [melancholy], *Beschämung* [shame]), they form a configuration and result in a deeply moving paragraph.

The grief and melancholy that arise through the unexpected breakthrough of the unnamed dialectal word from the paternal hometown, and that Adorno approximates through a series of foreign-derived words, recall the expulsion from that home in a moment when Adorno is still in exile from Germany. If foreign-derived words are a means to express such injury, then, what is their function after the return from exile? As we have seen earlier, the functions and contexts of the foreign-derived word, as Adorno sees them, change with the historical circumstances to which he relates them. The focus on the lure of foreign-derived words as similar to that of exotic girls is recounted in the postwar essay "Wörter aus der Fremde," yet it recalls a much earlier moment. That simile stands for the "*frühe[n]* Drang" (*early* craving, or, more psychoanalytically: pressure) towards words of foreign derivation. When that same essay turns to the function of *Fremdwörter* in the postwar moment, the similes and affects radically change.

In the postwar period, foreign-derived words no longer function to lure and seduce for Adorno. Instead, they can at times function to shock. Shock, Adorno says in this context, "may now be the only way to reach human beings through language" (224; tr.192). The *Fremdwort* can at best be a site of shock that arouses the speakers from their numbness, a numbness facilitated by the false depth of the "jargon of authenticity."[62] Meanwhile, the seductive exotic girls of his adolescence turn into *Totenköpfe* (skulls; literally: death's heads) who await their resurrection:

> In this way foreign-derived words could preserve something of the utopia [*Utopie*] of language, a language without soil [*Sprache ohne Erde*], without subjection to the spell of historical existence, a utopia that lives on unawarely in the childlike usage of language. Hopelessly, like death's-heads, foreign-derived words await their resurrection in a better order of things. (224; tr. 192, trans. modified)

The emphasis on desire in adolescence gives way to a melancholy state within the same essay. The gap between the figuration of the *Fremdwort* as seductive other, on the one hand, and the skulls of the postwar era, on the other, indicates a deadly caesura. The hope that foreign-derived words would carry an explosive power, the explosive force of enlightenment even ("Wörter" 221), has now turned into the insight that they themselves have been the victims of explosive forces. It is difficult not to read this image as an implicit post-Holocaust reference, particularly in light of the apothegm on foreign-derived words as "the Jews of language." As death's heads, *Fremdwörter* would seem to turn the (German) language into a cemetery. As I noted earlier, Adorno, unlike critics such as Steiner, does not decry the postwar, post-Holocaust condition of the German language as a "hollow miracle." The death's heads are not simply empty, devoid of life; they are the most material remnants of the dead. As such, they do not mark the German language as unlivable territory, but rather guarantee that the German language retains the memory of those deadly historical events. For Adorno, German in the postwar years "is suitable for expression" because of the presence of foreign-derived words and their ability to disturb, shock, retain, and remind as they are situated both in a Beckett-style postapocalyptic scenery and within a Benjaminian weak messianic hope.

Nonetheless, the utopia that this passage evokes before a seemingly dystopian image has to do precisely with leaving such territories behind. The "language without soil" is akin to the "hidden language that is unknown in the positive sense" that the earlier *Fremdwort* essay had envisioned (645; tr. 291), albeit now shrouded in a mournful rather than assured mode.[63] *Utopie*, the single *Fremdwort* of this passage, is itself a topographical expression, as it literally means "no place" in Greek. It thus corresponds to the notion of a "language without soil."[64] Yet the foreign-derived word and the Germanic phrase do not simply repeat the same content in different forms. Utopia, as the imagination of an unreal but desired state, parallels the function of the subjunctive mode in language (*Konjunktiv*) that we encountered in *Minima Moralia*, though it is more future-oriented. It expresses the desire for an order that does not (yet) exist, and this desire may break the "spell of historical existence" as a first step. The notion of a "language without soil" provides a glimpse of what the content of that utopia might be. *Erde* as an image of both organic rootedness and territory, rather than place, is what needs to be left behind. Both "utopia" and "language without soil" express the desire to break the link between language and territory and to transcend history.

Although the utopian language to which Adorno refers does not correspond to or cannot be circumscribed by actual languages in existence, the essay is nevertheless engaged in working on the German language as well as notions of the "mother tongue." Instead of blaming historical events on the language, Adorno sees it as the site that registers historical dynamics and can express them. Through his focus on the *Fremdwort* as an unassimilated category within the language that can register the desire for something beyond the native and the familiar, as well as preserve the memory of deadly events, he imagines the German language as a site of nonidentity. The presence of the word of foreign derivation—even if it no longer holds the same promise it once did for him, because it has been touched and transformed further by history—makes the German language a repository and a site of possible resurrection. Though the foreign-derived word is said to be emotionally distant, this distance can express an emotional condition of mourning and melancholia. The affective quality of foreign-derived words is not something fixed but produced and reproduced. Adorno does not simply suggest replacing the negative affective quality of these words with positive ones. Instead, he follows his own maxim to use the "foreignness" of the word, not deny it. *Fremdwort*, affect, and history are closely entangled in Adorno's critically postmonolingual practice.

With all its vicissitudes, the centuries-long discourse on words of foreign derivation in German language usage has centered again and again on the question of what is German, and how to demarcate what is German by excluding elements deemed nonnative. This form of internal multilingualism was thus primarily perceived as a disturbing threat from the outside, and the German language was imagined as endangered or contaminated, rather than as flexible and capable of absorbing and assimilating new elements. The fact that internal multilingualism is a component of all languages, but that the degree of a wide-spread consciousness about it varies from one community to another, underscores that the linguistic level itself does not automatically give rise to the kinds of turns we can observe in German discourses. That even Austrian language usage and consciousness differ in this regard and have been relatively more comfortable with foreign-derived words, further suggests that the issue is not about *the* German language, but rather about the non-Austrian German political, social, and cultural sphere. Intervening in this discourse has thus been a means to participate in a struggle over what is German in a German national context.

As the complaints following Adorno's radio lecture prove, the anti-*Fremdwort* attitude continued to exist in the postwar years. When Peter Braun edited his volume *Fremdwort-Diskussion* in 1979, he could still state that the topic was a current one and that there was public interest in it beyond circles of linguists (7). Since at least the 1990s, Latinate and French-derived words are no longer the primary targets of purist endeavors. Rather, the focus has shifted to the presence of English words and phrases in German usage. While many of these words, such as *cool*, *kids*, and *Handy* (cell phone), have become widely used everyday *Fremdwörter*, the animosity of contemporary purists is directed at the perceived rise in the use of unincorporated English phrases in public life, particularly in the domains of advertising and media. The object of the complaints has thus changed somewhat from foreign-derived to foreign words (such as *task force*, *account manager*, *call a bike*). At the same time, the openly chauvinistic rhetoric of earlier times is studiously avoided in favor of a more moderate-sounding appeal to the preservation of linguistic and cultural difference in the era of globalization.[65] What today's discourse nevertheless shares with the earlier ones is the sense of urgency and threat to the German language, as some critics see the integrity and even the very survival of the German language endangered by the dominance of English.[66] This shift suggests that the issues and particularly some of the affects around the foreign-derived word have not necessarily been resolved but rather displaced, albeit in a significantly transformed manner. Internal multilingualism continues to be a charged issue today.

Writing against the backdrop of this long-standing debate, Adorno takes the position that the foreignness of the *Fremdwort* should not be downplayed or denied but used. Yet what he understands as that foreignness changes with his analyses of the social totality in which he locates the discourse and the words. His early essay on foreign-derived words offers a framework for understanding the anti-*Fremdwort* discourse as something other than an expression of nationalism, which most other critics had identified as its core. Instead, Adorno situates the *Fremdwort* in the framework of modernization and capitalism and reads it allegorically as testifying to the overall societal process of reification. His early perspective expands the understanding of "foreign" from simply encompassing what is not native to describing the general social condition of alienation. Later, when he begins to account for and integrate antisemitism into his understanding of modernization and capitalism, he is led to articulate the relationship between foreignness and alienation more explicitly. Therefore, foreign-derived words do not simply mark the boundaries between native and foreign, pure and impure, but rather chart the tension between foreignness and alienation as two distinct but intersecting categories within the German language. This distinction helps to analyze how one is at times translated into the other, or how they are sometimes conflated with each other. Beyond the discourse on foreign-derived words, the distinction is useful in such areas as contemporary discourse on minority literature, where minorities are frequently reduced to expressing, if not embodying, foreignness, and denied the possibility that they might in fact be addressing issues such as alienation.

Besides this more ideological dimension, I draw attention to the role of affect in *Fremdwort* discourse and its intersection with the ideological. Adorno is also well aware of the "affective tension" in the German language connected to the presence of foreign-derived words and makes use of it in his own writing. In my readings of his writing, I demonstrate that Adorno's use of foreign-derived words is very deliberate and that it always functions to heighten and intensify the content of his discourse. All of Adorno's texts, I suggest, can be read through the lens of the configuration of foreign-derived, foreign, and native words. The types of foreign-derived words that he prefers are of a technical, emotionally aloof kind, yet he uses them as distancing and disruptive elements of linguistic configurations in a way that produces and conveys affective as well as emotional intensity. While other critics have suggested that the *Fremdwort* is a privileged site of nonidentity, I argue that nonidentity in Adorno's writing is best grasped in the affective tension that results from the interplay of foreign-derived, foreign, and native words. This configuration, which is neither fully monolingual nor explicitly multilingual, manifests the postmonolingual dimension of Adorno's theory and practice.

Writing with *Fremdwörter* is a mode of reasserting the internal multilingualism of a language, and, in the case of Adorno, produces an internal multilingualism that registers social and historical dynamics. Under the thrall of the monolingual, even this limited move to reassert multilingualism constitutes a significant move beyond the mother tongue. Insofar as moving away from the mother tongue notion means moving away from any notion of the homology between language, nation, culture, and ethnicity, writers who employ *Fremdwörter* deliberately partake in such a break with the homology.

As noted, Adorno's writing also partook of another form of multilingualism besides the use of foreign-derived words: he wrote some texts in English. This bespeaks, in however small a way, a bilingual writing practice. For Adorno, this practice was a matter of necessity and arose out of the situation of exile. He did not consider himself a bilingual writer as a result, but continued to hold on to the concept of the primacy of a single native language, albeit a primacy underwritten by the foreign-derived word. Where Adorno produced only a small amount of his voluminous writing in another language, other writers have turned to bilingualism as the basis of their poetics. The next chapter takes up a deliberate bilingual writing practice as a more explicit move beyond the mother tongue.

CHAPTER THREE

Detaching from the Mother Tongue

Bilingualism and Liberation in Yoko Tawada

WRITING A GLOBALIZED LINGUASCAPE

What form do confrontations with the monolingual paradigm take in the late twentieth and early twenty-first century under conditions of globalization? The heightened, accelerated interaction between different parts of the world due to new information, transportation, and financial technologies that goes by the name of "globalization" produces a new framework in the latter half of the twentieth century in which languages circulate, change, and accrue meaning. If one may supplement Arjun Appadurai's model of disjunctive "flows" (of people, goods, ideas etc.) that constitute the new "scapes" of globalization, one could speak of languages and shifting linguistic practices as comprising part of a new "linguascape." In this linguascape, heretofore uncommon language combinations emerge on a significant scale due to mass migrations and refugee movements (in Europe, for example, Turkish and German, Kurdish and French, Arabic and Swedish), while postcolonial migrations bring formerly colonized languages to the colonial centers (French and Arabic, Indonesian and Dutch). The virtual realm of the Internet, meanwhile, allows for languages to circulate, meet, and change irrespective of territorial moorings, and thus, even of the physical mobility of people. As with other realms affected by globalization, this linguascape is marked by both heterogenizing and homogenizing tendencies. On the one hand, new hybrid codes emerge out of this situation (such as the Stockholm-based urban youth slang, Rinkeby Swedish); on the other hand, smaller languages disappear at an accelerated rate (the phenomenon of "language death") while the global dominance of English increases. Whether the focus is on the losses or gains of this process, however, thinking on a global scale beyond the confines of the nation-state has fostered a new awareness of multilingualism, which in turn has provoked both affirmative and concerned responses. This situation constitutes a radically new context in which to bring multiple languages together in one's writing.

The following three chapters turn to three contemporary authors who engage multilingualism within a globalizing context. Their writing relates to social changes, especially modes of displacement such as travel, exile, and migration, but it also transforms and works through these phenomena by creating novel multilingual forms. These authors—Yoko Tawada, Emine Sevgi Özdamar, and Feridun Zaimoğlu—are part of the reemergence of multilingualism that characterizes the period since the 1990s. They allow insight into this period and its new linguistic configuration. They are evidence of this new visibility, and also of the fact that this new visibility occurs in different forms, with different agendas, addressing different contexts and issues, choosing different paths. The present chapter traces the manner in which bilingual writing, defined as writing an oeuvre in two or more languages separately, can be a means of going beyond the mother tongue.[1]

The playful bilingual writing of Yoko Tawada, an author of works in Japanese and in German that engage both thematically and formally with the monolingual paradigm in an age of globalization, offers a unique perspective in this regard. Born in Japan in 1960 and living in Germany since 1982, Tawada initially wrote in Japanese, before beginning to write also in German in 1988. Since then, she has produced two large, entirely separate corpuses in Japanese and in German simultaneously.[2] Instead of writing in one language and then translating into the other (like English-French writer Nancy Huston, for example), Tawada writes unreplicated texts in each of the languages.[3] She even prefers different genres in different languages: she tends to write poetry and novels in Japanese, and plays, short prose, and literary essays in German. In both languages, though, travel, myth, and bodily metamorphoses are recurring and interlocking themes. Also in both of them, linguistic experimentation and observations about language are regular features. The stylistic characteristics of her writing, particularly the easy slide from realist setting into dreamlike states, have led critics to describe her writing as surreal or situate it more generally within an avant-garde tradition.[4] The particular form of Tawada's literary bilingualism ultimately has three main characteristics: she writes in a rare language combination with relatively few joint readers, she continuously switches between her two languages, and she inscribes bilingual perspectives into each of her oeuvres in subtle, deconstructive ways. For this oeuvre—or rather: these oeuvres—she has received numerous awards in both Japan and Germany.

The particular form and context of Tawada's literary bilingualism, this chapter will show, aims at a critique of the monolingual paradigm and the concept of the mother tongue from within. This critique takes the firm inclusion into the monolingual paradigm as a problematic state. That is, the monolingual paradigm is not just problematic because of the exclusions it produces, as chronicled in the previous chapters on Kafka and Adorno and the upcoming chapter on Zaimoğlu, but also from the vantage point of the inclusions it enforces. Tawada's writing unearths the restrictions that monolingualism and the mother tongue produce for monolingual subjects and experiments with bilingually derived ways of loosening those strictures. In conjunction with real and imagined transnational mobility, she uses bilingualism as a literary strategy of detachment from any language's claim on the subject, rather than as a basis for a claim to double belonging. The strictures of the mother tongue that Tawada's writing of the 1980s and 1990s reveal have much to do with the reproduction of gender and kinship in a national framework. In her more recent work since the 2000s, meanwhile, bilingual forms become a means to interrogate the inscription of race via language. Through these forms, Tawada's writing opens up unexpected paths across a globalized linguascape. A brief visit to bilingual writing before and after the monolingual paradigm will throw the particularity of her innovation into sharper relief.

BILINGUAL WRITING

Like many forms of multilingualism, writing in two or more languages was more common prior to the rise of the monolingual paradigm. In seventeenth-century Europe, for instance, it was common for the small literate elite to be polyglot and to write at times in Latin, and at times in Dutch, Italian, French, or German. The choice of language was primarily guided by the topic at hand, as some languages were considered more appropriate for some topics than others, such as Latin for sciences, and Italian for love poetry.[5] A framework in which aesthetic and generic criteria included a consideration of appropriate language thus fostered the production of oeuvres in multiple languages. The monolingual paradigm arising in the eighteenth century gradually, but radically, changed this framework and put the—assumedly singular—native language and ethno-national identity of the writer into the forefront, until it became unimaginable for many to write in anything but their "mother tongue." To return to a key phrase, Friedrich Schleiermacher asserted by 1813 that "every writer can produce original work only in his mother tongue, and therefore the question cannot even be raised how he would have written his works in another language" ("On the Different Methods" 50). As Schleiermacher's emphasis on "original work" indicates, this attitude derives from a particular conception of originality and creativity as rooted in authenticity, with authenticity in turn deemed possible only in a singular native language.

Asserting the impossibility of writing in a second or third language alongside a sanctioned "mother tongue" has been effective in downplaying these practices throughout the nineteenth and twentieth centuries, but not in fully discouraging them. A quick glance reveals numerous canonical authors who, for one reason or another, produced literature in more than one language: besides the best-known cases of Vladimir Nabokov (Russian/English) and Samuel Beckett (English/French), one could list Oscar Wilde (who wrote his *Salomé* in French), August Strindberg (whose French literary production was consequential for his Swedish works), Isak Dinesen (who gained fame in Danish and, under the pseudonym Karen Blixen, in English) or Halide Edip Adıvar (one of the founders of modern Turkish literature, who also wrote in English), and the numerous postcolonial writers of the second half of the century, such as Ngugi wa Thiong'o (English/Gikuyu).[6] Albeit motivated by different reasons and in different contexts, writing in two or more languages has thus flourished in this period and, if anything, continues to increase.

One of the primary conditions that has weakened the monolingual paradigm's deterrence of writing in anything besides the "mother tongue" has been displacement outside the nation-state. Many of the writers in the twentieth century who produce bilingual oeuvres have experienced some form of displacement outside the nation-state, whether voluntary or involuntary. This is true for the two major bilingual writers of the century, Beckett and Nabokov. The Anglo-Irish Beckett voluntarily moved to France and found his literary voice and fame first in French before returning also to English, while the trilingually raised Nabokov wrote his major Russian works in German exile and decided to write in English during a stay in France.[7] As noted in the previous chapter, even Theodor Adorno reluctantly decided to write some essays in English during his more than decade-long exile in the United States, while he otherwise resisted changing his language.[8] To be sure, displacement in itself does not necessarily lead to bilingual writing, as demonstrated by the case of numerous exiles and expatriates who continue to write in their first language. Under the continued force of the monolingual paradigm, however, it is displacement that opens up the possibility of writing in more than one language. Globalization, understood as a process of increased displacement, makes such writing thus more likely, as the case of Yoko Tawada also underscores.

BECOMING BILINGUAL: A JOURNEY
FOR MONOLINGUALS

Writing in Japanese and in German, Tawada is an author in two languages and national contexts in which the monolingual paradigm is deeply ingrained. Just as in the case of Germany, the myth of the homogenous, monolithic, and monolingual nation has governed the imagination of Japan both inside the country and elsewhere.[9] This view dates back to the self-imposed rapid process of modernization that Japan underwent beginning in the late nineteenth century.[10] As part of this process, authorities devised a linguistic standard based on the Tokyo dialect that the newly established school system enforced with great success. As a result, the widely diverse linguistic landscape that predated this monolingualization—the mutually incomprehensible dialects across the islands, the languages of indigenous populations such as the Ainu on Hokkaido—almost disappeared, along with awareness of their existence. The ideological genre of *Nihonjinron* (literally: writing about Japan) that emerged in the period after 1945 was entirely dedicated to claiming the unique homogeneity of the Japanese nation and its language. Both becoming modern and becoming a nation thus entailed monolingualization of the population and restructuring of the society and culture according to the precepts of the monolingual paradigm.

As in other places, however, forms of multilingualism have become more assertively visible in contemporary Japan, thus confronting the governing monolingual paradigm with a reemergent multilingualism. Accelerated processes of globalization under conditions of post–Cold War reorientation in the 1990s have led to the destabilization of the national myth of homogeneity and confronted Japan with its de facto linguistic diversity. Among these processes were the emergence of new social movements that led to the visibility of the languages of formerly assimilated indigenous people such as the Ainu and of ethnic minorities such as Korean immigrants, the return of the descendants of Japanese emigrants from Latin American destinations such as Brazil and Peru and their divergent linguistic practices, and an overall increase in the number of Japanese with international experiences, perspectives, and linguistic competences. The literary realm, in the meantime, saw for the first time the rise of non-Japanese writers writing in Japanese. The prominence of an author such as American emigrant Hideo Levy constitutes a phenomenon that the *Nihonjinron* genre with its insistence on the unmasterability of Japanese by foreigners had declared impossible.

Yoko Tawada's writing actively participates in this politically charged, reemergent multilingualism, albeit in a manner that does not wear its political stakes on its sleeve.[11] With two actively developed literary languages, Tawada challenges the assumption of the monolingual writer solely able to write in the mother tongue. She thus contributes to the destabilization of monolingual certainties. By writing even her Japanese oeuvre abroad, she also expands what it means to be a Japanese writer, just as her German oeuvre adds new dimensions to the notion of the German writer. That her second literary language is German, rather than an indigenous or immigrant language in Japan or the global language of English, begins to signal, however, the particularity of her bilingual intervention. With German, she chooses a language that is geographically, culturally, and linguistically distant from the Japanese context. The number of speakers of both Japanese and German is small and there is little overlap between the languages, or even their scripts. This bilingual constellation, therefore, does not emerge out of or refer back to any sociolinguistic community and does not even assume readers who are familiar with both languages. It is thus a bilingualism addressing itself to "monolinguals"—that is, an audience most likely only fluent in one of those languages—and confronting them with perspectives gained in an unfamiliar language. Enabled by this configuration, Tawada's writing time and again explores the process of monolinguals leaving monolingualism behind, a process which in her writing often entails departing from the national realm.

The 1998 bilingual play *Till* stages this focus on monolingualism and its overcoming in experimental theatrical form. Set in a medieval German town in Lower Saxony, with the title character's name and characteristics alluding to the legendary German trickster figure Till Eulenspiegel, the nonrealist play loosely revolves around a visit by a small group of twentieth-century Japanese tourists.[12] Neither side is particularly surprised at the other's presence or linguistic, physical, and temporal difference as they go about their own business and interact with each other only minimally. Tawada's staging of different time periods as coexisting in this manner deliberately reverses and ironizes the Western gaze that situates its Others as existing in an earlier time, even as she takes up the stereotypical figure of the Japanese tourist in the West.[13] The bilingual play thus unfolds an ironic attitude towards both sides simultaneously, albeit differentially. Underscoring the radical difference between the two sides are their languages: the German characters speak only German, while the Japanese characters speak only Japanese, so that neither side understands the other.[14] There is one figure with bilingual competence, the female Japanese tour guide who is billed as *Dolmetscherin* (interpreter) and who does on occasion approximately render some of the German dialogue for the two tourists she is accompanying and with whom she carries on a general conversation in Japanese. Yet she herself never speaks in German and does not engage with the German figures directly. While the play is bilingual, its characters effectively are not.

The play thus brings two languages together, yet it does not "mix" them to produce a hybrid linguistic form, or even make them intelligible to each other. Its bilingual makeup emphasizes the difference and separateness of the figures, rather than any commonalities. Fully aligned with the characters' national backgrounds, the languages seem to imply an unbridgeable gap between German and Japanese sides. No "intercultural dialogue" takes place among the characters.[15] Rather than envisioning a dialogue, the form of the play's bilingualism denies the possibility of overcoming national, linguistic, and epochal difference, even if those differences do not give rise to any conflicts between the sides. This bilingual staging appears to reinforce the monolingual nature of nationalities.

The highly isolating monolingualism that Tawada produces in this play, however, also constitutes the means to break with monolingualism. The absence of a mediating language between the two sides is a deliberate choice on her part. In her stage directions, she emphasizes that any staging of the play should aim to make do without translations into the other language. She elaborates: "Through gestures, facial expressions, tone of language, or choreography a common world has to be created on the stage. For the audience members who understand only one of the two languages, part of the stage remains a secret, yet musical and visual access must be possible" (*Till* 44). Instead of translation between languages, she thus suggests translations into other, nonverbal, forms of expression, a process that linguist Roman Jakobson has termed "intersemiotic translation" or "transmutation" and distinguished from interlingual translation ("On Linguistic Aspects of Translation" 145). Translation thus does occur, just not necessarily between verbal languages. On the level of languages, Tawada consciously produces a degree of opacity. By conceiving of this opacity as a "secret" that might be approached through other channels of understanding and perception, though, she aims to cast it as an enticing mystery, rather than a form of exclusion and inaccessibility. The reported positive audience reactions to the stagings in Germany (Hanover, 1998) and Japan (Tokyo, Kyoto, Kobe, 1998), respectively, suggest that the play accomplished this goal.[16]

One of the Japanese characters in the play explicitly articulates the possible benefit of this linguistic opacity. Inondo, the male Japanese tourist, states that he wanted to travel to a place whose language he does not understand: "I thought I might get a different view for the world if I do not understand the language anymore" (*Till* 94). The inability to comprehend the surrounding language promises new perceptions and experiences. Rather than feeling excluded by this linguistic opacity, Tawada's figure seeks out this condition as productive. Travel to another place and language environment is thus not based on the desire to encounter new cultures and peoples and to communicate with them, but rather on the desire to experience the world anew. The "world" that this passage invokes is not the social "world," the world of different cultures and peoples, but rather the proximate material "world."[17] The most proximate material of this world, upon which Tawada's figures stumble time and again and which they thereby experience anew, is language. When one does not understand a language on the semantic level, one is forced to listen to sound and tone, when it is spoken, and wonder about the shape of the script, when it is written. In this manner, language ceases to be a purely communicative tool and takes on material quality.

Through the bilingual configuration of *Till*, Tawada raises the metalinguistic awareness of both her characters and her audience. This metalinguistic awareness, in turn, constitutes one of the hallmarks of bilingualism in general. Elizabeth Klosty Beaujour, one of the leading scholars of literary bilingualism, summarizes neurolinguistic studies that show how "bilingualism confers a continuing advantage for tasks involving metalinguistic awareness, or separating word sounds from word meaning, generating synonyms, being sensitive to communicative needs, and perceiving new sounds" (*Alien Tongues* 16).[18] Bilingual subjects, in other words, are continuously reminded of the contingent relationship between sound and meaning, signifier and signified. It is this denaturalizing sense of contingency that appears threatening to some monolinguals and leads them to consider bilingualism as pathological. Transposing the split between signifier and signified that the bilingual may expose onto the bilingual subject herself, such critics assert that "often bilinguals have split minds [. . .]. Bilingualism can lead to a split personality and, at worst, to schizophrenia" (Max Adler, quoted in Beaujour, *Alien*

Tongues 44).[19] In contrast to such depictions of bilingualism as a threat to mental health and the integrity of the subject, bilingual writers have used the metalinguistic awareness it brings as a poetic resource. Beaujour cites Jane Grayson's observations on Nabokov's style to this end:

> He sees patterns of sound and potential meanings in words which the [monoglot] native speaker, his perception dulled through familiarity, would simply pass over. He deviates more readily from set modes of expression and conventional registers of style, inventing new and arresting word combinations, employing high-flown, recherché vocabulary alongside the most mundane colloquialisms. (quoted in Beaujour, *Alien Tongues* 105; brackets added by Beaujour)[20]

Although Tawada's style differs from Nabokov's in many regards—from her preference for short, essayistic prose form and her more explicit thematization of bilingualism in her writing to her greater affinity to surrealism than to late modernism—she shares with him the tendency to find "patterns of sound and potential meanings" in unexpected places. Her narrators and her characters, such as those in *Till*, search precisely for a new perception that is not "dulled through familiarity" and find it in bilingual constellations where they do not, or do not want to, understand the other language. By withholding translations in the staging of the play, Tawada also seeks to achieve this effect, at least partially, for her audience. Rather than furthering their bilingual competence in two languages, she thus offers them the heightened metalinguistic awareness of bilinguals. For a moment, even monolinguals thus potentially gain a bilingual perspective on language. Drawing on avant-garde and modernist strategies of defamiliarization, Tawada adapts them in her globalized bilingual writing to destabilize monolingualism from within and from without.

YEARNING FOR THE FOREIGN: THE EXPATRIATE
BILINGUAL WRITER AND THE PROBLEM OF INCLUSION

In her play *Till* and in many other texts, Tawada identifies travel
as the first step out of the "mother tongue" and into new language environments that hold the promise of revealing new perspectives on the world.[21] This move situates her in a tradition of
writers who depart from both the nation and the monolingualism of the mother tongue. As Beaujour explains, citing one of the
most prominent twentieth-century examples:

> For Beckett, as for many others, the study of French, Ital-
> ian, and German, which allowed him to grow beyond the
> Procrustean limits of Fatherland and Mothertongue, was
> the first step in psychic liberation; and one could argue that
> he did not change languages because he had changed places
> but, rather, that he changed places in order to be able to
> change languages [. . .]. In France and in French, Beck-
> ett is not expected to belong completely. This is why he
> is more "at home" there—that is, nowhere. [. . .] [Beck-
> ett] leaves [English] behind and takes up the language of a
> tribe to which he does not belong. Having done this, being
> thoroughly detached, he can ultimately return to his first
> language without the original emotional servitude. (*Alien
> Tongues* 165, 170)

Like Beckett, Tawada views the move to a new language environment, undertaken individually and voluntarily, as liberating
and enabling. Again like Beckett, she does not seek to establish
the new language as a substitute mother tongue, but uses it as
a means of detachment from the restrictions and enclosures to
which the mother tongue gives rise. The additional language in
fact helps to undermine the mother tongue's claim to singularity
and exclusivity.

The common denominator that facilitates this liberatory view
of bilingualism lies in both authors' relationship to the monolingual paradigm. Both Beckett and Tawada start out as monolingual subjects in a structure that recognizes their relationship

to the "mother tongue" as an unquestioned given. In contrast to the situation of exclusion from the "mother tongue" and the monolingual paradigm, which, as I have shown, is constitutive for Kafka, these two authors are thus firmly *included* in the monolingual paradigm.[22] Their situation also differs from that of multilinguals, such as George Steiner or Feridun Zaimoğlu, who grow up with two or more languages from the beginning and thus never knew a purely monolingual state.[23] Beckett and Tawada's turn to another language is thus a response to the problematic of *inclusion* into the monolingual paradigm. As the earlier discussion of *Till* began to show, for Tawada this problematic is in fact central to her writing and to the literary strategies she employs. Whether staging it in her bilingual play or inscribing it into her prose, as discussed below, Tawada's identification of and attention to the problem of inclusion constitutes her most important contribution to the struggle of going beyond the mother tongue in the postmonolingual condition. It is a problematic that is rarely so emphatically raised by other writers or explicitly recognized by critics who instead generally focus either on forms of exclusion or stress multiple belongings.

While Tawada then shares much with her fellow expatriate bilingual writer Beckett, there are also significant differences. First, her two literary languages are much more radically different from each other than are his and they have relatively few readers in common. As we have seen, Tawada uses this situation—encapsulated in *Till* as the salutary possibility of incomprehension—as a central aspect of her poetics, a situation much less possible in Beckett. Second, unlike Beckett, Tawada does not move to one language for a period of time, before returning to the other. Rather, she develops her oeuvre in parallel, writing completely different texts—often in different genres—in both languages concurrently, as her publication history amply demonstrates. This accelerated move between the two languages is constitutive of her writing as it helps to maintain detachment from both languages and prevents settling into either one. Finally, as the next section elaborates, for Tawada the question of gender is a major component of the move outside the nation and the problems attendant to the mother tongue and the monolingual paradigm.

YEARNING FOR THE FOREIGN: JAPANESE WOMEN LEAVING MOTHER TONGUE AND FATHERLAND

While the character in Tawada's bilingual play *Till* who desires a new perspective on the world in a foreign language environment is a Japanese man, most of her traveling characters "yearning for a foreign language" (*Talisman* 14) are female. This yearning is in surprising proximity to an historically specific cultural and social phenomenon that is closely intertwined with globalization, gender, and language. The "yearning" expressed in Tawada's writing echoes a "desire" for "the foreign" that motivated numerous middle-class Japanese women in the 1980s and 1990s to leave Japan in order to study, live, and work abroad in the United States and Europe—something that anthropologist Karen Kelsky has identified as a distinct, highly gendered phenomenon, since the number of women in this pursuit grew demonstrably in that period and dwarfed that of men leaving Japan by far (*Women on the Verge* 6).[24] Kelsky's study reveals that the central motivation behind this phenomenon was not simply practical but also tied up with what the women consistently articulated as "desire" and "longing" (*akogare*) for a different female existence: "the turn to the foreign has become perhaps the most important means currently at women's disposal to resist gendered expectations of the female life course in Japan" (*Women on the Verge* 2). Leaving the national realm behind is thus entwined with imagining a different gendered existence. The possibility of this existence is projected onto the foreign, specifically onto the "West," whose modernity and ideals of universalism many of the subjects in Kelsky's study assert and contrast to a "backward and benighted Japan" (*Women on the Verge* 3–4, 6–7). They relate this "backwardness" principally to the arena of gender relations. Resistance to hierarchical gender relations thus takes the path of alliance with the "West" as a powerful phantasmatic structure.[25] The desired result is not just the relocation of female subjects outside the national realm but a reconfiguration of gendered subjectivity based on a new affiliation: "women's narratives of internationalism advocate the absorption of the West into the female self, yielding a 'new self' (*atarashii jibun*) that represents a detachment of women's subjectivity from the Japanese nation-state" (*Women on the Verge* 3). Subjectivity is thus identified as a site where belonging to nation and gender are potentially reconfigured in new ways through a process of detachment.

Language has played an important role in this phenomenon, as many women left Japan for foreign language study, and many others worked as "interpreters, translators, bicultural and bilingual consultants [. . .] and other facilitators of Japan's business, media, and cultural relations with the world" (Kelsky, *Women on the Verge* 3). That is, language was not just an incidental aspect of this phenomenon but its means and often its justification. Exposure to a foreign language is hence part and parcel of the process of producing a desired new female subjectivity, even as the situation is ironically aided by the fact that many of these professions are traditionally regarded as feminine.

Awareness of this phenomenon provides a new perspective on Tawada and her writing that has so far been overlooked in scholarship.[26] Having left Japan for Europe in 1982, her biography situates her as part of the early wave of this phenomenon, though her choice of Germany is unusual.[27] More importantly, her texts record the move away from Japan time and again. The vast majority of her texts feature single Japanese or East Asian women in Europe, detached from any collectives, and instead engaged in close considerations of language and translation. Her early poem "Absturz und Wiedergeburt" (Crash and Rebirth, 1987), for instance, surreally describes a female Japanese interpreter's departure from the realm of the mother tongue in a plane as life-threatening and catastrophic (leading to a plane crash) but survivable (she awakens in a postapocalyptic landscape in which a new story awaits her). Likewise, the protagonist in the short novel *Das Bad* (The Bath, 1989) is a young Japanese woman who initially works as an interpreter and loses her tongue during a meeting with Japanese businessmen and their German business partners. In other texts, the female Japanese protagonists are travelers, tourists, or displaced individuals, who explore their immediate surroundings, frequently with an eye toward gendered structures.

While these thematic elements put Tawada in proximity to the discourse that Kelsky describes, other aspects of her writing set it apart from that discourse. Part of the idealized image of the "West" in this discourse is the view of white Western men as less sexist and more likely to embrace an equitable relationship between the sexes. Kelsky argues that the "liberatory potential of the West," as these women define it, "is intertwined with desire for the white man as fetish object of modernity" (*Women on the Verge* 4). In contrast, Tawada's frequent and unflattering depiction of the more or less subtle violence of German men in their interactions with East Asian women—as in her novel *Das nackte Auge* (The Naked Eye, 2004), in which a German man kidnaps a Vietnamese woman and holds her hostage—debunks the notion of a more enlightened, less sexist Western masculinity.[28] This divergence in part stems from the fact that Tawada's writings are simultaneously in dialogue with multiple discourses and (national) preoccupations. *Das Bad*, for instance, takes aim both at Japanese men's misogyny in business settings and at European men's sexist Orientalism in personal relationships. Written in Japanese, but published solely in translation in Germany, the novel engages with these two different discourses at the same time. This simultaneity constitutes an important dimension of the transnationalism of Tawada's writing. Specifically, it constitutes an instance of the practice that theorist Naoki Sakai terms "heterolingual address," referring to a mode of writing with divergent audiences in mind (*Translation and Subjectivity*). The recognition that a mere switch from the Japanese to a "Western" social and linguistic structure is not sufficient for liberated subjectivity explains Tawada's critical stance towards inclusion, whether it be into the "mother tongue" or into any new substitute language. Her German-language prose texts, the focus of the remainder of this chapter, demonstrate this critical, "heterolingual," attitude and its bilingual means.

FROM A BILINGUAL PERSPECTIVE: REREADING MOTHER TONGUE

How does a bilingual and transnational reading of the problem of gender, nation, and inclusion, which seems partially to emerge from the Japanese context, take shape in Tawada's German-language texts? Frequently set in the German everyday in which the female Japanese narrators observe the new environment as incipient bilinguals, these texts use a bilingual perspective to bring to light gendered structures in the German language in order to denaturalize them. Neither Germany nor the German language are thus per se solutions to problems first encountered in the Japanese context, but rather provide one further site and language in which to engage these problems and pursue the literary project of going beyond the mother tongue.

The opening text from Tawada's most successful German volume to date, the 1996 collection *Talisman*, exemplifies this inscription of a bilingual perception into a seemingly monolingual text and the surprising recodings it makes possible. In the short prose piece "Von der Muttersprache zur Sprachmutter" (From the Mother Tongue to the Language Mother), the female Japanese narrator recounts her observations during her first year in Germany, primarily focusing on the small environment of the office. Her impressions circle around linguistic experiences and the discovery that her relationship to the objects around her is mediated by language. While there is no real difference between a pencil in a Japanese or a German office, the narrator states that the new name—*Bleistift* instead of *enpitsu*—made it appear different at first. More significantly, she reflects on the fact that her German colleagues speak differently to and of these objects, such as one coworker who gets mad at her pencil constantly breaking and refers to it as "the stupid pencil." In one of the subtle indications that the text, seemingly fully grounded in a quotidian reality and a recognizable world of references, conjures something beyond this familiarity, the narrator casts this anthropomorphizing act as a form of "German animism" ("Sprachmutter" 10). With fine irony, Tawada thus turns the description of the sober office environment into the fieldwork setting of a reverse linguistic ethnography. Identifying the attitude towards the pencil with an anthropological term usually applied to so-called primitive peoples imbues the seemingly rational workplace with hidden magic belief. This ethnographic lens, enabled by a bilingual perspective, functions to destabilize the familiar linguistic behavior by reinterpreting it in a new, unexpected framework. Similar reinterpretations occur throughout the brief text, with the titular "mother tongue" a particular focus.

The bilingual gaze of the "Sprachmutter" text leads to the narrator's observations about gender in the German language. It is the explicit comparison with and the contrast to the Japanese language—about which the narrator says that "all words are without gender"—that provokes the reflection on the presence of gender in German ("Sprachmutter" 11). That is, the focus on gender in German grammar comes out of an explicitly invoked bilingual gaze. Noting that language textbooks state that "to a mother tongue speaker grammatical gender appears as a natural part of a word" (11), the narrator tries to mimic this naturalization of gender in an exaggerated act of literalization.[29] She attempts to envision all objects on her desk as somehow masculine by nature if they carry the masculine article *der*: "The small realm on the desk gradually became sexualized: [*der*] pencil, [*der*] ballpoint pen, [*der*] fountain pen—the male beings lay there in a masculine way and stood up in a masculine way when I took them in my hand" (12).[30] This new gaze humorously reveals a world of writing that is thoroughly masculine in its very means, thus subtly commenting on a constellation in which the very tools a female writer has at her fingertips are already gendered.

In this text as in many others throughout her writing, Tawada focuses on the ways in which gender is inscribed into language and thereby becomes naturalized. The referentiality of gender in language is a complex one, of course, as literary theorist Barbara Johnson reminds us: "in all languages that are structured by grammatical gender, gender both is and is not referential. [. . .] Gender is thus somewhat arbitrary in all languages (who would have thought that 'girls' were neuter in German?), but that arbitrariness may nevertheless have an unconsciously internalized referential effect" (*Mother Tongues* 23).[31] By parodically literalizing gendered structures in language, Tawada thus lays bare the "unconsciously internalized referential effect" of grammar. It is Tawada's bilingual gaze that brings these unconscious dimensions to the surface, thereby enabling a first step toward their denaturalization for those considered native speakers.

In this context it is significant that the language that is being destabilized in the "Muttersprache" text is not so much the Japanese language, the presumed first language of the narrator. The text rather uncovers unconscious effects encoded in the German language. Yet it would be even more accurate to say that most significantly the text targets the very concept of "mother tongue." While referring to the surface level of German in this specific case, the titular "mother tongue" in fact primarily figures as a naturalizer of linguistic structures and relations, as when that narrator reads that "to a mother tongue speaker grammatical gender appears as a natural part of a word." By not defining "mother tongue" as a particular language, and particularly not as her own native language, Tawada's bilingualism addresses a larger structural issue and opens up room for flexible interventions. The "mother tongue" is thus not just something to intervene against in the Japanese context, but also in the German context. In both interventions, Tawada's writing is directed against inclusion into the monolingual paradigm and the mother tongue structure.

Much of the power of the concept of the mother tongue lies in the singularity and exclusivity ascribed to it, based on the notion that the *mother* is unique and irreplaceable. As suggested throughout this book, the notion of a "mother tongue" can productively be understood as a "linguistic family romance" because it produces a fantasy about the natural, bodily origin of one's first language and its inalienable familiarity that is said to establish kinship and belonging. The insistent singularity also strongly discounts any possible new affiliation. In an age that does not just witness globalization but also new reproductive technologies and new social arrangements ("Heather has two mommies") that throw age-old certainties into question, the singularity of motherhood is no longer guaranteed, however. The shift away from "Muttersprache" towards something called "Sprachmutter" in Tawada's title in fact turns to technology to undermine the primacy of origin and authenticity in thinking about linguistic affiliations. Using the bilingually inspired literalizing gaze on grammatical gender, her narrator interpellates a typewriter as a new "mother":

> There was also a female being on the desk: a typewriter [*eine Schreibmaschine*]. She had a big, broad, tattooed body, on which all letters of the alphabet were visible. When I sat down in front of her, I had the feeling that she offered me a language. Her offer did not change the fact that German is not my mother tongue, but instead I received a new language mother.
>
> This female machine which gave me the gift of language I called a language mother. I could only write the signs which she already carried in and on herself, that is, writing for me meant nothing but repeating her, but that way I could be adopted by the new language. (12–13)

The feminine gender of "typewriter" in German—*die* Schreibmaschine—functions as the enabling starting point for an ironically reconfigured linguistic family romance in which all elements are in play. This alternative family romance has language come from a source that is a machine imagined as organic body. The body is interpellated as feminine yet does not follow conventions of femininity in its "big, broad, and tattooed" shape. Instead of uniqueness, the machine-body offers endless repetition and mechanical reproducibility of language. "Adoption" finally suggests a mode of kinship that is not underwritten by blood relation. This alternative linguistic family romance does not replace the mother tongue or reconstitute it ("it did not change the fact that German is not my mother tongue"), but functions as a supplement to it.

The crossing of technology and organic body, of mechanical reproduction and social adoption that Tawada suggests in this passage as well as in many others in her writing is remarkably close to ideas developed in feminist approaches to technoscience, most prominently by Donna Haraway. As Shannon Winnubst, commenting on Haraway, writes: "Virtually all boundaries are crossed here—human/nonhuman, organic/inorganic, biological/chemical, chemical/mechanical and, yes, alive/undead, male/female, white/black, straight/queer" ("Vampires, Anxieties, and Dreams" 13). Winnubst continues: "Leaving behind the natural/unnatural dichotomy, and all of the (sexual, racial, religious, national) violences it has brought upon us, can we not at last engage kinship, as Haraway encourages, as 'a technology for producing the material and semiotic *effect* of natural relationship, of shared kind' (1997, 53; italics added)? Can we not at last rethink relation as a set of open-ended affections, affinities, and possibilities, rather than a predetermined, closed set of (often incompatible) organic bonds?" The bilingually enabled alternative linguistic family romance of "language mother" aims to do just that.

Tawada's version of the quest for rethinking relation as neither purely organic, nor purely mechanical repeatedly centers on a rereading of "mother" in her texts. In *"Sieben Geschichten der sieben Mütter"* (Seven Stories of the Seven Mothers), also in the volume *Talisman*, none of the "mothers" refers to a biological mother. Instead, the series of vignettes takes up compound words that contain the word *Mutter*, using it in a metaphoric or indirect way. *Stiefmutter* (stepmother), *Gebärmutter* (uterus; literally: birthing mother), *Doktormutter* (female doctoral advisor; literally: doctoral mother), *Perlmutter* (mother-of-pearl), *Muttermal* (birth mark; literally: mother's mark), *Muttererde* (mother earth), *Mutterseelenallein* (utterly alone; literally: mother soul alone). While this collection of "mothers" already expands the concept, each of the vignettes also rewrites conventional notions

of motherhood and mothering by referencing writing and subject constitution in unexpected ways. *Gebärmutter* (uterus), for
instance, is the name the narrator gives to the room in which she
writes ("Sieben Geschichten" 101). These systematically decon-
textualized and then newly recontextualized readings of *Mutter*
derive from a play with compound words that treat their elements
as material for mechanical reassemblages. Such play and reassem-
bly is enabled by a language mother who does not in fact insist on
monolingual boundaries but allows for different constellations of
letters in any alphabetic system.

Tawada extends the implications of this alternative linguistic
family romance to the new childhood it enables: "When one has
a new language mother, one can experience a second childhood"
("Sprachmutter" 13). With this notion, Tawada supplements the
more prevalent trope that the mother tongue and childhood are
inextricably tied to each other and forever fixed in the past. The
eminent German Romance scholar Harald Weinrich, who was
instrumental in establishing the high profile Chamisso prize for
non-Germans writing in German—which Tawada received in
1996—for instance, reproduces the old trope: "We must first acknowledge that Chamisso authors live with the permanent handicap (unlike native writers) of having passed their childhood and
youth in a milieu that speaks a different language. Consequently,
they lack a certain depth of experience in their German that people used to try to capture with the word *temper*" ("Chamisso"
1340; emphasis in original).[32] Weinrich, who also asserts the organic nature of the native language, "which, as we often say,
'is absorbed with one's mother's milk,'" casts a writer's additional languages only in terms of disability ("permanent handicap") based on this "lacking" childhood ("Chamisso" 1339).
Tawada departs both from the organic nature of such thinking
and from the concept of childhood it produces. As the narrator
in the "Sprachmutter" text continues: "In childhood, one per-
ceives language literally. That way, every word takes on its own
life and makes itself independent of its meaning in the sentence"
("Sprachmutter" 13). Rather than associating childhood with be-

longing and embeddedness in a familial and social history, she presents it as a developmental period in perception. The literalism on which the text is built is now legible as a result of mimicking this childlike perception. In this way, the "second childhood" is yet another means of independence and detachment and not one of double belonging and the assertion of roots and memories in two languages. This notion of childhood does not carry any memories, but sees the world—or at least language—as if for the first time. What is a "permanent handicap" for critics like Weinrich, still thinking in the categories of the monolingual paradigm, is an opportunity for a writer like Tawada to seek to go beyond it. To this end, Tawada puts the promise of bilingual perception—as staged in *Till*—in proximity to a childlike perception and rediscovery of the world.

Yet while the typewriter, interpellated as the "language mother," occupies a privileged position through its titular appearance, it is another office item—namely, the staple remover, "der Heftklammerentferner"—that abandons the family romance as such: "Its wonderful name embodied my yearning for a foreign language" ("Sprachmutter" 14). The staple remover lies outside the chiasmus of the title "From the mother tongue [*Muttersprache*] to the language mother [*Sprachmutter*]"; it detaches what the chiasmus still holds together—namely, kinship figured through both the mother language and the language mother. This utensil, not able to write or erase, is fully detached from the act of writing itself. It is "Analphabet" (14; illiterate) and does not function to reproduce language or writing. In contrast to the other objects on the desk, the narrator also does not imagine this item as male or female in a human sense. Rather, she compares it to a snake's head with teeth, thus also reversing the move from the organic to the inorganic that the "mother tongue—typewriter" sequence exemplifies (14). This object and its name are no longer viewed through a literalizing gendered lens. With that, the object breaks the chain of human reproduction and even alternative modes of kinship based on technologically enabled affiliation. It becomes the ultimate means of detachment and liberation:

> In the mother tongue words are attached to people so that one cannot playfully enjoy language. There, thoughts cling so closely to words that neither the former nor the latter can fly freely. In a foreign language, however, one has something like a staple remover: it removes all the things that are attached to each other and cling to one another. (15)

Against the naturalizing restrictions of the mother tongue, the foreign language offers a new space for creativity and freedom. Drawing on the terminology of earlier chapters, Tawada's bilingualism becomes legible as facilitating language depropriation while shunning appropriation of a second or even of a first language. This depropriation is strongly motivated by a desire to bring the deep structures of gendering inscribed into any language to the fore in order to disable them and make room for alternate visions of being and perception.

BILINGUALISM AND NEW "FRAMEWORKS" OF GLOBALIZATION

If the question of language and gender begins in a national framework, its unfolding takes Tawada on a transnational path towards the creation and elaboration of an unusual "linguascape." In the process, Tawada's playful, depropriating engagement with language yields a unique perspective on multilingualism, globalization, and subjectivity. In her essay "Schreiben im Netz der Sprachen" (Writing in the Web of Languages), Tawada describes globalization thus:

> Nowadays one frequently sees words and images from different worlds juxtaposed [*nebeneinanderstehen*]. Through migration, world travels, or Internet surfing, people often find themselves in a situation where the juxtaposition [*Nebeneinander*] already exists but a corresponding frame of mind has not yet been developed. Sometimes I ride the bus through a city and am surrounded by several conversations in several languages. Two sentences where one right after the other penetrates my ears by chance don't yet occupy a

common space. You need a frame story [*Rahmenhandlung*]
to connect these sentences. ("Writing in the Web" 152–53,
trans. modified).

To explore linguistic configurations in a globalizing context,
Tawada focuses on the everyday of the urban metropolitan space
and identifies it as inhabited by multiple languages. These languages appear as distinct and set apart (*nebeneinander*), and do
not immediately point to hybridity and code-switching, one of
the most prevalent multilingual practices of everyday life. Yet
Tawada takes the side-by-side coexistence of languages only as a
starting point for developing new ways of thinking and for imagining new framing narratives (*Rahmenhandlung*). What is not
obvious in this passage is the fact that it contains in highly condensed form Tawada's response to the very question about con-
ceptualizing language and globalization that she raises. It is hidden in the "frame story" or *Rahmenhandlung* that she calls for:

> Eine Sorte Nudelsuppe heißt [auf Japanisch] zum Beispiel
> genau wie das deutsche Wort "Rahmen." Ein Laden, in dem
> man diese Nudeln kaufen kann, könnte "Rahmenhandlung"
> heißen. Die beiden Wörter haben natürlich historisch nichts
> miteinander zu tun. Deshalb wird ein solches Phänomen
> nicht ernst genommen und als Zufall abgetan. ("Schreiben
> im Netz" 41)

> [A kind of noodle soup, for example, is called [in Japa-
> nese] like the German word *Rahmen* [frame]. A shop in
> which one can buy these noodles could be called a *Rah-
> menhandlung*, a "ramen noodle shop" [although the word
> normally refers either to a "frame narrative" or a "picture
> frame shop"]. These two words have of course nothing to
> do with each other historically. Therefore such a phenome-
> non is not taken seriously and dismissed as coincidence. (my
> translation)][33]

By introducing the Japanese word *ramen* as a homophone of the
German *Rahmen*, the German word suddenly takes on new, surprising, and somewhat lighthearted meaning. Tawada achieves

this effect not by rewriting or adding anything obvious to the word. Instead, she *rereads* the word, or better still, she suggests listening to it differently—namely, bilingually. The German homonyms (*Handlung* as action, as plot, and as shop) are also mobilized in the same moment and add to the destabilization of the meaning one assumed to be clear in the first instance. As exemplified here, Tawada's bilingual reading practice intervenes in a subtle, unobtrusive, often humorous manner, not by altering words and languages themselves but rather by altering the *perception* of words and languages, as the play *Till* already suggested would be crucial, and the "Sprachmutter" text presented as affectively akin to experiencing a "second childhood." This new perception is not limited to one language alone but listens for new meanings and words both within and across languages.

Through such attention to the surface level of language—its sounds or shapes—Tawada reveals alternative moments of connection between two languages that are not related historically, genealogically, or even geographically, but come together accidentally as a result of globalization. Her traveling bilingual gaze focuses on finding such moments of linguistic contact hiding in plain sight throughout her writing. Thus she meditates on Else Lasker-Schüler's poem "Mein blaues Klavier" (My Blue Piano) through the letter sequence *la vie* in *Klavier* ("Zu Else Lasker-Schüler" 45). These frequent rereadings invite her audience to discover such unexpected connections for themselves. Her own name, for instance, can be reread via Turkish, as *yok o* (he/she/it is not there) *tavada* (in the frying pan), as I noticed belatedly.[34] These phenomena do not accumulate in an overt way, but remain primarily performative interventions that serve to release words and, with them, perception patterns from reified monolingual boundaries.

The "frame story" Tawada calls for as a means of connecting chance juxtapositions of words and images, then, turns out to be itself a medium of connection. While the purely phonetic dimension links the words to each other, the referential dimension of *Rahmen* as frame indicates that the homophone, which this passage highlights, is both an enclosure and an opening. As a picture frame, it focuses the gaze, while as a doorframe or a window frame, it opens unto other spaces.[35] Globalization, in Tawada's version, is then the meeting of unexpected points, of chance encounters, and new, fleeting, associations that require new, non-monolingual stories in order to make sense of them.

Such accidental correspondences of words from disparate languages stand against connections based on history, genealogy, or meaning. In contrast to a "historical way of thinking" about language on the model of etymology, a "new chain of words offers possibilities for associations that have a lot to do with the present and in which the elements from different cultures and realms come together in a surprising way" ("Writing in the Web" 151). This rejection of the historical, genealogical, and etymological is programmatic both for Tawada's conception of globalization and for her attempt to overcome the monolingual paradigm and its naturalizing, genealogical kinship metaphor of "mother tongue."

DREAMING IN AFRIKAANS: BILINGUAL HOMONYMS AND NEW TRANSNATIONAL PATHS

But where could such playful readings, devoid of genealogy and history or even proper "intercultural" contact, ultimately lead? A 2002 story from Tawada's German-language collection *Überseezungen*—a pun on the words *Übersetzung* (translation), *Übersee-Zungen* (overseas tongues), and *Über Seezungen* (about the fish sole) that unfolds on the basis of homonyms and homophones—provides one possible and unexpected answer. In the long prose piece "Bioskoop der Nacht" (Bioscope of the Night), which is the only text in the section titled "Südafrikanische Zungen" (South African tongues), bilingual homonyms move the narrator beyond a Japanese-German context to South Africa and lead to the exploration of repressed collective histories. Besides leaving behind the East-West axis that dominates Tawada's literary topography through the 1990s, the new and further globalized North-South and East-South constellation of *Überseezungen* also begins to address more explicitly the inscription of race, in addition to the heretofore primary preoccupation with gender.[36]

In a series of vignettes, "Bioskoop der Nacht" shifts between dream sequences, on the one hand, and the first-person narrator's attempts to find an answer to the question in which language she dreams, on the other. This question, we learn, is imposed on the narrator—a Japanese woman living in Germany—by complete strangers. The questioners seem to assume that the unconscious and involuntary articulations of dreams have an identifiable, national language. Demonstrating the effect of the monolingual paradigm, even the unconscious can only have one proper language in this view.[37]

Instead of overtly rejecting such a nationalization of dream-language, Tawada offers a parodically affirmative response in "Bioskoop." Yes, the protagonist's dreams are identifiable, the story says, but not as Japanese or German. Rather, they are partially decipherable as Afrikaans ("Bioskoop" 65). The suggestion that the Japanese-German protagonist may dream in Afrikaans challenges an ethno-cultural conception of linguistic belonging and the imposition of identities from the outside. In contrast to conventional reinscriptions of bounded identities and the continuing correspondence between language, ethnicity, and culture, Tawada breaks that homology.

Tawada's use of the dream form in this context is no doubt on the one hand parodic. It ridicules the essentialist logic of the ubiquitous question about the language of bilingual subjects' dreams.[38] On the other hand, however, taking up the dream as a form points to something more complicated about affiliation and belonging. Tawada does not dismiss the idea that dreams are productive sites of investigation. In contrast to the assumption that the dream will transparently reveal something about the dreamer, however, the story reminds us that dreams are overdetermined. As we recall from Freud, dreams mobilize multiple mechanisms of displacement and condensation. They also transform turns of speech and tropes—from all available languages—into scenes and narratives, and thus offer another model for much of Tawada's writing, which develops through literalized formulations of metaphorical language. These mechanisms help to explain what to make of the unexpected shift to Afrikaans.

The story establishes the link to Afrikaans through bilingual homonyms. "Bioskoop" itself is a near homonym that refers on the one hand to an early cinematographic apparatus (*Bioskop* in German), and on the other is simply the Afrikaans word for movie theater.[39] "Bioskop der Nacht" thus can be read as "cinema of the night," a technologically infused metaphor for dreams. The story itself fittingly begins with a surreal sequence that is only retrospectively revealed as a dream. In that dream, the "I" encounters a man who refers to himself as "die Mann" and explains "ich arbeite in einem Winkel" (I work in a corner), before pointing to the sky and calling it "lecker" ("Bioskoop" 61; yummy). In a later part of the story, in the course of party small talk, a Dutch psychoanalyst finally explains to the protagonist that her dreams take place in Afrikaans, since a number of these words are homonyms. *Winkel*, for instance, means "shop" in Afrikaans, while *lecker* means pleasant, so that the sky can indeed be *lecker*. These homonyms are hinges that transport the story from one language to another though they, like the *Rahmenhandlung*, at first mask this quality.

In "Bioskoop," these homonyms lead the narrator to journey to South Africa to begin learning the language, in order to translate her own dreams (76). That is, the homonyms transport the story not just from one language to another but also from one territory to another. This spatial move is significant, since it does not take the protagonist to an untainted third alternative to Germany and Japan, but rather to a language that is associated with the racist program of apartheid, which literally means "separation."

But why Afrikaans? This dream-language, which the protagonist claims not to know, corresponds neither to her nationality nor to her adopted home, but rather follows its own logic of displacement. As the initial dream sequence suggests, the imperceptible move to Afrikaans is possible because of the combination of homonymic identity and semantic difference between

German and Afrikaans, via the intermediate step of Dutch, the language from which Afrikaans developed. In asking herself how she ended up dreaming in Afrikaans, the narrator in fact recalls a scene in Amsterdam in which she wakes up to the sounds of a conversation outside her window, which she can almost understand, if it weren't for the way in which the words are *geheimnisvoll verschoben* (mysteriously moved or displaced). Historically, the difference between German and Dutch, which shared a common origin, is the result of a separate development following a vowel shift, in German *Lautverschiebung* (literally, "sound displacement"). *Verschiebung*, however, is also the word Freud uses in German for the mechanism of "displacement" in a dream. *Verschiebung*, then, refers separately to a linguistic and a psychic process, both of which move through contiguity. Tawada mobilizes these diverse processes in her own literary path, using both the new directions enabled by dis-placement and facing up to the entanglements created in this chain of associations by contiguity.

Afrikaans as a third term displaces the German-Japanese binary in which the narrator finds herself trapped in Germany. Yet because of the inextricable association of the South African language with colonialism and racism, this displacement does not lead to an untainted alternative. In his study of South African literature, Mark Sanders writes about the language: "Whereas modern Afrikaans emerged in the late nineteenth century with the emergence of a united Afrikaner volk in the struggle against British imperialism, when the schoolchildren of Soweto rose up against the imposition of Afrikaans as medium of instruction in 1976, Afrikaans, not English was regarded as the language of mental colonization" (*Complicities* 150). Afrikaans thus began as an "anti-imperialist" language, before becoming the very symbol for and means of racist oppression.

In Tawada's story, displacement offers an occasion to reflect on the legacy of apartheid. It prompts the narrator, for example, to recall high school discussions on Japan's relationship to the apartheid regime and its implication in it ("Bioskoop" 68). The narrator's journey to postapartheid South Africa further highlights the aftermath of racist policies, as in a visit to an impoverished township (77–80). The question of how Japanese people would have figured in the racial categorizations of apartheid preoccupies the protagonist repeatedly. Would she have been one of the "Blankes," the Whites (68, 74–75)? Because of the economic ties between the countries, the text correctly acknowledges, Japanese were indeed considered white (68, 75). The South African apartheid government designated them officially as "honorary whites." This designation resulted from the fact that Japan was South Africa's primary trading partner (Ivy, *Discourses of the Vanishing* 7). Neither the financial transactions between the countries, nor the linguistic traffic are thus innocent indicators of globalization. Guided by the "dream language," the protagonist not only engages with apartheid but also with its language, Afrikaans, rather than rejecting the language and turning to the languages of the regime's victims. Linguistic playfulness, the impetus for these moves, thus does not mean that a multilingual form is naïve or purely celebratory. Instead it reveals that complicity might be one of the forms of contact on a global scale.

The text offers its resolution in a new form: the making of a contingent collective of language learners. In contrast to the staging of isolated individuals, such as the protagonist in "Sprachmutter," who merely mentions a textbook and self-study, the protagonist of "Bioskoop" becomes part of a collective language learning experience. This collective, significantly, comes alive when speaking about the traumatic legacy of unredeemed injustice. The uncanny presence of violence is inscribed even into the textbook of the Afrikaans language course in Cape Town. In the form of a ghost story, the text incorporates a narrative that deals with the demands of the dead and of justice. The interpolated story tells of the ghost of a murdered girl whose corpse periodically appears by the side of the road until the police finally resolve her murder some one hundred years after the deed. The story's closure comes with the act of locating the bones of the murder victim at the site where she reappeared ("Bioskoop" 88–89). In contrast to the transnational moves that the framing text otherwise stages, this recounted story insists on marking the exact place of a violent death and a reconstruction of the events that led to it, since, as Dominick LaCapra elaborates in another context, "losses would have to be specified or named for mourning as a social process to be possible" ("Trauma, Absence, Loss" 716).

Though the textbook story itself ends with a resolution, the murdered girl nevertheless makes her way to the classroom: "The murdered girl sat in our classroom, she interfered, although she did not belong to the class. [. . .] The girl wanted to tell us her story, her encounter with her murderer" ("Bioskoop" 89–90). The girl's presence affects the language that the students produce in trying to respond: "Whenever the girl opened her mouth, everyone spoke incorrectly. [. . .] We were confused and hastily formed sentences that were crooked, full of gaps, and jumbled" (90). Yet these sentences are rewarding since they are part of a conversation, rather than an empty exercise: "It was satisfying. Because a correct sentence was usually banal" (90). In the students' response and in the structure of the "Bioskoop" story, the uncanny quality of the inserted story is replaced by a form of satisfaction in which Afrikaans sentences come out crooked—that is, marked by an ongoing, paradoxically lively conversation with the dead. This satisfaction comes also at a point where the narrator is able to say "we."

With this contingent collective, Tawada approaches the ideal that Naoki Sakai describes as a "nonaggregate community": "In a nonaggregate community, therefore, we are together and can address ourselves as 'we' because we are distant from one another and because our togetherness is not grounded on any common homogeneity." In such a community, "the heterolingual address is the rule" (Sakai, *Translation and Subjectivity* 7). A language class as a model for a community means a model in which the constitution of the group is accidental, temporary, and goal-specific. The individuals come together and then leave again, after language learning.

By persistently rereading words through the lens of other languages, Tawada offers a form of multilingualism that affects the monolingual paradigm from within. Through homophones and homonyms, Tawada points to structures that look alike but are not, and that look like one word but are not. Multiplicity and multilingualism are thus not necessarily visible, yet they constitute our world. In this way, Tawada's writing offers a multilingualism that does not just reproduce the preexisting boundaries of cultures, ethnicities, and nationalities, but imagines subjects as intricately, if invisibly tied to other places, languages, and histories. In contrast to the assumptions of the questioners in the beginning of "Bioskoop," a Japanese woman in Germany may dream in Afrikaans. That final example, however, also indicates that the turn to the multilingual is not a simple, harmless act, but harbors new insights about the self that might force a rethinking of the subject, its communities, and its modes of belonging.

What the focus on language learning also indicates, is this: If in the phenomenon of Japanese women's internationalism that Kelsky describes language learning was a central motivation and means of leaving behind the mother tongue and its national territory, then we notice here that Tawada is reenacting the same move in "Bioskoop." Her protagonist leaves Europe to go to South Africa in order to learn a language, just as many Japanese women left Japan for the West for language learning. Yet while Japanese women's internationalism was a means to escape restrictive gender norms, Tawada's protagonist seeks to escape imposed ethno-cultural, national, and racialized forms of identity. That is, her transnational move in this case is a means to resist the pressures of identifying herself unambiguously as Japanese in response to questions about her affiliation and "dream language" posed in the German context. The reenactment of the linguistic and transnational move indicates that the problem that initiated the original move—namely, the imposition of an identity and of social expectations arising from it—continues, albeit now more as a problem of race, ethnicity, and national identity, rather than solely gender. The reenactment also indicates that Tawada continues to privilege a move outside national contexts as a solution to this problem. However, while the strategy remains the same, new locations and new contingencies have to be found, as the previous ones—the unusual conjunction of Japanese and German—eventually produce their own pressures of determinate identification. In order to maintain the critical edge and imaginative space opened up by contingency, Tawada finds herself seeking out ever new transnational links and expanding into new linguistic, cultural, and geographical territories.[40] The postmonolingual condition, in other words, is not resolved by a one-time move beyond the mother tongue, but requires constant reinvention and questioning of the underlying concepts of language and identity. It requires constant exit strategies.

CHAPTER FOUR

Surviving the Mother Tongue

Literal Translation and Trauma
in Emine Sevgi Özdamar

LITERAL TRANSLATION

In 1990, Turkish-German writer Emine Sevgi Özdamar published her first book, *Mutterzunge*. To a German-language reader
encountering it for the first time, this title word is at once familiar and unfamiliar. Both parts, *Mutter* (mother) and *Zunge*
(tongue), are clearly German, as is the principle of linking two
nouns to create a new word. Yet this neologism departs from
the idiomatic expression *Muttersprache* (mother tongue, literally
"mother language") and thus inscribes difference into the word.
As the title story of the same name instantly signals, Özdamar's
Mutterzunge is to be read as a literal translation from another
language, where, like in English, "tongue" means "language."[1]
Through the coordinates presented in that story, that other language is identifiable as Turkish, even if it is not initially named.
Many other phrases in the book confirm and follow this pattern:
"Tongue has no bones" (Zunge hat keine Knochen), for instance,
translates *dilin kemiği yok*, an expression that means speaking
without thinking about the effects first; "I sat with my *twisted
tongue* in this city Berlin" (*Mutterzunge* 7; emphasis added; Ich

saß mit meiner gedrehten Zunge in dieser Stadt Berlin) invokes the Turkish phrase *çevrilmiş dil*, meaning "translated tongue."[2] Writing in literal translation, then, Özdamar presents a form of multilingualism that is both visible and invisible in the text.[3]

This chapter pursues literal translation as a postmonolingual writing strategy, gesturing towards and unfolding in the tension between monolingual paradigm and multilingual practice. The term "literal translation" is widely used in the field of translation, describing a mode of translation that stays (too) close to the wording of the original, privileging individual words over other aspects of the text, such as overall meaning, function, or rhythm (Bassnett, *Translation Studies*). Yet in contrast to literal translation as a mode employed by a translator, passages directly written as "literal translation" do not rely on the existence of an original text, but rather on a reader's recognition of linguistic forms as stemming from elsewhere. Such recognition, in turn, is only possible, if the phrases in question are familiar—a situation that only applies to linguistic forms fully established in a language. That situation in turn applies not to idiosyncratic and unique formulations but to repeated figures of speech, idiomatic expressions, and well-known proverbs—in other words, to the archive of ready-made phrases that constitutes the scaffold of every language. But just as familiarity with the invoked language is a key dimension of "literal translation," so is difference, for the new words in which these idioms are rendered make them seem strange—both to monolingual and to bilingual readers. In literal translation, the familiar undergoes an alienation effect.

The languages which Özdamar puts in a relationship of familiarity/unfamiliarity through her form of literal translation occupy a particular relationship to each other in the linguascape of postwar Europe. As a result of mass migration following the 1961 labor recruitment agreement, workers from Turkey brought the language to Germany.[4] Today, Turkish is the second-most-spoken home language in the country. Turkish-Germans, meanwhile, have come to be considered the country's primary Other. Constellating Turkish and German thus has a very different resonance in the German context than pairing Japanese and German, as Tawada does. Besides different associations with the languages and the relatively low prestige of Turkish as an immigrant language, the sociolinguistic constellation also means that there are more potential bilingual readers for Özdamar's writing, mostly but not exclusively Turkish-Germans themselves.[5]

Özdamar has been part of this Turkish-German history from early on, albeit in different guises. One of the most critically acclaimed German-language writers of Turkish descent, she is the recipient of important literary prizes and the subject of extensive scholarship.[6] She initially came to Germany as an eighteen-year old guest worker in 1965, in order to earn money for acting school in Istanbul. At the time of her first arrival, she did not know any German; she only actively acquired it during a second stay as a language student. After moving back and forth between the two countries and also spending some time in France, she finally settled in Germany in the late 1970s. There she worked as a theater and film actress, a playwright and theater director, before establishing herself as a major literary voice in the 1990s. Indicative of the representative status she at times holds in Germany, Özdamar was invited to read from her works at the 2002 opening of the new German chancellor's building in Berlin, along with Christa Wolf and Günter Grass, the prime representatives of postwar "East" and "West" German literature, respectively.[7]

To date, Özdamar has published three novels, two prose collections, a number of plays, and numerous short essays in German. Most of her prose writing, in contrast to her plays, has an autobiographical basis. Her three novels consecutively tell the story of a young girl growing up in Turkey in the 1950s (*Das Leben ist eine Karawanserei hat zwei Türen aus einer kam ich rein aus der anderen ging ich raus*, [1992]; translated as *Life Is a Caravanserai Has Two Doors I Came in One I Went out the Other* [2000]), and follow her migration to Germany and her frequent travel between Turkey, Germany, and other countries (*Die Brücke vom Goldenen Horn* [1999]; translated as *The Bridge of the Golden Horn* [2007]), and finally chronicle her stay in both

East and West Berlin in the tumultuous late 1970s while working in the Brechtian tradition at the *Volksbühne* theater (*Seltsame
Sterne starren zur Erde* [Strange Stars Stare to Earth, 2003]).
Many of the themes of the novels also reappear in various forms
in her two collections *Mutterzunge* (1990); translated as *Mother
Tongue* (1990) and *Der Hof im Spiegel* (The Courtyard in the
Mirror, 2001). In 2007, Özdamar published her first book written in Turkish, *Kendi kendinin terzisi bir kambur* (The Hunch-
back as His Own Tailor), thus also becoming a "bilingual writer"
in the sense elaborated in the previous chapter.[8] Based on this
oeuvre, Özdamar is widely read as an author of migration, be it
internal migration in Turkey (*Caravanserai*) or transnational migration to Germany (*Bridge*).[9]

Many critics have commented on Özdamar's technique of literal translation, which is a feature of all of her German-language
publications, although it is most pronounced in her earlier work,
gradually receding in the later books. It has been interpreted as
a mode of preserving and presenting authentic Turkish culture
(Aytaç; Kuruyazıcı), as encapsulating an alternative and affirmative Turkish memory culture capable of countering official history (Seyhan), as enriching German culture (Wierschke), as an
exploration of the foreignness of Germany (Şölçün), as a mode of
intercultural dialogue (Mecklenburg), or as an aesthetic experi-
ment (Brandt). As this list indicates, critics differ even in the evaluation of the linguistic and national orientation of this technique:
Is it a form that expresses something about Turkish culture and
the Turkish national context? Or should this technique be read
as relating primarily to experiences in Germany? Or, alternately,
could it be read outside such national ascriptions? In the present
chapter, I propose to read her employment of this multilingual
form as a means of working through traumatic (trans)national
histories.[10] In Özdamar, I show, literal translation plays a crucial
role in the affective negotiation of traumatic recall. It specifically
participates in the working through of the memory of political violence and its traumatic effect on the "mother tongue." My reading of Özdamar also stresses that a new language can be a site

of affect in a way that the "mother tongue" is not, and that the affective charges of one language can be recoded through the affective charge of another. As a result, Özdamar's literal translation transforms both Turkish and German simultaneously, albeit differentially.

The primary focus of this chapter is Özdamar's short but key text "Mutterzunge," along with relevant passages from her other works, principally *Das Leben ist eine Karawanserei*. The guiding motif of "Mutterzunge" is the loss of the "mothertongue." A female Turkish narrator situated in the divided city of Berlin asks herself repeatedly when it was that she lost her mother tongue. In response to her own question, she recalls seemingly disjointed scenes from the past that all figure as possible moments of loss. By analyzing particular instances of literal translation, which emerge in this text, both thematically and formally, I demonstrate the traces of trauma that inflect Özdamar's employment of literal translation. After identifying the particular political trauma that is at stake in "Mutterzunge," I turn to the concept of trauma itself to understand the affective work that the form of literal translation accomplishes. In the final part, I suggest how this affective reworking also functions to resituate the post-Holocaust German language as a site of relief. First, however, it is worth considering the resonance of literal translation in other contexts as well as zeroing in on the particular form that the monolingual paradigm takes in modern Turkish history.

LITERAL TRANSLATION: BETWEEN ACCOMMODATION AND RESISTANCE

Mother tongue, *Muttersprache, langue maternelle*: although these words have come to be read as signs of authenticity, origin, and uniqueness, their origin lies elsewhere—namely, in translation. They are literal translations of the Latin *lingua materna*, which initially referred to the vernaculars over against the learned language Latin.[11] "Mother tongue" is thus, ironically, always already a translated concept. Where *Muttersprache* and

Mutterzunge diverge from each other is in the status of the resulting word. The former has long been integrated into the language
as a "loan translation," its translational origin entirely forgot-
ten. The latter, on the other hand, loudly announces its difference. This in/visibility of translation is the dividing line between
"loan translation"—a widespread form of expanding the lexicon
of any language—and "literal translation"—a potential poetic
resource precisely because of its marked eccentricity. Only where
it functions as a form of multilingualizing estrangement rather
than monolingualizing support for an evolving standard may literal translation function to challenge the monolingual paradigm.

Writing in literal translation also differs from writing with
words of foreign derivation, the subject of chapter 2. In contrast to
Fremdwörter, literal translations are not readily available, if hos-
tilely treated words, but rather coinages of the author usually not
encountered before. As a critically postmonolingual writing strategy, writing with *Fremdwörter* relies on words that have moved
"from abroad" in the past, whereas in writing literal translation,
the expressions are fresh new arrivals in the present. They therefore startle, rather than call up long-held resentments or desires.

The multilingualizing estrangement of literal translation has
been a much-discussed literary strategy especially in postcolonial
contexts. Since the 1960s, postcolonial writers such as Gabriel
Okara have advocated for literal translation as a resistant strategy by writing in the colonizer's language while literally translating from the colonized one. For Okara, this form is a means of
expressing "African ideas, African philosophy, and African folklore and imagery to the fullest extent possible" ("African Speech"
476).[12] Critic Waïl Hassan refers to this mode of writing as
"translational" and likewise underscores its potential as a technique that can serve to "Arabize, Africanize, Indianize" the colonial language ("Agency and Translational Literature" 754). West
African literature specialist Chantal Zabus describes the same
phenomenon as "relexification" and defines it as "the making of a
new register of communication out of an alien lexicon" (*The African Palimpsest* 112). To be part of "larger strategies of cultural

decolonization," such a strategy has to be intentionally accompanied by "the glottopolitical will to do violence to the dominant language," Zabus asserts (113, 133). All these forms follow an appropriative model in response to linguistic dispossession.

Özdamar herself has invited a postcolonial reading of German literature of Turkish migration by suggesting that the situation of *Gastarbeiter* (guest workers) was a form of belated internal colonialism.[13] However, although her literary employment of literal translation shares much with postcolonial models, and although Turkish has low prestige in Germany due to its status as an immigrant language, such a hierarchization does not account for her own textual strategies or the histories she tells through this form, as we will see. Her acts of literal translation are not set against German as an imposed language, but against violence in the "mother tongue" itself. That mother tongue, in turn, is a result of monolingualizing strategies of the nation state.

THE MONOLINGUAL PARADIGM IN THE TURKISH NATION-STATE

In one of the most quoted passages from Özdamar's work, the female narrator of "Mutterzunge," situated in East Berlin and pondering the loss of her "mothertongue," resolves to learn Arabic as one possible path to retrieve the lost language, Turkish:

> Ich werde Arabisch lernen, das war mal unsere Schrift, nach unserem Befreiungskrieg, 1927, verbietet Atatürk die arabische Schrift und die lateinischen Buchstaben kamen, mein Großvater konnte nur arabische Schrift, ich konnte nur lateinisches Alphabet, das heißt, wenn mein Großvater und ich stumm wären und uns nur mit Schrift was erzählen könnten, könnten wir uns keine Geschichten erzählen. Vielleicht erst zu Großvater zurück, dann kann ich den Weg zu meiner Mutter und Mutterzunge finden. (12)

> [I will learn Arabic, that was once our script, after our liberation war, 1927, Atatürk forbids the Arabic script and the

Latin letters came, my grandfather knew only Arabic script,
I knew only Latin alphabet, that is, if my grandfather and I
were mute and could only tell each other something through
script, we could not tell each other any stories. Maybe first
back to grandfather, and then I can find the way to my
mother and mothertongue.][14]

This rich passage, with its gendered account of language, writing,
and memory, introduces Turkish national history into the text
and through an imagined scene in the family sphere dramatizes
the implications of this radical linguistic break for the nation.[15]
In a way typical for Özdamar, it overlays official history and private storytelling.[16] In order to understand the particularity of this
overlay, it is useful to revisit the history of linguistic interventions
by the Turkish state to which Özdamar draws attention here.

Founded in 1923, the Turkish Republic, the successor state
to the multilingual, multiethnic Ottoman Empire, remade itself as a nation-state in the European mold. For the architects
of the new nation, this move entailed embracing and enforcing
a monolingual structure. During Ottoman times, the language
of the elites and the bureaucracy was Ottoman Turkish, a hybrid
language incorporating a large amount of vocabulary and even
syntax and morphology from Arabic and Persian, which differed
significantly from the Turkish spoken by the mass of the Anatolian population—those who later made up much of Turkish citi-
zenry—and was not readily intelligible to the latter. The Ottoman state did not impose this language onto its subjects and was
in fact relatively indifferent to the languages spoken by its people,
in this regard somewhat resembling the Austro-Hungarian Empire. The Ottoman Empire, then, was multilingual in terms of the
numerous languages spoken by the different peoples it ruled, and
diglossic in terms of the distinction between (Ottoman) Turkish state language and Turkish popular language.[17] The state language, finally, was itself a multilingual hybrid. The new Turkish nation-state sought to replace such multilingualism, diglossia,
and hybridity all at once, in its place creating a purely monolingual situation, as it declared the unity of language a necessary

condition for the unity of the country. To this end, the state spent enormous energy on the creation of the national language.

Although Turkish was put at the center of imagining the nation, the preceding bifurcation between Ottoman Turkish and folk Turkish meant that the national language had to be developed anew. In that way, Turkish nation-building follows the classic model of "invented traditions." The new language was produced in acts of linguistic invention, mostly undertaken by bureaucrats and others allied with the state, including in acts of literal translation.[18] Yet this invention was presented as mere language purism, allegedly returning to a purer *Öztürkçe* ("originary" Turkish). In addition to the change in writing system from Arabic to Latin script, the Türk Dil Kurumu (Turkish Language Institute), an official body founded in 1932, began the process of removing Arabic and Persian loanwords from the language in a highly successful undertaking of linguistic engineering. The underlying language purism targeted primarily these two languages, while accepting French loanwords, underscoring how closely linguistic politics was tied to the larger political goal of "Westernization" and "De-Orientalization." This process continued to alter the language from above in radical ways until the mid-1980s, when it slowed down, but did not fully stop. Because of it, today's standard Turkish is largely a state invention that did not exist in its current form even just a few generations back. The difference in vocabulary is so significant, in fact, that the original speeches of Turkey's founder, Mustafa Kemal Atatürk, from the 1910s, '20s, and '30s are no longer intelligible to today's speakers. Officials repeatedly "updated" them—that is, they translated them into current language usage in order to make them accessible for new generations, particularly schoolchildren. A parallel situation in the United States context would mean that current Americans could not understand any speeches by Theodore Roosevelt or Woodrow Wilson without translation.

The effect of this radical engineering, which did not leave any area of the language untouched—inventing, for instance, entirely new names for the months of the year[19]—is a cut that makes the written archive of a nation inaccessible to its subsequent citizens. Parts of cultural memory are deliberately cut off and oblivion deliberately produced. Although the hypothetical scene with the mute grandfather that Özdamar invokes is somewhat fanciful, she articulates this disruption as one that runs through the family, through the generations. Yet in Özdamar, the family is both a privileged space and a disjunctive one vis-à-vis the state. There is no uncomplicated, harmonious, unified family from where to oppose the state.

MOTHERS, MOTHER TONGUES, AND THE STATE

In many of Özdamar's texts, the female protagonist's own mother—like her "mother tongue"—is not a site of unproblematic origin and belonging. A key scene in her first novel *Das Leben ist eine Karawanserei* illustrates this point particularly well and is worth dwelling on. Upon returning from an extended stay with relatives in an Anatolian small town, the young female protagonist of *Karawanserei* begins to pronounce the word "mother" (*anne* in Standard Turkish) in dialect. Her own mother rejects this version of the word: "My mother said: 'Don't talk like that: you have to speak Istanbul-Turkish again, clean Turkish, you understand, in two days school is starting again. [. . .] Say Annecigim [my dear mother]! Not Anacuğum [my dear ma].' [. . .] The two words fought in the middle of the room" (*Karawanserei* 53). This passage undermines the conventional linguistic family romance of the "mother tongue" as language emanating naturally and in unmediated fashion from the mother. As the invocation of the school indicates, this "mother tongue" is closely linked to the nation and its claims on the formation of its citizens—a process of formation that reaches into intimate familial relations. In this passage, the mother acts to enforce a version of the "mother tongue" that adheres to the standard imposed by nation-state institutions. Although she does so finally in tears and with the best of protective intentions (*Karawanserei* 53; "In school they will put life on you like a tight shoe. I cry for you."), it is she who most vigorously polices her daughter's speech.

Through the mother, Özdamar reveals women's, and in particular mothers', potential implication in the reproduction of the dominant linguistic and political structure. The relationship between women and nation is, of course, a complicated one. On the one hand, women can be utilized as the embodiment of the nation and as keepers of tradition. On the other hand, they can be viewed as outside male domains of domination, and therefore imbued with the potential for subversive resistance to hierarchy. Özdamar represents these different relationships of women towards the state in generationally differentiated forms. In the above scene, a third figure, the grandmother, joins the fight between the mother and daughter and takes clear sides by declaring: "'Istanbul words don't leave any sweet taste on the tongue, the words are like sick branches, they break one after another.' My mother said: 'Don't you hear how she says Anacuğum?' Grandmother said: 'Yes, she says Anagi,' which is 'mother' in her village dialect from Cappadocia. Her Anagi, my Anacuğum stood next to each other across from the Istanbul Anneciğim" (*Karawanserei* 53). In this constellation, the mother becomes the prime ally of the state while the (paternal) grandmother stands out as a subversive counter force. Both the grandmother in *Karawanserei* and other illiterate or rural mothers in Özdamar's books (such as the protesting mothers in "Mutterzunge" [8] and in *Brücke*) try to resist state power, while the narrators' own mothers often try to fit in.[20] This generational alignment has a particular political connotation. The urban mother belongs to the first generation to have grown up in the Republic and to share Kemalist dreams and values such as secularism and modernization.[21] The grandmother, on the other hand, represents traditional folk wisdom. She is not aligned with the Ottoman Empire or any state, however, but with strands of anarchic Anatolian popular culture. The daughter, as the youngest generation, time and again allies herself with the spirit of folk resistance embodied by the grandmother.

With two different vernaculars (Anacuğum/Anagi) asserting themselves against the standard, Özdamar underscores the pluralism of the nonstandard and the heterogeneity of the vernacular. To put this in Bakhtinian terms, the conflict staged by Özdamar is that between the dispersion of heteroglossia, on the one hand, and the strictures of unitary language imposed by official institutions (the state, schools, grammars, dictionaries) on the other. Yet, like the state language, the vernacular is acquired in a socially mediated process—in this case travel to the peripheries of the nation—rather than being naturally present. The "mother tongue" is in either case not a private, authentic site of belonging, but rather is contested affectively, as well as institutionally, between state-sanctioned language and multiple vernaculars.

VIOLENCE AND THE MOTHER TONGUE

Most scholars to date have presumed that the loss of the mother tongue that Özdamar's narrator in "Mutterzunge" laments is related to, if not actually caused by, migration.[22] Kader Konuk asserts: "The 'Mother Tongue' got lost in migration" (*Identitäten im Prozeß* 88). Regula Müller lists the "loss of the mother tongue" as part of the "consequences of migration" ("Ich war Mädchen" 134). Seyhan sees a similar cause: "After her long sojourn in Germany, [the narrator] feels that when she thinks of her 'mother sentences' spoken by her mother in her mother tongue, they sound like a foreign language she has mastered well" (*Writing* 118). Isolde Neubert speaks of "culture shock"—again implicitly related to migration—as leading to "speechlessness" ("Searching for Intercultural Communication" 158). Other scholars, who do not directly comment on the reasons for the loss, still emphasize migration to Germany as the pivotal reference point for understanding Özdamar's translational form (Şölçün, "Gespielte Naivität"; Horrocks, *Turkish Culture*). In most of these cases, migration is primarily understood as a cultural experience or a cultural challenge. A closer look at the text, however, reveals that the presumption linking the loss with migration and the realm of cultural difference does not quite capture the text's treatment of loss.

Before offering an alternative reading, it is useful to consider why migration has been so frequently seen as the ready and obvious answer to the narrator's question. This is in part due to the text itself. Immediately after locating herself in a Berlin café, the narrator recalls two fragments of conversations with her mother. In both of these her mother tells her that she has physically changed in Germany: "My mother then said: 'You have left half of your hair in Alamania' [. . .] I also asked her why Istanbul had become so dark, she said: 'Istanbul always had these lights, your eyes have gotten used to Alamania lights.'" (7).[23] It is the mother who sees the daughter's loss of hair and her changed visual perception as having been caused by her migration to Germany. While she does not explicitly dispute this interpretation, the narrator nevertheless continues her search, thereby indicating that this answer is not yet satisfactory. Assumptions about the link between migration and loss are thus formulated in the text itself, but as conjectures of the mother that the daughter does not share.

The structure of "Mutterzunge" also provides a clue that this is not a straightforward story of migration from Turkey to Germany and its effects on the language of the migrant protagonist. The text consists of two parallel series of vignettes. One series of vignettes is set in the narrative present, in divided Berlin, and frames the overall text. In this framing, the text ends with the narrator resolving to learn Arabic in order to recover more than the three words in the "mothertongue" that surface in the course of "Mutterzunge."[24] In the subsequent, much longer text "Grossvaterzunge," that resolution leads to a more clearly discernible story line, involving an unhappy love affair with the Arabic teacher. The second series of vignettes in "Mutterzunge" records remembered scenes such as brief exchanges, snapshot-like images, and surreal dream sequences.[25] The vignettes move from scenes in Turkey to scenes in Germany and back to scenes in Turkey. Arrival in Germany is by no means the endpoint of the story, but rather represents a stop along the way, albeit a central one. Thus, while migration to Germany is an important reference point, both thematically and poetically, the moments prior to that migration are structurally much more prominent in the text than is generally acknowledged by current scholarship. These moments also relate in a distinct manner to the loss of language, yet they do not do so on the grounds of culture or identity, but of politics.

The "Turkish" vignettes of "Mutterzunge" primarily recall the impact of political violence. Despite the concluding moment of "Mutterzunge," which explicitly invokes the politics of the early Turkish Republic regarding language and writing, in the vignettes relating to Turkey, Özdamar returns to a different period and issue: she turns time and again to the subject of the political persecution of young leftists during the 1970s. Following a period of broadening democratic participation partially enabled by the left-leaning military coup of 1960, the 1970s in Turkey, as elsewhere in the world, saw an intense politicization and an increased polarization of society. The right-wing military coup of 1971, which attempted to limit civil rights and the spread of socialist ideas, was followed by increased repression and violent crackdowns on leftists. Throughout the 1970s, leftist youth in particular were the target of both arrests and abuses by the state and of brutal attacks and killings by state-sanctioned fascist death squads.[26] Much of the second part of *The Bridge of the Golden Horn*, Özdamar's second novel, describes this historical moment and generational experience in great detail, while the same history also provides the backdrop to her third novel, *Seltsame Sterne starren zur Erde* (Strange Stars Stare to Earth).[27]

In "Mutterzunge," the first extended memory vignette suggests a very precise moment in Turkish political history. The narrator remembers a mother's story about losing her son to anti-leftist political persecution. Although Özdamar renders the remembered monologue of the mother in very personal terms, focusing on the mother's experience of the police searching her house and of her son being sentenced to death, one detail—death by hanging—

links this story to history. While many young leftists died in the early 1970s in different ways, only three were sentenced to death by hanging. The hanging in May 1972 of the iconic leftist student leader Deniz Gezmiş, along with two of his comrades, had a profound impact on Turkish politics of the 1970s and beyond.[28] Özdamar invokes this background by specifically mentioning the hanging, but otherwise remains within the domestic perspective of the illiterate mother who attempts to resist the police in vain.

The final recalled vignette in "Mutterzunge," rarely discussed in detail by critics, establishes the intricate relationship between political violence in the Turkish nation-state, language, and migration to Germany most explicitly. The vignette reads in its entirety:

> In den Polizeikorridor haben die auch den Bruder von Mahir gebracht, Mahir, der in den Zeitungen als Stadtbandit bekannt gemacht war. In den Tagen hatten sie Mahir mit Kugeln getötet. Mahirs Bruder saß da, als ob er in seinem Mund was Bitteres hatte und es nicht rausspucken konnte, er hatte ein sehr dünnes Hemd, ich hatte einen schwarzen Pulli mit Hochkragen. "Bruder, zieh es an." Mahirs Bruder sah mich an, als ob ich eine fremde Sprache spreche. Warum steh ich im halben Berlin? Geh diesen Jungen suchen? Es ist siebzehn Jahre her, man hat ihnen die Milch, die sie aus ihren Müttern getrunken haben, aus ihrer Nase rausgeholt. (11–12)

> [They have also brought the brother of Mahir into the police station hallway, Mahir, who was made known as a city bandit in the newspapers. In those days they had killed Mahir with bullets. Mahir's brother sat there as if he had something bitter in his mouth and could not spit it out, he had a very thin shirt, I had a black sweater with high collar. "Brother, put it on." Mahir's brother looked at me as if I speak a foreign language. Why do I stand in half Berlin? Go searching for this youth? It is seventeen years since they pulled the milk that they drank from their mothers out of their noses.]

This passage, too, contains implicit historical references. Given the publication date of 1990, the reference to "seventeen years" identifies the historical moment in question quite precisely: it is around 1972–73, in the aftermath of the second military coup. The insistently repeated name "Mahir" further recalls the well-known radical student leader Mahir Çayan, who was killed by police bullets in March 1972. Çayan explicitly emulated tactics of urban guerrillas, a stance pejoratively encapsulated in the word "city bandit" (*Stadtbandit*).[29] The focus on the nameless brother rather than on "Mahir" himself indicates, however, a perspective on this period that shifts once again to the familial. In this passage, the narrator recalls a scene of utter alienation in the hallway of a Turkish police station many years earlier, before abruptly moving to the text's present in divided Berlin. In the remembered scene, the alienation manifests itself in the failure of a caring gesture to soothe, or even to be communicated to, the nameless young man. This alienation deeply affects language: "Mahir's brother sat there as if he had something bitter in his mouth and could not spit it out." What seems to be stuck and become bitter in the young man's mouth is language, specifically Turkish, the language in which this scene presumably takes place. In the context of this scene, the bitterness is produced by state violence, political repression, and familial loss.

While "Mahir's brother" is unable to produce any language at all, the narrator's own language is affected differently. In a sentence that functions as a crucial pivot for the entire text, the narrator's language turns foreign: "Mahir's brother looked at me as if I speak a foreign language." (Mahirs Bruder sah mich an, als ob ich eine fremde Sprache spreche.) On one side of the pivot is the silent gaze of a young man situated in the past. On the other side, the narrator is suddenly situated in the present, and the status of her language is in question. The uncomprehending gaze of the past (*looked* at me [*sah* mich an]) provokes a radical temporal jump into the present (as if I *speak* a foreign language [als ob ich eine fremde Sprache *spreche*]). The sentence thus testifies both to a radical caesura and to its lingering linguistic effect. The second part of the sentence is remarkable as well. It offers a hypothetical (as if) and a metaphor (speaking a foreign language), yet what it says is in fact literally true for the narrator in the present. She does speak what Mahir's brother would have considered a foreign language—namely, German. The metaphor "speaking a foreign language" becomes literalized, so that the sentence pivots not simply from past to present but also from the figurative to the literal. This literalization of the act of speaking a foreign language is indeed enabled by migration, yet the crucial sentence indicates that the turn to the literal use of language is provoked not by culture shock, but rather by the unredeemed moment in the police station hallway.

The turn to the literal mode enables a new perspective, as well as the establishment of a new mode of recalling this trauma. Although the object of the narrator's quest seems to be changed for a moment from the "mothertongue" to the persecuted young leftists ("Why do I stand in half Berlin? Go searching for this youth?"), the odd sentence about young men and their mother's milk reconnects these two subjects by means of a literal translation: "It is seventeen years since they pulled the milk that they drank from their mothers out of their noses." (Es ist siebzehn Jahre her, man hat ihnen die Milch, die sie aus ihren Müttern getrunken haben, aus ihrer Nase rausgeholt).[30] This sentence plays on colloquial Turkish expressions that mean "making someone regret something they did, making someone pay for their transgression."[31] The sentence thus can be understood to mean "it has been seventeen years since these young men were made to suffer for their actions, that they had to pay a price for their beliefs." Yet through literal translation, the text not only recalls the fate of the young men who suffered thus, but also encompasses the mothers along with their milk and the bodily experiences of mouth and nose that the Turkish idioms conjure up.[32] In German, these elements produce an odd, and even an unsettling, image that invokes an incongruous torture scenario.[33] In this manner the translated form refers obliquely to the tortures to which many young leftists of that generation were subjected. In addition, it suggests the impact of the violence in the familial realm.

The operations of literal translation, though relying to a degree on an underlying Turkish matrix, also cast that language in a new light, as being both necessary and insufficient to the text. When spoken in Turkish, the idiomatic expression about the mothers' milk lacks the unsettling connotations it has in German. It gains this at once threatening *and* evocative quality only when defamiliarized in literal translation. An actual retranslation into Turkish erases the poetic and critical edge of the text. The initially unenthusiastic reception of the Turkish translation of *Karawanserei* (as *Hayat bir Kervansaray* in 1993) seems to bear this out. Turkish Germanists have suggested that this was due to the fact that, retranslated into Turkish, Özdamar's literary language simply sounded colloquial, and thus lost its suggestive quality (see Aytaç; Kuruyazıcı). Gürsel Aytaç also relates the intriguing anecdote about the well-known Paris-based Turkish writer Nedim Gürsel, who was not impressed with Özdamar's first novel after reading it in Turkish, but had a completely different reaction after reading it in French translation (176). Literal translation, therefore, is not a means of simply recovering a lost mother tongue that would have been better able to articulate these experiences. Instead, the "loss" pertains to the mother tongue itself just as much as to the protagonist of the text. What the text testifies to—namely, a deep-seated defamiliarization and estrangement in the mother tongue—is expressed in "Mutterzunge" through simultaneous recourse to both Turkish *and* another language.[34]

The alienation and pain in this "Turkish scene" differ substantially from that recorded in the encounter with the cathedral in Cologne, one of the vignettes from the middle of the text that many critics have commented upon. In it, the narrator recalls a physical reaction to the moment when she opened one eye to the sight of the Kölner Dom from a train window: "in that moment I saw it, the cathedral looked at me, suddenly a razor blade came into my body and also ran inside, then there was no more pain, I opened my second eye also" (10–11). The razor in this surreal image has an anesthetic effect, as Bettina Brandt points out.[35] The pain recorded here thus does not last, but rather passes as the razor is incorporated. This scene in particular has been read as signifying the arrival of the migrant as she is confronted with one of the most iconic landmarks of Christian religious and German national identity. Yet the text does not end there, but rather moves back to Turkey and to the scene in the police hallway. This latter scene, in contrast to the one set in Cologne, ends in pain and necessitates a radical jolt from the past to the present. That "razor" is not incorporated; instead, a sudden temporal caesura cuts into the remembered scene. The cuts of state violence, and those of migration, differ from each other: the violence of the state continues to haunt as a loss, while a sharp new tool is gained in migration.

LITERALITY AND TRAUMA

While the previous section has considered the implicit reasons for the loss of the mother tongue, this is actually not the main question that the text itself pursues. The question that the narrator asks repeatedly is not *why* she has lost her mother tongue, but rather *when* this has happened: "If only I knew when I have lost my mothertongue" (7), "if only I knew in which moment I have lost my mothertongue" (9). Rather than being a minor difference, this explicitly temporal focus points to a core concern of the text. The recurrent search for a specific moment of loss and the concomitant turn to literal translation can be elucidated, I suggest, through trauma theory.

Following Cathy Caruth, one of the leading theorists in the field, trauma refers to the impact of an injurious event that is too unexpected and overwhelming to be experienced at the moment it occurs and is therefore not fully integrated by the subject. Because of its unassimilated nature, it returns, albeit with some delay, repeatedly and insistently. What characterizes this traumatic recall above all—and distinguishes it from memory—is the "literal return of the event against the will of the one it inhabits" (Caruth 5). Rather than actually remembering the event and being able to reflect on it, the subject is revisited by the event in the form of flashbacks. Caruth emphasizes that "it is this literality and its insistent return which thus constitutes trauma and points towards its enigmatic core: the delay or incompletion in knowing, or even in seeing, an overwhelming occurrence that then remains, in its insistent return, absolutely true to the event." (5). Trauma is thus a mode of recall in which the exact return of the event coincides with amnesia: "the vivid and precise return of the event appears [. . .] to be accompanied by an *amnesia* for the past" (152; emphasis in original).

Read in that light, "Mutterzunge" therefore does not just recall "traumatic" events on the level of content—the death sentence of a young man, the murder of another, the unbearable loss felt by families—but is itself constituted by a traumatic structure: the paradoxical coexistence of literal recall and amnesia. The narrator recalls monologues, snapshots, and dreams in vivid detail, yet at the same time she insists that something is amiss in her memory. A newspaper headline, "Workers have spilled their own blood themselves," for instance, is recalled and even explained (9; "Strike was forbidden, workers cut their fingers, put their shirts under the blood drops, in the bloody shirts they wrapped their dry bread, sent it to the Turkish military"). But rather than comment or reflect on this bloody history, the narrator is preoccupied with the strangeness of her mode of recall. The headline appears like a "foreign script" (*Fremdschrift*), the moment of reading it seems "photographed," not experienced (9). Even though the scene thus returns to the narrator, it does so as something alien and unassimilated. The dimension that is missing from it and is staged as affected by amnesia is the very experience of that moment itself. "Mutterzunge," in other words, does not simply tell the story of a lost language, or of state violence, or of migration, for that matter, but rather enacts the "delay or incompletion in knowing, or even seeing, an overwhelming occurrence." As Caruth further emphasizes, trauma "does not simply serve as record of the past but precisely registers the force of an experience that is not yet fully owned" (151). The text's repeated focus on the missing dimension of its memory functions therefore as its primary testimony. It testifies to the excessive, incomprehensible nature of the recalled events.

Trauma, however, is also tied to survival in multiple ways. Again, Caruth's elaboration is helpful: "for those who undergo trauma, it is not only the moment of the event, but of the passing out of it that is traumatic; [. . .] *survival itself*, in other words, *can be a crisis*" (9; emphases in original). The pivotal sentence in the police hallway scene stages this moment. The second part of the sentence that jolts the narrator into the present leaves out the moment of leaving the scene. That "passing out of" the scene remains only silently captured in the caesura, but not narrativized. What is missing is the remainder of the scene with Mahir's brother, whose fate—survival, death?—we do not learn. Missing moments are thus constitutive of trauma. The narrator's search for a lost moment, rather than for any underlying reason for loss, itself thereby points to the predicament of trauma. Yet the structure that constitutes trauma also contains the elements that "can make survival possible" (Caruth 10). This is the case because trauma is a "temporal delay that carries the individual beyond the shock of the first moment. The trauma is a repeated suffering of the event, but it is also a continual leaving of its site." It thereby testifies to a *"departure"* (10; emphasis in original). In its sudden jump from a time, place, and language of state violence to a much later state of migration, "Mutterzunge" testifies to this simultaneity of trauma and survival and, within that, to the particular means of its departure.

In Özdamar's text, literal translation enacts the link between trauma and survival, between acting out and working through, in the most condensed form.[36] Literal translation is in fact the means of working through. Because trauma is constituted by literal return—in other words, by a pure form of repetition—the ability to work through relies on distorting that literality—that is, on repetition with a difference. This difference can come in various forms. Caruth, considering the workings of testimony, mentions geographic and temporal dislocation, a new addressee made available through translation, a slight change in narrative.

Translation, with its potential of addressing a new audience in a new place and time, for instance, can enable "the passing out of the isolation imposed by the event" (Caruth 11). On the one hand, as the carriers of greatest—that is, "most literal"—literality, the passages rendering Turkish idiomatic expressions in German words record exactly the combination of literal recall and amnesia. In other words, they attest to a traumatic structure. On the other hand, translation into a new linguistic context necessarily dislocates the words and images from their usual signifying networks and produces entirely new associations, addressed to a new audience. Thus, no matter how literal the translation, literal translation is always about difference and about telling the "slightly different story" that the working-through of trauma requires (Pierre Janet, cit. in Caruth 154). As the sentence with the mother's milk has demonstrated, in translation the same idiomatic expression begins to tell a different, in this case much more ominous, story.

In the process of translation, what is recalled is both preserved and altered, not just in its meaning but also in its affective quality. This conjunction explains why Özdamar's writing, despite referencing traumatic histories, does not ultimately read like a lamentation. Instead, her language is evidently "playful," it displays "irony and humor" and has a "comical and absurd tone," as Sohelia Ghaussy correctly notes ("Das Vaterland verlassen" 6). A closer look at a passage from "Mutterzunge" demonstrates how the text produces divergent affects in its translational response to trauma. The first Turkish vignette, in which the narrator recalls the story of a "mother of a hanged man," once again registers more than just the story told. The woman describes how she felt after hearing about her son's death sentence: "we cried together, our hodja from streetmosque stood on his knees like half a man, cried, the ashtray, which was two fingers thick, jumped from the middle into two pieces on that day, I heard a 'shasht,' the ashtray lay straight in front of me" (8–9). The effect of the state's death sentence is to cause splits and breaks in the familiar environment. The *Hodscha* is likened to a *halber Mensch* (half a man), the ashtray is in two pieces. These splits, in turn, signify other splits. For the mother whose story it is, the ominous splitting apart of the ashtray, an everyday object, signifies the force of an emotional rupture due to her loss. For the narrator who is retelling this story in response to her own question about the loss of the "mothertongue," on the other hand, it is one of the possible moments in which her loss might have occurred. In both cases, the split relates to grief over state violence against leftist youth and the loss it caused in the familial realm.[37]

The more fundamental split to which the narrator ultimately draws attention, however, is the split between recall and amnesia, the characteristic structure of trauma that we already encountered earlier: "These sentences of a mother of one who was hanged I also only recall as if she had said the words in German" (9). With that, the passage as a whole is explicitly marked as translation. In this translation the split runs between two different linguistic units, the *sentences* of the mother and the *words* supplied by the narrator.[38] Although signifying a split, this separate attribution of sentence and word also serves to highlight a double perspective. While the mother's story expresses death and grief in its recalled sentences, the words used to recount it in German are highly original, creative, and lively. By speaking of an ashtray that "jumps" (*springt*), rather than as having a "crack" (*Sprung*) or, more accurately, as breaking into two pieces, the narrator enlivens the object, which now sounds more active: it jumps instead of merely cracking or breaking. Whereas the sentences of the mother tell a story of loss and grief, the words in the new language produce an enlivened environment full of suggestive movement. It is in these German words—that is, in the form of a nonnormative translation—that new affects are produced.

RECODING TRAUMA, RECODING GERMAN

The affective transformation that occurs *via* the German language on the textual micro-level in Özdamar's writing is accompanied by her reconsideration of discourses *on* the German language on a macro-level. Özdamar's critical perspective on Turkish and her mobilization of German as the language of "working-through" are both enabled by the manner in which she constructs the German language as a historical entity. Özdamar draws on the history of German in two interrelated moves. On the one hand, she references the discourse on the post-Holocaust German language that aims to come to terms with a tainted language, yet she transfers this problematic to Turkish. On the other hand, she constructs a genealogy of German that situates it as an oppositional language, rather than as an oppressive majority language.

Özdamar's focus on the conjunction between language and political violence recalls the debates around the German language after the Holocaust. This implicit invocation becomes apparent in key passages in her third novel *Seltsame Sterne starren zur Erde,* where she explicitly thematizes the effect of anti-leftist politics on the Turkish language. The protagonist, a Turkish theater actress who is unable to continue working under the military regime, explains to a Swiss friend in Istanbul why she is in despair:

> I am unhappy in my language. For years we only say sentences
> such as: they will hang them. Where were their heads? One
> doesn't know where their grave is. The police has not released
> their corpses! The words are sick. [. . .] How long does a word
> need in order to become healthy again? One says, people lose
> their mother tongue in foreign lands. Can you not also lose
> your mother tongue in your own country? (23)

For the narrator, the words are "sick" because of the things to which they must refer. Here the narrator explicitly suggests the possibility of a loss of the mother tongue that is not caused by migration, but rather by "one's own country." To escape this loss, the protagonist goes to Germany and begins working in the Volksbühne in East Berlin. Just as this chapter argues with regard to "Mutterzunge," migration in Özdamar's third novel does not constitute the cause of the loss, but rather represents a potential solution for it. Yet this description of the linguistic situation of the Turkish language in the 1970s in *Seltsame Sterne,* and more implicitly in "Mutterzunge," invokes discourses about the German language in the aftermath of Nazism and the Holocaust. As the "language of the perpetrators" (*Sprache der Täter*) German has had to carry "undeniable historical burdens" (*unabweisbar[e] historisch[e] Hypotheken*), as Stephan Braese put it (8). Paul Celan, for instance, for whom the language remained "unlost, yes, despite all" (*unverloren, ja, trotz allem*), nevertheless characterized it as "enriched" (*angereichert*) by—that is, unalterably marked by—the events and experiences of which it was a part, and grappled with this tainted medium throughout his writing ("Ansprache" 185–86). Though radically different both in the scale of the violence involved and in the extent to which the status of the language was affected, this specifically German discourse provides a language for a Turkish historical experience in Özdamar's translational writing. This discursive transfer might be best described as a "touching tale," rather than a simple equation of histories, to use Leslie Adelson's concept.[39]

Despite the invocation of this burdened historical dimension of German, the protagonist of *Seltsame Sterne* does not see that language as tainted and, instead, eagerly embraces it as an alternative idiom.[40] This positive view of the language is enabled by the genealogy of German that the book constructs throughout—beginning with its title, which is a quotation from an Else Lasker-Schüler poem. German is invoked as the language of Lasker-Schüler, Brecht, Heine, and Kafka—that is, as the language of canonical, yet minoritarian and/or oppositional figures.[41] This mode of constructing an alternative, minoritarian and, in particular, German-Jewish genealogy of German can be found in other contemporary minority writers as well. Walter Benjamin and Celan play a prominent role in Tawda's writing. Dilek Zaptçıoğlu's 1998 youth novel *Der Mond isst die Sterne auf* (The Moon Eats the Stars) features a discussion of Heine at a key moment in the story; Celan is an important reference point for Zafer Şenocak's poetry; and Hilde Domin for José F.A. Oliver's. Iranian-German novelist Navid Kermani offers a programmatic construction of this genealogy, with a strong emphasis on

Kafka, in his essay "Was ist deutsch an der deutschen Litera-tur?" (What Is German about German Literature?)[42] Through this genealogy, minority writers reclaim German for themselves. In this perspective, German is neither a tainted post-Holocaust language, nor is it the dominant majority language oppressing minority languages. It is also not a "colonial" language.

In "Mutterzunge," as in many of Özdamar's other texts, German is the language in which a traumatic story can be told, rather than being a traumatized or traumatizing language. The translational exchange between the two tongues creates a con-stellation in which German offers the means to remember and re-work a Turkish trauma—a trauma brought on by state violence, but brought to language in migration. Literal translation is thus a multilingual form that can affectively recode all involved lan-guages. The "mother tongue," in the end, is not lost due to the confrontation with another language—that is, due to increased multilingualism. It is instead marked by the impact of the mono-lingualizing state forces that created it, in violent and creative acts, in the first place. Not restoring the mother tongue is the task at hand, but surviving it. A postmonolingual writing strategy, holding together amnesia and recall, death and pleasure, finally reveals the violence inherent in the mother tongue and the mono-lingual paradigm, but also shows libratory ways to go beyond it.

In the altered linguascape that migration has created, Ger-man and Turkish have been mingling together for the last fifty years. While this chapter has focused on the relation between these two languages in the form of literal translation fashioned by Özdamar, a far more prevalent multilingual mode has been that of switching between and mixing of languages. This every-day practice has inspired writers of many multilingual constella-tions, most famously in the American context, Gloria Anzaldúa. Özdamar, too, has at times employed such code-switching.[43] The next chapter takes up an author who has turned a provocative mixing of codes into his principal aesthetic and postmonolingual strategy.

CHAPTER FIVE

Inventing a Motherless Tongue

Mixed Language and Masculinity in
Feridun Zaimoğlu

RACIALIZATION AND MOTHER TONGUE IN A POSTMIGRANT CONTEXT

What happens to the linkage between language and ethnicity in the postmonolingual condition—that is, in a situation of the re-emergence of multilingualism against the backdrop of the monolingual paradigm? The changed linguascapes of globalization in particular bring this question to the fore, as people and languages circulate along new paths and commingle in novel ways. Migrations produce multilingual communities and practices, but just as importantly, they quickly begin to produce speakers of languages that are not supposed to be "their own" by right of inheritance. Suddenly there are "Turks of German language," as one German publication from 1984 declares.[1] As this title, belonging to one of the first literary anthologies of the writings of young Turkish-Germans, indicates, the seeming disjuncture between "language" and "ethnicity" is intriguing for the German editors of the volume, but it is also a disjuncture that their formulation helps to keep in place. These "disjunctive" speakers, if one will, raise the very question of "nativity" in language.

Through their existence and visibility such speakers reveal that "one's 'mother' tongue is not necessarily the language of one's 'real' mother," as Etienne Balibar notes with regard to "second generation immigrants" (99). Although this point would appear to be a truism, the mother tongue metaphor has functioned to disavow precisely this discontinuity and, in its place, holds on to the fetishistic fiction of a natural birth into a language. In fact, the unsettling disjuncture between "language" and "ethnicity" that such speakers expose is often warded off by denying nativity to them while claiming it for others on the basis of perceived congruence between the categories. Instances of speakers being told "Du sprichst aber gut deutsch" (But your German is so good!), for example, signal a presumed nonnative relationship to the language. Such exclamations do not just foreclose the claims of other speakers to a rightful relationship to their language, however. Rather, these utterances instantiate, reassert, and safeguard the linkage between a language and an ethnicity in an everyday reproduction of the structure of the monolingual paradigm.

The speakers who come to live out this ambivalent structure today, the "second-generation immigrants," do not so much mark the phenomenon of migration as that of the *aftermath* of migration. Some cultural agents in Germany thus refer to them as "postmigrants."[2] What does migration, after all, mean to children and grandchildren who did not themselves move from one country to another yet continue to be conceived under the sign of this phenomenon rather than as fully belonging in the new home as fellow citizens? This situation appears specific to nation-states such as Germany that have not conceived of themselves as "countries of immigration" and therefore lack inclusive categories for all their residents and even citizens.[3] Yet the category "postmigrant" might be analytically useful in any context in which subjects and communities are considered under the sign of migration rather than arrival and settlement. The experience of Hispanics in the United States, for instance, shares many points of contact with that of Turkish-Germans, particularly in their—at times—contested relationship to their languages.[4] These commonalities have much to do with the essentialization of real or imagined linguistic difference in processes of racialization.

The position of the postmigrant reveals once again that the monolingual paradigm does not simply assert that a subject can only have one true language but also that this language has to correspond to particular ethnic properties. The link between language and ethnicity, in other words, is always shadowed by racialization. In that way, the postmigrant potentially occupies a position vis-à-vis the monolingual paradigm that has similarities with that of Kafka—that is, of a "monolingualism of the Other" (Derrida). Yet in contrast to the force of nationalism ruling Kafka's time and place, the postmigrants of a transnational age do not necessarily remain in such a monolingualism but rather may actively mix multiple languages.

Growing up with multiple languages from the beginning, rather than belatedly becoming bilingual—as Tawada and Özdamar did—young postmigrants tend to make creative use of these often socially unequally situated languages. In the process, they create new collective codes, such as the much-studied Rinkeby Swedish, the multilingual youth language drawing on Swedish, Turkish, Arabic, and other sources that emerged in the suburbs of Stockholm and spread to other urban settings in Sweden. Postmigrants' hybridized, novel ways of mixing linguistic material make the complex flows of the linguascape palpable, even as they are frequently castigated by the proponents of linguistic purism and monolingualism as aberrant, deficient, and inadequate speakers.[5] They live out the tension between reemergent multilingualism and the dominance of the monolingual paradigm as creative but not fully legitimized speakers of the languages they use; it is partly this avant-garde position that makes them so attractive for others who appropriate their practices for their own ends.

This chapter turns to an emblematic 1995 work that takes up these questions of ambivalent nativity, linguistic racialization, and creative mixing in a startling mode. Turkish-German author Feridun Zaimoğlu (b. 1964), who himself arrived in Germany as an infant and grew up bilingually in Turkish and German, almost single-handedly propelled young postmigrants' linguistic practices into the public sphere of post-unification Germany with his book *Kanak Sprak: 24 Mißtöne vom Rande der Gesellschaft* (Kanak Speak: 24 Discordant Notes from the Margins of Society).[6] The book started Zaimoğlu's rapid career as the best-known Turkish-German writer in Germany today.[7] Consisting of twenty-four first-person monologues attributed to young men of Turkish background in Germany, *Kanak Sprak* presents an array of provocative voices from the "margins of society," such as pimp, garbage collector, rapper, junkie, transsexual, and Islamist. Their monologues frequently provide polemical responses to dominant discourses rather than telling life stories suited to satisfying ethnographic or even biographical curiosity. The figures expound on their lives and their views of German society in a striking, often abject language that instantly drew public attention and made the book into a cult hit. In response to the author's question "How is life in your skin?" the figures speak scathingly but without self-pity about the stigmas they face and the racism they experience, as well as ruminating about the underlying problems they see in German majority society, from troubled human relationships, to a perceived lack of values such as mercy and compassion, to the traces of past racialization and the Holocaust. The problem of racialized masculinity, caught between hypermasculine self-staging and fear of castration, emerges time and again in this volume explicitly dedicated to male voices.[8]

Already with his title, which has since become a household term, Zaimoğlu signals the centrality of language and racialization and his book's means of responding to this problematic.[9] *Kanak* is a contraction of the racist slur *Kanake*, which has been primarily directed at migrants from Southern Europe and especially Turkish-Germans.[10] *Sprak* reads as a condensed form of *Sprache*—language. Where the 1984 volume *Türken deutscher Sprache* (Turks of German Language) staged the disjuncture of language and ethnicity in response to migration, Zaimoğlu's title a decade later inscribes racialization into language as a deformative force, but also signals the transformative potential of postmigration for any language. In contrast to the authors I have previously discussed in this book, Zaimoğlu thus relies more strongly on defiant appropriation as a response to linguistic dispossession, rather than on depropriation—the questioning of language as anyone's property—as a critical tool. The hyperbolic nature of this appropriation, however, provides hints that its excess may lead to a position of depropriation after all. This depropriative moment is underscored by the fact that in *Kanak Sprak* Zaimoğlu creates a distinct linguistic style that is not actually found on the streets, even as it mimics some characteristics of postmigrants' linguistic practices.[11] Consequently, *Kanak Sprak* can be described as a "synthetic vernacular," to use Modernism scholar Matthew Hart's helpful term. Like the synthetic vernaculars in Anglophone writing that Hart focuses on, *Kanak Sprak* conjoins the local and the global in its language, thereby inventing a new transnational code that is both rooted and not rooted, that affirms and challenges the link between language and ethnicity.[12] Reading the particular form of Zaimoğlu's stylized language, its strategies, inclusions, and exclusions, this chapter charts especially the book's engagement with racialization at the site of language as a difficult and contradictory one that does not fully escape the pressures of the monolingual paradigm. The most significant exclusion in this regard is the absence of Turkish in *Kanak Sprak*. In an attempt to resist the monolingual logic that would consider Turkish to be these figures' proper "mother tongue" and their "natural" property, Zaimoğlu excludes Turkish altogether from his inventive style.[13] Instead, he casts the *Kanak* vernacular as a result of male self-generation without sources elsewhere.

While the code-switching practices of postmigrants in Germany and elsewhere have come to the foreground, this most widespread form of reemergent multilingualism in the globalized everyday continues to confront monolingual judgments, which make it an object of derision as well as fascination. The tension between the monolingual and the new multilingual might in fact be greatest vis-à-vis code-switching. That this form of multilingualism comes from speakers frequently cast in racial terms indicates that the challenge goes beyond a linguistic one to the very realignment of race and ethnicity as clear-cut markers in a transnational age. As the following discussion of *Kanak Sprak* demonstrates, however, this negotiation of racialized language may come with a strongly gendered dimension as well. If, as suggested earlier, the continued force of the monolingual paradigm derives from the embedded linguistic family romance of the mother tongue—that is, from the conjunctive mobilization of gender, kinship, and affect—then a closer look at the realignment of this conjunction in imagined vernaculars of male postmigrant youth might be necessary for a critical assessment of postmonolingual gender politics.

CLAIMING GERMAN, DISJUNCTIVELY

In the early 1990s, in the aftermath of unification, widespread racist attacks took place across Germany against individuals and groups that appeared to be non-German. Besides open mob violence in Rostock against Roma and Vietnamese families (1992) and numerous firebombings of refugee shelters, the firebombing of homes of long-term Turkish-German residents in Mölln (1992) and Solingen (1993), in which women and children died, provoked mass protests against racist violence. This moment also coincided with the coming of age of Turkish-German postmigrants, the so-called second generation, who sought to intervene politically in this situation. They formed some of the new social movements that have come to be seen as characteristic of the early 1990s globally. These subjects represented themselves as actively oppositional to a society to which they nevertheless belonged. Their self-positioning differed from that of their parents, who often continued to consider themselves "guests" even after twenty or thirty years of living in Germany. Their children's claims to belonging, however, were constantly rebuffed by a majority society in the process of rethinking Germanness across the East-West divide.[14]

Kanak Sprak comes out of this moment and gives literary form to social assertion in the face of exclusion. It does so primarily by claiming the German language for its figures—and its author. With its linguistic focus, it recognizes the long-standing function of language as a boundary marker in the German context. In its language and attitude, *Kanak Sprak* articulates in particular the complex positioning of Turkish-German male youth, about whom different, gendered stereotypes circulate than about young Turkish-German women.[15] Turning the abjection ascribed to this racialized and gendered group into an aesthetic program, Zaimoğlu creates his linguistic style as a means of intervention.

Deliberately assembling figures from the "league of the damned" (84), Zaimoğlu engages directly with the linguistic and social abjection of young postmigrant men but does so in a way that inscribes them into German. As part of a strategy of defiant appropriation, *Kanak Sprak* embraces stereotypes about young male postmigrants—such as low social status, lack of formal education, sexism, criminality, and violence—rather than pointing to positive counterexamples to combat these negative associations. Through this hyperbolic embrace, Zaimoğlu seeks to provoke reflection on the emergence of these images. As he puts it in his second book, *Abschaum: Die wahre Geschichte von Ertan Ongun* (Scum: The True Story of Ertan Ongun) (1997), which chronicles the story of a drug addict and petty dealer: "We are the Kanaks you Germans have always warned about. Now we exist, precisely corresponding to your image and your fears" (183; Wir sind die Kanaken, vor denen ihr Deutschen immer gewarnt habt. Jetzt gibt es uns, ganz eurem Bild und euren Ängsten entsprechend). The appropriation of the racist term *Kanake* with its negative connotations also constitutes the point of departure for an attempted resignification.[16] Such a move is similar to acts of reclamation practiced by other marginalized groups. As Judith Butler notes about the term "queer," for example, "the apparently injurious effects of discourse become the painful resources by which a resignifying practice is wrought" (Butler, *Bodies That Matter* 224).[17] But while affirming the negativity associated with racist images of minority youth, Zaimoğlu eschews another component of the German stereotype of migrant youth: their alleged speechlessness. Zaimoğlu's figures may be pimps, garbage men, or drug dealers, but they are not mute or inarticulate. Their form of articulation instead highlights overwhelming linguistic inventiveness in German coupled with defiant analyses of their own lives and German society.

This language is a "synthetic vernacular" that nevertheless claims authenticity.[18] In his preface to *Kanak Sprak*, Zaimoğlu reports that he collected the voices of these figures in extended quasi-ethnographic research in the locales of the youth scene in his hometown, the northern German provincial capital Kiel.[19] He explains how he gained entry to this scene in popular bars and clubs, but also on the street and at a psychiatric unit through "guarantors" who assured their acquaintances that he was trustworthy. Rendering the material he collected in monologue form, Zaimoğlu further foregrounds the voice and individual presence of his figures in a theatrical linguistic performance. The short monologues that make up the book are based on his notes and tape recordings, according to the author. While this description underscores a strong claim to authenticity, Zaimoğlu also openly admits that the monologues are ultimately "Nachdichtungen," his poeticized takes on the collected material (18). In his description, he even implicitly acknowledges that his informants spoke both German and Turkish and thus practiced a type of interlingual code-switching that is characteristic for postmigrants, but absent in this text, as we will see (13).

In *Kanak Sprak*, the German language is the primary site for the articulation of the *Kanak*'s existence, but in a way that is and is not "German" at the same time. A look at particular passages indicates how this functions and gives a first sense of the texture of Zaimoğlu's language. Referring to the dominant trope of being stuck between two cultures, the youngest figure, "Hasan, 13, vagrant and student," for instance, declares: "This bullshit about two cultures, i've had it up to here, what's that crap, what am i supposed to do with this smart natter about two pieces of pelt, where there isn't enough room even for my butt; one pelt i'll spread over my body, so that i don't get scared, but under my butt i need just some damn-me solid ground, where i crouch and end" (*Kanak Sprak* 97; Diese scheiße mit den zwei kulturen steht mir bis hier, was soll das, was bringt mir'n kluger schnack mit zwei fellen, auf denen mein arsch kein platz hat, 'n fell streck ich mir über'n leib, damit mir nich bange wird, aber unter'm arsch brauch ich verdammich bloß festen boden, wo ich kauer und ende).[20] Hasan rejects the clichéd narrative of betweenness circu-lating about his situation and offers a counter-analysis of his life in which he calls for "solid ground" under his feet, even if merely to "crouch and end."[21] This analysis is put forth in a language that is both thoroughly German and not an easily comprehensible form of German at all, provoking a dizzying reading experience for any German-language reader, which an English translation can only approximate.

Zaimoğlu even provides an intralingual translation from this *Kanak* style into standard German, underscoring the fundamen-tal internal difference inscribed in this German: "Gott fickt jede Lahmgöre" (god fucks every lame brat), he explains, is one way of saying "Wenn man weiterkommen will, muss man sein Schicksal selbst in die Hand nehmen" (*Kanak Sprak* 14; If you want to get further in life, you have to take your fate into your own hands). While the individualist can-do ethos expressed in the translated statement is surprisingly mainstream and socially conformist, the provocative, neologistic language in which it is put performs the true transgression. This highlighted intralingual translation also marks the German of the text as not immediately comprehensible to other "native" speakers unfamiliar with this code, even though all the words are in German. It thus destabilizes the sanctioned "native speakers'" access and taken-for-granted relationship to the language.

What marks this style is its extraordinarily fine-tuned play with the resources of the German language, to which it lays claim in this manner. In one of the few passages within the monologues explicitly commenting on language, "Abdurrahman, 24, rap-per," even criticizes the dominant subject's language as weaker: "the heady type bears a kinda mark of cain between his blond

brows, you recognize him by his talk which, larded with foreign vocabulary, fast approaches a level where image-speaking
croaks and words roll by like pot lids." (*Kanak Sprak* 21; Der
kopfler trägt so ne art kainsmal zwischen den blonden brauen, du
erkennst ihn daran, dass sein reden mit welschen vokabeln ge-
spickt scharf kurs nimmt auf ne ebene, wo das bildsprechen verreckt und die worte wie topfdeckel vorbeikullern). Conjuring the
image of words as playfully rolling pot lids, the passage contrasts
the rich metaphoricity of this speech with its alleged absence in
the speech of the German—here represented synecdochically in a
racializing image as "blond brows." Ironically, the minority subject accuses the majority subject, at least a certain type of majority subject, "the heady type," of dangerously overusing "foreign vocabulary," suggesting an alienation and impoverishment
of majority German's German.

The *Kanak* figure's speech, on the other hand, draws out images from the resources of the German language rather than turning to foreign vocabulary, we are told *and* we are shown. Neither
of the passages from "Hasan" and "Abdurrahman," for instance,
contains foreign words or *Fremdwörter*, thus ironically performing a type of language purism that rejects words of foreign derivation.[22] Instead, *Kanak* style unfolds in newly coined neologisms
based on German words (*kopfler* [heady type], *Lahmgöre* [lame
brat]) and moves wildly between registers, drawing on biblical
images (*Kainsmal* [mark of Cain]), archaic forms (*welsch* [out-
dated word for foreign, primarily referring to French]), colloquial-
isms (*bange werden* [become afraid], *verreckt* [croaked]), Northern German dialect (*schnack* [natter]), and vulgar expressions
(*scheiße* [shit] and *arsch* [butt]). Ellipses and contractions typical of spoken speech (*ne* and *wie'n* instead of *eine* and *wie ein*)
underscore its vernacular quality. The unexpected appearance of
some of these registers—such as biblical language, older or dialectal forms of German and, in many places, high literary language—in the speech of postmigrants from the "league of the
damned" situates these figures in a broader linguascape than is
generally afforded to them.

While the broad range of vocabulary and register that constitutes this speech produces a sense of the *Kanak* figure's linguistic mobility across the whole spectrum of the German language, the constant jump between these divergent and incongruent registers introduces a recurrent element of surprise and even shock. The persistent juxtaposition of registers that would not appear to belong together prevents the text from settling into any one of them as dominant and thereby conveys a sense of restless linguistic movement and disorienting linguistic stimulation. It can provoke a visceral reaction in the reader trying to absorb such register jumps present in nearly every passage of the book. What this switch between registers mimics and points to in the external linguascape that inspired it is the switch between different languages. The text renders the multilingualism of the postmigrant linguascape to which it refers not through a transcription of that language but primarily through a mixing of registers drawn from German. In this form, it transposes code-switching from an *interlingual* practice to an *intralingual* one in German. This transposition makes *Kanak Sprak* both more "monolingual" and less so at the same time. In fact, it makes *German* both more monolingual and less so. The monolingualism that this strategy produces is unsettled and full of jump cuts, a monolingualism, in other words, with a multilingual affect.

This juxtaposition of registers is held together at a level other than the semantic—namely, at that of sound. Alliteration and assonance create continuity and connectivity throughout the text. The passage from "Abdurrahman," like many others, features both alliteration *blonde brauen, welsche vokabeln*), and assonance (the repetition of *o* in *kopfler/so/blonden/vokabeln/wo/ worte/topfdeckel/vorbeikullern*). Recurring throughout *Kanak Sprak*, these devices lend a poetic and playful, at times musical, dimension to this language, even when the content described is abject. The materiality of the language asserts itself and provides a sensual, physically affecting dimension to the text.

While the particular language of *Kanak Sprak* is unique, its use of nonstandard language and stylized vernacular resembles strategies used by writers in other linguistic contexts and thereby indicates a larger transnational and postmonolingual literary landscape in which the book participates. The "synthetic vernacular poetics," which Hart describes and to which I have alluded earlier, marks one such strand.[23] Dohra Ahmad, borrowing Ken Saro-Wiwa's term "rotten English," argues that such vernacular literatures share an "anti-institutional stance, a wicked sense of humor, a deep engagement with history, and a constant preoccupation with language" (*Rotten English* 26). Speaking of this writing's "clear purpose of reclaiming and valorizing codes that had thus far been presented (even frequently, by their own speakers) as substandard," she notes that their "puns, neologisms, musicality, orality, all function as weapons against cultural domination" (*Rotten English* 29). Zaimoğlu's book could also be described as a German version of what another critic, Evelyn Ch'ien, labels writings in "weird English," which for Ch'ien stretch from Nabokov's *Pnin* to Junot Diaz's *Oscar Wao* (*Weird English*). These tendencies are not limited to English, however, but also can be found in other languages. Emily Apter, for instance, discusses numerous further examples of writers radically appropriating and deforming French, such as Martiniquan Raphael Confiant, who "revels in rubbing high literature's face in this linguistically biodegradable material" (*The Translation Zone* 167). Even smaller languages participate in this global trend, as Corina Lacatus describes with regard to contemporary Swedish literature (*The (In)visibility Complex*). There, Tunisian-Swedish postmigrant author Jonas Hassen Khemiri's manipulations of Swedish transpose the country's newly globalized linguascape into literature for the first time.

Yet while *Kanak Sprak* shares much with these versions of "weird" or "rotten" literature aesthetically, it differs from them in its relationship to its primary language, German. For many of those writing their version of "rotten English," for instance, whether it is Saro-Wiwa, Gloria Anzaldúa, or Irvine Welsh, the standard language is an imposed and enforced language, closely connected to colonization, conquest, and cultural imperialism.

The postcolonial context, in particular, has given rise to numerous such versions.[24] Yet, the situation is different for postmigrants and disjunctive speakers such as Zaimoğlu or Khemiri. The emphasis in that context is not so much on the imposition of a dominant language as on the withholding of claims to a language experienced as one's own. *Kanak Sprak*'s attitude to German is thus not colored by animus against a forcibly imposed language, but by a response to a context in which the disjunctive speaker's relationship to that language is not culturally sanctioned. The problem is thus not "making an *imposed* language one's own" (Ahmad, *Rotten English* 29; emphasis added), but claming a *withheld* language as one's own.

In that vein, the problematic that Zaimoğlu addresses is closer to that of Kafka, who could not lay claim to his "mother tongue"—which was also his "mother's tongue"—due to a racialized conception of the German language. The different historical circumstances and aesthetic frameworks of these writers, however, produce different linguistic family romances in response to this problematic. In his memorable image of German as someone else's baby stolen from the crib and made to walk the tightrope, Kafka, we recall, articulates a sense of having illegitimately appropriated the language. Zaimoğlu, on the other hand, links the language the young postmigrant produces to his own body: "the word force of the *Kanak* expresses itself in a squeezed-out, short-breathed, and hybrid stammer without period or comma, with arbitrary pauses and improvised turns of speech" (*Kanak Sprak* 13; Die Wortgewalt des Kanaken drückt sich aus in einem herausgepressten, kurzatmigen und hybriden Gestammel ohne Punkt und Komma, mit willkürlich gesetzten Pausen und improvisierten Wendungen). This description turns the *Kanak*'s language production into a painful physical process that ambivalently invokes both giving birth and defecating. In this linguistic family romance, the language emanates directly from the body of the young male postmigrant instead of stemming from a "mother" or "father." He himself becomes the charged source of a language that constitutes his identity. The double quality of this *Wortgewalt*, where *Gewalt*

can mean both "power" and "violence" (hence my translation as
"word force") signals the ambivalent nature of this linguistic self-
generation. Making German itself visibly postmonolingual seeks
to register and to undermine this continued racialization of the
language in order to claim it.

Zaimoğlu's linguistic family romance is thrown into even
sharper relief when compared to Gloria Anzaldúa's version for
the Chicana writer from the borderlands. Zaimoğlu's direct and
defiant address to the majority society cited earlier ("we are the
Kanaks you Germans always warned about") echoes a similar one
by Anzaldúa: "We are your linguistic nightmare, your linguistic
aberration, your linguistic *mestisaje*, the subject of your *burla*.
[. . .] Racially, culturally, and linguistically *somos huerfanos*
—we speak an orphan tongue" (Anzaldúa, *Borderlands/La Frontera* 58). Zaimoğlu and Anzaldúa both express the experience
of subjects being cast out by a racialized system to which they
respond with a forceful in-your-face self-assertion via language.
But while Anzaldúa's "orphan tongue" invokes language as a
child who has lost her parents, Zaimoğlu focuses solely on male
self-generation without reference to parents or other affiliations.
To this end, he asserts that the language of the *Kanak* figure is
composed "out of 'hotchpotched' vocabulary and idioms [. . .]
that do not occur in this form in either of the two languages"
(*Kanak Sprak* 13; emphasis added; aus "verkauderwelschten"
Vokabeln und Redewendungen [. . .], *die so in keiner der bei-
den Sprachen vorkommen*). While this is indeed true and leads to
a creatively disruptive postmonolingual German, the absence of
Turkish has more problematic, gendered dimensions.

NO TURKISH SPOKEN HERE: LANGUAGE, AFFECT, AND MASCULINITY

According to the monolingual paradigm, Turkish *should* be Turkish-German postmigrants' "mother tongue." Zaimoğlu's struggle
against this aspect of the monolingual paradigm takes the form
of marginalizing the ascribed language, Turkish. In *Kanak Sprak*

Turkish is present only in indirect ways. An expression such as *Jung-blutbengel* (young blood rascal) is not immediately recognizable as an evocation of the Turkish word for young man, *delikanlı*, though it may draw on the word's literal meaning "crazy blooded" in addition to the German phrase *junges Blut* (*Kanak Sprak* 28; young blood). The most visible "Turkish" word in the text is *der Alemanne*, which plays with the Turkish word for German (*Alman*) but also with the German name of a Germanic tribe (*Alemannen*). The Turkish presence is ironically made visible in the naming of the German. This naming produces the majority German counterpart of the *Kanak* as a projection of the subcultural imagination and thus asserts agency and naming rights. But such Turkish-derived expressions remain the exception and do not account for the many striking neologisms and word plays of the text. Though *Kanak Sprak* is written in a language that requires intralingual translation into standard German, this is not due to a translated, bilingual nature in Turkish and German, so characteristic for Emine Sevgi Özdamar's writing, as discussed in the previous chapter. To the contrary, in *Kanak Sprak*, Turkish is marginal to the make-up of the text. Why is that so? A consideration of the only actual Turkish words in the entire book provides the key to the answer.

The only place in *Kanak Sprak* to feature actual Turkish words is the preface, and there they appear only to indicate the author's deliberate decision to avoid Turkish and Turkish-inspired expressions. Zaimoğlu explains that he did not incorporate certain features of the language of his interlocutors even in translation. The words he specifically mentions are terms of endearment: "gözüm (mein Auge), gözümün nuru (mein Augenlicht)" (*Kanak Sprak* 14; my eye [. . .] light of my eye). These expressions would indeed be unusual modes of address in German, particularly between men. They evoke an affectionate relationship, and more importantly, conjure a mode of masculinity in which such an expression of affection between presumably heterosexual men would be acceptable.[25] Since Zaimoğlu does not shy away from expressing himself against the grain of German discourses, this specific aversion appears significant. He explains that he replaced such terms because he wanted to avoid the "folklore trap" and not let his language be misunderstood as the "flowery language of Orientals" (14). This explicit distancing gesture from Turkish expressions used by his interviewees casts the Turkish language in a specific mould: Turkish is correlated with folklore, floweriness, homosocial tenderness, all of which are presented in a negative light. Through this strategy, Zaimoğlu produces a particular image of Turkish as inherently "Oriental"—that is, ornamental, sentimental, and feminized—while asserting the opposite for the Turkish-German male figures of his text.

Zaimoğlu's rejection of actual Turkish words or Turkish-derived expressions, then, is linked to the desired construction of the *Kanak* figure. What is at stake here is that figure's masculinity and agency. Zaimoğlu dismisses Turkish as unsuitable for representing the *Kanak* as he wants to construct him because of the affective charge of the language he ascribes to it. In this construction, the affective charges of languages are highly significant since they are the mode through which the masculinity of the minority subject is postulated and with which it is invested. Zaimoğlu replaces the term of endearment "light of my eye," for example, with *Bruder* (14; brother). That is, he replaces the tenderness that might be expressed through the Turkish phrase with a fraternal relationship and a renewed emphasis on masculinity. Though expressions for "brother" are also frequent forms of address in Turkish, Zaimoğlu does not identify those expressions as his source or give the Turkish equivalents in the text. Through his linguistic choices, the author abandons affectionate moments in favor of a more aggressive masculinity that shuns elaborate expressions of endearment towards other men.[26]

The deliberate exclusion of Turkish from the linguistic mix of *Kanak Sprak* is moreover part of a generational struggle over racialized masculinity. Zaimoğlu presents his style as a rejection of the dominant representation of Turkish-German men as hapless, victimized, and mute figures in previous discourses. He specifically blames first-generation migrant writers for colluding with this image. Writing about *Gastarbeiterliteratur* (guest worker literature) in his introduction to *Kanak Sprak*, he complains: "The Turk turns into the quintessence of 'emotion,' of a sloppy nostalgia and fake exotic enchantment" (*Kanak Sprak* 12; Der Türke wird zum Inbegriff für "Gefühl," einer schlampigen Nostalgie und eines faulen exotischen Zaubers). The emotionality with which "the Turk" is identified according to Zaimoğlu is one of cheap sentimentality. He also associates this literary tradition with emasculation and feminization. The subtitle of a separate essay on *Gastarbeiterliteratur*, "Ali macht Männchen" (Ali plays begging dog; literally: Ali makes a little man) illustrates his position succinctly.[27] It turns the generic guest worker/Turk and writer of guest-worker literature "Ali" into a submissive dog, willing to perform acrobatics for the master as trained.[28] This submissiveness is coded as emasculating: it turns men into diminutive *Männchen*. As Moray McGowan notes, the exploitation of migrant workers was indeed sometimes articulated through the trope of feminization: "Frequently these [. . .] Turkish-German texts of migrant labour experience portray labour-narrators, feminised in the sense that they are 'no longer the actor, but the acted upon'" ("Multiple Masculinities" 298).[29] Yet, while these writers reacted to the victimization discourse in a—highly problematic—gendered manner, Zaimoğlu holds them responsible for this gendering and for having contributed to a paralyzing identity of Turkish men as victims.

Zaimoğlu's *Kanak* aesthetics counter this perceived emasculation with aggressive masculinity, proclaiming to the majority society, even if in quotation marks: "'Ihr habt Angst vor unserem Sperma'" (You are scared of our sperm).[30] Consequently, Zaimoğlu links resistance to cultural expectations and the hegemonic gaze of the majority culture to the reassertion of aggressivity and masculinity. Such a combination of gendered aggression with a particular linguistic style is widespread in "vernacular literature" in "rotten English," as Ahmad remarks. She notes that this literature's "often shocking and almost never decorous content [. . .] had historically been something of a 'bad-boy' undertaking" (23).[31]

With its gendered attitude in its treatment of the signifier "Turkish," *Kanak Sprak* is not alone. As Barbara Mennel argues, Turkish-German films of the 1990s often "remain indebted to a masculinist discourse and tradition that, in turn, enabled [their] national
and transnational success" ("Bruce Lee in Kreuzberg" 3). In these
films, the masculinist discourse draws on a transnational aesthetics, frequently a U.S.-derived "ghetto aesthetic" that "features a
highly gendered discourse of criminality" (7).[32] Specifically, Turk-
ish-coded spaces, practices, and aesthetics are not invoked as viable alternatives to dominant German discourses. About the final scenes of Fatih Akin's first feature film *Kurz und Schmerzlos*
(Short Sharp Shock, 1998), the story of three friends and small-
time criminals in Hamburg-Altona, for instance, Mennel observes:
"The image and soundtrack express loss and melancholy, which
are narratively connected to [the Turkish-German protagonist's]
return to his speechless father as well as his imminent departure
for Turkey. The sequence mourns the loss of the friends [who die
violent crime-related deaths] and reinstates a circumscribed Turkish identity" (23). Like Zaimoğlu, the film reinforces the association of a pointedly Turkish sphere with the specific affects of loss
and melancholy, and with first generation migrant men.

In a social context in which Turkish is assumed to be the property of Turkish-German postmigrants, Zaimoğlu's deliberate
avoidance of Turkish challenges the monolingual paradigm. But
the particular way in which Zaimoğlu *casts* Turkish in his preface reproduces negative associations with the language circulating in the German cultural sphere—associations that necessitated
Zaimoğlu's disavowal in the first place. As Turkish is dismissed as
unsuitable for constructing the *Kanak* figure, the language that
appears to supplant it is English.

BELONGING TO A TRANSNATIONAL POSSE? RACIALIZED MASCULINITY VIA HIP-HOP ENGLISH

In today's globalized linguascape, English occupies a privileged
place as lingua franca and as a powerful symbolic marker. Some

observers consider this prevalence of English as a threat to all other languages and worry that it is leading to linguistic homogenization. English, in that view, is an agent of a dangerous monolingualization of the globe. Other commentators, meanwhile, emphasize the many different forms this global English takes, and in fact speak of "Englishes" in the plural.[33] In that view, English itself is undergoing a process of multilingualization. Behind both perspectives lie different conceptions of language and ethnicity, and the role a global language can play in their potential realignment. Those who fear linguistic dispossession through English see that link endangered, while others emphasize acts of appropriation and the possibility of forging new links. Although these divergent perspectives may appear to be two sides of the same coin, their divergence actually comes out of and gestures towards a larger conceptual difference. In both cases, radically different subjects are imagined as the speakers of English that serve as the point of departure for the respective discourse. Those who see the language as a threat are more likely to align it with globally hegemonic subjects and equate it with Americanization and American hegemony more generally.[34] A very different evaluation emerges when English is viewed as the language of a postcolonial Indian or Nigerian speaker who speaks it with her own inflection. The meaning ascribed to English, then, varies with the subjects who are primarily associated with it in a given discourse.

In *Kanak Sprak*, English primarily, though not exclusively, enters through hip-hop—that is, through a cultural form developed by African-Americans.[35] Although actual English words and phrases constitute only a minimal portion of *Kanak Sprak*, English is of strategic importance for the book. The placement of the monologues that foreground hip-hop at the very beginning of the volume (as the first, third, and fifth monologues) gives them particular weight and creates the impression that these voices are representative for the volume as a whole.[36] Associating English with African Americans and specifically with hip-hop serves to imagine the place of the *Kanak* figures in a simultaneously racializing and de-ethnicizing, but always gendered, manner.

The very first monologue of *Kanak Sprak* establishes rap as an oppositional and resistant force and contrasts it favorably to pop, another English-language form. Abdurrahman, the rapper of the first monologue, declares that "Pop is ne fatale Orgie" (pop's a fatal orgy) because it functions as a dulling ideology: "pop is was für kostgänger der illusion" (pop's a thing for boarders of illusion) that breeds uncritical acceptance of the status quo (*Kanak Sprak* 19, 20).[37] The fostering of an oppositional attitude is instead ascribed to rap, which in turn is linked to African-American English. In the monologue attributed to "Bayram, 18, breaker," the connection between English phrases, German postmigrant discourse, and hip-hop takes this shape:

> Ich bin'n *breaker* und hab meine gute *posse*, die alle *peace* wollen und *peace* stiften, weil *peace* is schon das, was man aus sich machen sollte, hüter über deinen bruder und die *posse* und über die kleinen, die schon ne wehr brauchen vor den verdammten verderbern im dunkeln. Rap is'n harter kodex, auf schlaffem posten bist du im nu'n toter posten. [. . .] Der rap sagt: sieh dich vor vorm untersten wie obersten chargen, vor dem der garantiert im falschen pelz rumläuft, um dich auf lamm zu polen. Bist du'n lamm fressen sie dich. [. . .] hier bei uns, bei den breakern und rappern, bei den brüdern und schwestern, ist schluss mit dem stuss, wir schwimmen nicht mit dem strom, wir machen nen eigenen strikten strom, wo jeder'n fluss is und aufhört 'n gottverschissenes rinnsal zu sein. (*Kanak Sprak* 41–42; emphasis added)

> [I'm a break-dancer and I have my good posse who all want peace and do peace 'cause peace is what you should make of yourself, guardian of your brother and the posse and of the little ones who already need some defense against the damned ruiners in the dark. Rap's a tough code, on a slack post you're fast a dead post. [. . .] rap says: beware of the lowest and the highest ranks, of the one who runs around in a false fur, to rewire you into a lamb. If you're a lamb, they'll eat you. [. . .] here among us break-dancers and rappers, among the brothers and sisters, we're done with that

bullshit, we don't swim with the tide, we make our own strict tide, where everyone's a river and stops being a god-damshitty rivulet.]

The English or pseudo-English words "breaker," "posse," and "peace" stem from the vocabulary of African-American hip-hop culture and in the speech of this figure invoke an identity (breaker), a community (posse), and a vision (peace), respectively.[38] Beyond the referential meaning of the words, they offer a mode of orientation and of making sense of the world, of one's own position within it as well as a "code" of conduct. This orientation and sense-making activity draw on a social analysis implicit in the terms themselves. Because of these implicit meanings, German words could not take their place. Instead, the English words and the specific minority culture to which they refer in this context make the young Turkish-German break-dancer part of a much larger "posse"—namely, one that is transnational.

In citing the English vocabulary of hip-hop, the figures in *Kanak Sprak* participate in one of the prime transnational cultural forms of our time. Though globally dominant, hip-hop carries with it the association of oppositionality and minority resistance, on which Zaimoğlu's figures draw and with which they identify.[39] With this appropriation of the globalized language of hip-hop, they also go beyond the tired cliché of being stuck between two cultures that we saw the thirteen-year-old "Hasan" rail against. As a third term and language, English breaks down the binary between one-dimensional affiliations with either Turkish or German. It seemingly affords the young postmigrant a more global and less ethnically determined position.

Yet, as ethnographer Ayşe Çağlar points out, hip-hop and rap culture and aesthetics have been actively promoted by German state institutions as an appropriate "language" and cultural practice for Turkish-German youth in particular. German social workers in youth clubs organize courses in rap and stage local graffiti and break-dance competitions (Çağlar, "Management kultureller Vielfalt" 226–27). Paradoxically, they see these forms of U.S. minority culture as a means of *integrating* young Turkish-

German men into *German* society (229–30). "English"-coded practices are thus aligned with "German" culture and society and set against "Turkish"-coded practices. Rather than denoting a place outside German culture, these cultural forms, mediated through English, function as a gateway to establish a place within German culture. At the same time, this particular path to "integration" leads through the appropriation of those cultural innovations of a minority elsewhere—African-Americans—which speak to marginalization and racist oppression.

Çağlar's observation about this paradoxical function of hip-hop culture is partially confirmed in another *Kanak Sprak* monologue entitled "Der direkte Draht zum schwarzen Mann" (The Direct Line to the Black Man) attributed to "Ali, 23, Rapper (von 'da crime posse')."[40] Considering rap as a means of *Aufklärung* (enlightenment) for the oppressed in the tradition of Zulu Nation, Grandmaster Flash, and Public Enemy, Ali sees his role as spreading an antidrug and anticrime message: "no drugs, no crime [. . .] wenn du echt bronx sein willst" (*Kanak Sprak* 28; no drugs, no crime [. . .] if you want to be real bronx). But if he does not succeed in his musical career, Ali continues, he will join the police force, since he pleads for "unbedingte teilnahme" (*Kanak Sprak* 32; unconditional participation in society). The Heidelberg hip-hopper Boulevard Bou seconds this attitude in his song "Geh zur Polizei" (cit. in Ayata, "Kanak-Rap in Almanya" 281; go to the police). These examples demonstrate that far from being simply an outlaw identity, hip-hop can also function as part of a state apparatus of law and order.[41] This transnational form, then, accumulates different meaning in a national context. It thereby adds to the postmigrant's implied access to the global a dimension of being fixed within a racialized global margin.

The foregrounding of the "black man" in rapper "Ali's" monologue further indicates that the source for and point of access to an appropriation of American English is the expression of an oppositional male minority existence. Although the passage cited earlier refers to an inclusive, almost utopian, community of "brothers and sisters," hip-hop signals a predominantly male domain (Ayata, "Kanak-Rap" 276; Menrath, *Represent What* 11). In his study of the everyday language use of Asian-British youth, Roxy Harris likewise finds the young men's penchant for what he classifies as African-American Vernacular English to lie in their "strong affiliation to black masculinities," represented in hip-hop (*New Ethnicities* 12). The English fragments in *Kanak Sprak* thus help to appropriate this masculinity, often figured as hard and tough, while disavowing the femininity that Zaimoğlu ascribes to Turkish. These language strategies construct the masculinity of the *Kanak* youth as oppositional, active, globally mobile, and non-Oriental.

In this linguistic and stylistic manner, *Kanak Sprak* participates in a general trend whereby postmigrants in Germany can be heard primarily through the vehicle of hip-hop, which appears as the state-designated and state-legitimized means of minority articulation.[42] While this does not mean that the young people who embrace this style are manipulated, it does point to the fact that in the "German" imagination there is a link between the minorities in Germany and those in the United States.[43] This imagined link between Turkish-Germans and African-Americans is by no means new. In a 1973 feature on Turkish migration to Germany, *Spiegel* magazine raised the specter of German cities turning into "Harlem."[44] Experiences with cultural differences have been repeatedly articulated through reference to a U.S. context, and seem to suggest that no useful German precedents are available.[45] Yet the linguascape of *Kanak Sprak* also houses a different, unexpected memory of the German past.

BUT IS IT KOSHER? THE KANAK'S YIDDISH
AND HEBREW WORDS

In contrast to the highly visible presence of English in *Kanak Sprak*, Yiddish and Hebrew words appear in more subtle, dispersed fashion throughout the text. While the insertion of African-American hip-hop vocabulary can be read as negotiating present racialization in Germany, the occurrence of Yiddish loanwords in German speaks to a memory of past racialization. Throughout *Kanak Sprak* we find expressions such as *schlamassel* (36, 47; mess), *mischpoke* (121; family, clan), *meschugge* (62, 92, 117; crazy), and *schofele* (136; paltry)—all words with origins in Yiddish via *Rotwelsch*.[46] Although these words today are used in everyday German speech, Zaimoğlu's citation of these "Germanized" Yiddish words is nonetheless intriguing. His use of such words suggests the presence of unconscious histories embedded in language. Furthermore, their use tells us something about immigrants' relationship to the history and cultural memories with which they come into contact and into which they necessarily enter, not the least through language.[47]

References to Jews, and particularly to the German historical memory of the Holocaust, surface throughout Zaimoğlu's text.[48] The most explicit reference in this regard is embedded in the monologue of the gigolo who encounters a female German customer wanting him to play a Jew. The fantasy of the "christ lady" (*christenlady*) centers on the fact that the Turkish-German man, unlike most Germans, is circumcised—that is, it centers on his marked masculinity. Even in this case, then, racialized masculinity is at stake. But unlike the self-identification of some of the *Kanak* figures with black masculinity, this interpellation as Jewish comes from the outside and points to contact with unresolved national histories, not desired transnational mobility. In his reflection on this encounter, the gigolo specifically links this fantasy to the haunting presence of murdered Jews, for whom he is made to stand in.[49] Though *Kanak Sprak* at first seems like a social critique of present circumstances, "complex histories are as much at stake as social conflicts in these discursive palimpsests," as Adelson argues ("Against Between" 251). The linguascape thus can have historical depth.

Some of the other Jewish references in *Kanak Sprak* are ironic, as when Zaimoğlu has the Islamic fundamentalist say "Ich, der ich mich [gottes] wort ergeben, esse koscheres, geschächtetes fleisch" (141; I, who has submitted to god's word, eat kosher, properly slaughtered meat). By using the Hebrew term *kosher* rather than the Turkish *helal* (from Arabic *halal*) or even simply the religiously neutral *geschächtet*, Zaimoğlu blurs Jewish and Muslim practices within a German text and linguistically criss-crosses minority subject positions within Germany.

In the particular instance of the Islamist, Zaimoğlu undermines a discourse of purity and properness to which the utterance confesses ideological allegiance. The text is thus marked by a tension between the recurrent appeal to purity in the content of the monologues and their "impure," abject language. This conflict between the statement and the language in which it is articulated signals ironic distance between the figures and the authorial voice.[50] It also leads us to the special significance of abjection for the entire text and its "impure" linguistic strategies.

ARTICULATING ABJECTION: LIFE OUTSIDE THE MONOLINGUAL PARADIGM

Abjection as a debilitating condition as well as a potential resource animates the stylized language of *Kanak Sprak* throughout. As Julia Kristeva argues in *Powers of Horror: An Essay on Abjection*, the abject is "neither subject nor object" but rather a non-object (1). This non-object—such as waste matter and bodily fluids—nevertheless is linked to subject formation by its very exclusion. It "marks out a territory" in which subjects and objects emerge in the first place (*Powers of Horror* 10). Judith Butler draws out the social implications of this structure most clearly:

> The exclusionary matrix by which subjects are formed thus requires the simultaneous production of a domain of abject beings, those who are not yet "subjects," but who form the constitutive outside to the domain of the subject. The abject designates here precisely those "unlivable" and "uninhabitable" zones of social life, which are nevertheless populated by those who do not enjoy the status of the subject [. . .]. The notion of *abjection* designates a degraded or cast out status within the terms of sociality. (Butler 3; 243n2)

This underlying structure of sociality—the relationship between the domain of those deemed subjects and those abjected—also informs *Kanak Sprak* and its project of linguistic resignification. The production of the *Kanak* figure does not occur in isolation but in relation to the social space from which he is abjected, a space still governed by the monolingual paradigm. Similarly, Zaimoğlu's turn to abjection does not occur in isolation but at a specific historical moment. Indeed, Uli Linke has demonstrated the importance of abjection in the construction of German identity in the 1980s and 1990s as part of a rhetoric of bodily incorporation and the excretion of waste ("Murderous Fantasies").

The *Kanak* figure has a special relationship to abjection, one that is connected to his social status and his aesthetics. As one figure puts it: "As long as this country refuses us real entry, we will soak up the anomalies and perversions of this country like a sponge and then spit out the dirt. The soiled know no aesthetics" (*Kanak Sprak* 113–14; Solange uns dieses land den wirklichen eintritt verwehrt, werden wir die anomalien und perversionen dieses landes wie ein schwamm aufsaugen und den dreck ausspucken. Die beschmutzten kennen keine ästhetik). The abject space is where the refuse of mainstream society accumulates outside the domain of legitimized subjects. Soaking up that refuse, the abjected become points of density and in that density retain that which the subjects discard in order to mark their difference and their legitimacy. The dirt and abjection with which the book confronts its readers are thus resignified as emanating from mainstream society, rather than originating with the *Kanak* figures. Yet the *Kanak* figures are marked by their contact with it. Only by spitting it out, by aggressively reinserting the dirt into the domain of the subject, can they discharge it. This passage explicitly links aesthetics to social abjection and proposes that we read the language de-formations in *Kanak Sprak* in this light. Having soaked up the codes and languages circulating in multiple domains, the *Kanak* figures' language constitutes a highly condensed and concentrated form while its mode of articulation occurs in a spitting out of manifesto-like proclamations—that is, in an ambivalent *Wortgewalt*.

Yet despite the texts' defiant appropriation of the racist slur *Kanake*, the abject nature of the figures' status and self-reference cannot be fully redeemed, as many of the monologues suggest: "pal, I also see myself like some tiny ol' piece of insect shit who just has to get it into his head what's up" (*Kanak Sprak* 24; Kumpel, ich seh mich auch wie so'n oller mickriger insektenschiss, der nur tüchtig in den kopp kriegen muss, was sache ist). As a number of the figures observe, this social abjection results from racialized difference: "only the nappy hair turns me into a rotting fish" (*Kanak Sprak* 119; Nur's krause haar macht mich zum modderfisch). The monologues repeatedly articulate the debilitating side of this abjection. "Rahman," for instance, describes the experience of being suddenly overcome with fear in everyday life: "what I mean is a fucking horror that is deep down and comes shooting up like puke. The tariffs don't work any more in that case; you feel like you're muck or even more stinky waste or some tin can that one kicks away and it clanks like a riot" (*Kanak Sprak* 118; was ich mein, is so'n scheissgrausen, das tief drinsteckt und hochschiesst wie kotter. Da haun die tarife längst nicht mehr hin, dir kommt's vor, als wärst du'n frass oder eher schon stinkiger abfall oder so ne blechdose, wo man wegkickt, und's scheppert wie krawall). Filled with an abject horror, the figure itself turns into waste. The description of this horror is linked to the figure's sense of invisibility:

Schlimm is, dass die alemannen dich nischt für ne müde mark sehn, du bist gar nischt da, du kannst da antippen und sagen: mann, mich gibt's schon seit ner urlangen zeit, fass man an, dass du merkst, da is fleisch und knochen, für die biste gar nischt, luft und weniger als schnuppe luft, du hast eben kein sektor, wo man dich ordnen könnt, das sieht denn aus, wie wenn ne olle leiche rumliegt, und die machen mit nem stück kreide nen umriss. Im umriss is denn nix wenn se'n kadaver wegtragen, da siehste 'n strichmänneken aus teppich. (*Kanak Sprak* 118–19)

[What's terrible is that the teutons do not see you, you don't
even exist, you can tap them and say: man, I exist already
for a very long time, come on, touch me so that you realize
there is flesh and bones, for them you are nothing, air and
less then irrelevant air, that's because you have no sector
where one could put you, rather it looks like a stupid corpse
is lying around and they make a cutout with chalk. In the
cutout there is nothing once they carry away the cadaver,
you just see a stick figure made out of carpet.]

Lacking the substance and reassuring contours of a living body,
the male postmigrant is split between turning into a cadaver, one
of the prime figures of abjection, and the haunting emptiness of
his place. This emptiness and insubstantiality are brought on by
invisibility and the lack of an identifiable "sector." Abjection robs
him of existence as a live subject and casts him out into "'unin-
habitable' zones of social life" (Butler 3). While this *Kanak* figure
cannot be said to make *Männchen* (begging dog; literally: little
man), he turns instead into a corpse and a *strichmänneken* (stick
figure; literally: little man drawing). With this vernacular expression, he also caricatures his own masculinity.[51] Both the *Kanak*'s
very existence and his masculinity are affected by abjection. The
sound of "riot" caused by the kicked can, on the other hand, is an
audible trace of the abject figure. This sound signifies the trashing
of the discarded object that the marginalized postmigrant figure
becomes in a structure that assigns him no other place. What to
that figure is a reverberation of his existence may sound to the
surrounding social space like a riot that he has started. The sound
of this riot is what we hear in the language of *Kanak Sprak*. What
these passages also underscore, however, is that Zaimoğlu provides us with "images of transgressive Turkish men as both *occu-
pying and theorizing* the space of the abject in German society"
(Adelson, "Against Between" 250; emphasis added). This double-
function of the *Kanak* figure maintains a representational tension
between acknowledging the circumscribed status of the postmigrant subject and the act of speaking in spite of it, expressed in a
postmonolingual German.

This focus on and entanglement with the abject sets a different tone from familiar discourses around hybridity, which at first would seem applicable to *Kanak Sprak*. Abjection, by its very repugnant and blurry nature, does not lend itself to a facile pluralism or a celebration of abstract difference as hybridity does.[52] Much less affirmative, the abject recognizes and acknowledges the power of discourse under which these "subjects" are formed or deformed. Even the notion of subversion, while useful, distracts from the disabling nature of abjection that Zaimoğlu's writing records throughout.[53] Furthermore, as Adelson argues, "Zaimoğlu's discourse links flesh, filth, dirt, shit, and history in curious ways" ("Against Between" 249). This linkage is not merely a matter of subversion but rather, as Adelson further shows, a mode of thinking and writing the complexities of historical narrative in 1990s German discourse (see "Against Between"). By highlighting abjection, the text articulates both agency and powerlessness together. In her discussion of *Kanak Sprak* in *The Turkish Turn*, Adelson concludes that the "text teeters between a figural representation of iconoclastic Turks that occasionally reinforces stereotypes of migrant youth and a more iconoclastic mode of representation that excitedly gestures toward new ways of imagining a Turkish presence in Germany" (104). The new imagination toward which Zaimoğlu gestures, while ambivalent, has its productive side and this productive side is closely linked to language and a postmonolingual configuration.

That abjection should manifest itself in language is not a coincidence. Kristeva shows the intimate link between the abject, language, and aesthetics through a detailed reading of the writings of Louis-Ferdinand Céline, the principle source for her "essay on abjection" along with other modernist writers such as James Joyce. She specifies:

> The writer, fascinated by the abject, imagines its logic, projects himself into it, and as a consequence *perverts language—style and content*. [. . .] One might say that with such a literature there takes place a crossing over of the dichotomous categories of Pure and Impure, Prohibition and

Sin, Morality and Immorality. [. . .] Writing [such texts] implies an ability to imagine the abject, that is, to see one-self in its place and to thrust it aside only *by the means of the displacements of verbal play.* [. . .] the subject of abjec-tion is eminently productive of culture. Its symptom is the *rejection and reconstruction of languages.* (*Powers of Horror* 16, 45; emphases added)

Locating the cultural productivity of abjection in language, the "displacements of verbal play" both conjure and rescue the sub-ject from abjection. In *Kanak Sprak*, this is evident in the "sheer delight in play with the language" (Cheesman, "Akcam" 186). The "positive" side of abjection is precisely its close link to deliri-ous writing, which is another mode of "radical desublimation" (Jay, "Abjection Overruled" 148). This helps us to read the con-junction of the abject with the sense of linguistic pleasure that so clearly marks the text, its proliferation and mixing of expres-sions, registers, metaphors, alliteration and assonance. German as the language through which the dominant society stakes its identity and excludes minorities becomes, in the code-mixing configuration of *Kanak Sprak*, both the site of the articulation of abjection and the site of pleasure.

Decidedly neither pluralist nor simply hybrid, *Kanak Sprak* signals the existence of subjects that crisscross languages without obeying national boundaries or linguistic norms, but in a way that acknowledges these subjects as still circumscribed by a struc-ture of social abjection. The seeming deformation of German is thus a productive site for imagining the postmigrant's tense posi-tion within and without the realm of the local, the national, and the transnational. Reworked forms of code-switching and code-mixing are aesthetic resources in this regard that are capable of signifying belonging, resistance, ambivalence, and pleasure. They are also resources that can lead to a reshaping of social forma-tions and the subjects who are permitted to constitute them. This joyfully exhibited linguistic "deformation" of German, for in-stance, also serves to dislodge the connection between language and ethnicity on which the privilege of the ethnically sanctioned "native" speaker is based. By writing a German that is unfamiliar and jolting, the text undermines that presumed privileged access. Nativity does not necessarily give rise to familiarity, mastery, and access to one's language, the book signals performatively.

While the linguistic dimensions of the book stage a defiant existence outside the monolingual paradigm—the realm of proper subjects with proper languages—it is also partially caught up in the paradigm's logic. Its rejection of Turkish, a language to which nativity would be ascribed, indicates the limits of the strategies it adopts. That language is represented negatively as the code of feminization, homosociality, loss, nostalgia, and passivity and is thus rejected and marginalized. That this code is primarily associated with a father generation considered weak and powerless, rather than with mothers, underscores the manner in which the linguistic codes are engaged in negotiating racialized masculinity. The "motherless" tongue of *Kanak Sprak* is set against a language figured as a failed "father tongue." Rather than actively working through the conjunction of affect, gender, and kinship embedded in the "mother tongue," the text thus merely disavows it, while remaining mired in it. The transnational mobility and masculinity associated with English, on the other hand, appears to be so inviting and full of possibility because it seems to be outside any ascriptions of or desires for nativity. Between abjection and pleasure, appropriation and disavowal, this gendered imagination of the globalized linguascape is thus precariously situated in proximity to the monolingual paradigm from which its figures are excluded.

CODA: MEDIA REPRESENTATIONS VERSUS ZAIMOĞLU'S "WORD FORCE"

The linkage between ethnicity and language that *Kanak Sprak* aims to address and reimagine was immediately taken up by the German public and especially by the entertainment sector. There, it was used to reinstate the monolingual paradigm and to render harmless the disjunctive native speakers by turning them into comedy fodder. Today, the label *Kanak Sprak* is treated as descriptive of a style of postmigrant youth language, which is imagined quite differently from the literary language of the book itself but also from the sociolinguistic facts about postmigrants' actual linguistic practices.[54]

Although Zaimoğlu's book drew attention to Turkish-German postmigrant youth language as a culturally rich form and with his title *Kanak Sprak* coined a durable term, the innumerable versions it has spawned have represented this linguistic practice in entirely different ways. Particularly comedians, such as the duos Mundstuhl and Erkan and Stefan—white middle-class German men—have built entire careers out of their version of *Kanak Sprak*, or, as it has also been called, *Türkendeutsch*. British Germanist Tom Cheesman refers to the language of these comedy groups as *Kanakisch* and defines it as "a new highly successful quasi-dialect mimicking speech patterns of the urban multi-ethnic proletariat." Specifically, he characterizes it as relying on "impoverished vocabulary and a very small set of highly structured joke routines. *Kanakisch* grammar omits articles, and knows no case but the dative." ("Talking 'Kanak'" 98).

In this version, none of the "word force" that Zaimoğlu created for his figures remains. Instead, the figures who speak in such a manner are the butt of jokes. Even when the viewer is sympathetic to them (as in the films of Erkan and Stefan), there is also always a gap, a knowing superiority over the obviously dimwitted heroes. Comedy versions of *Kanak Sprak* build on the presumption of incompetence, perpetuating the deficiency premise of both *Gastarbeiterdeutsch* and *Türkendeutsch* and turning it into a joke, whereas, as we have seen, *Kanak Sprak* turns the tables on linguistic competence and joyful mastery of the German language, reclaiming it from the "blond brows." Cemented by these comedy versions in mass media, however, *Kanak Sprak* now is closely associated with "stupidity," as linguist Jannis Androutsopoulos documents in "Ideologizing Ethnolectal German," an association that is obviously deeply stigmatizing to postmigrant youth and a far cry from any notion of creativity or defiance.

Since the mid-1990s *Kanak Sprak* has become a lucrative commodity for those able to exploit it. Erkan and Stefan even requested a copyright on their version of *Kanak Sprak* in response to a similar style featured in an Austrian commercial for McDonald's. A German court ruled in early 2007 that these comedians could not claim a "monopoly on the marketing of the colloquial language of Turkish youth" because they did not develop this style but just mimicked an existing phenomenon (*FAZ.net*). Although the attempt at acquiring copyright was not successful, the very fact of the case indicates the strange place of postmigrant youth linguistic practices between stigma and creative resource for others. The struggle over the value of postmigrant creativity is not over.

The postmonolingual condition, as these examples show, is full of contradictions and does not proceed smoothly towards a multilingual paradigm in which language and ethnicity may be fully delinked. Yet closely considering attempts of going beyond the "mother tongue" can help to begin imagining that different structure. The particular forms of multilingualism discussed in this book all move into that direction, even if they do not arrive there yet.

Toward a Multilingual Paradigm?

The Disaggregated Mother Tongue

THE DISAGGREGATED MOTHER TONGUE

What is the relationship between language and identity today? According to the monolingual paradigm, there is one privileged language, the mother tongue. This language is special because one is born into it, one acquires it with the "mother's milk" (H. Weinrich, "Chamisso") or at least at the "mother's knee" (B. Anderson, *Imagined Communities*). The individual is connected to it through family and kinship ties and experiences childhood through it. The sounds of this language can stir something deep down inside a person; this is the language of primary attachments, the language in which one first says and becomes "I." It is a language that signifies belonging and reaffirms it. On a practical level, it is the language one masters best and has full command of. Other languages may be enjoyed but will never be mastered in the same way and can never attain the same deep meaning, they can never penetrate to the very core of the subject in the same manner. This story about language and identity, I have argued, can best be understood as a linguistic family romance that constructs a narrative of true origin and ensuing identity. The concept of the mother tongue and its rich connotations, in other words, offers a strong model of the exclusive link between language and identity.

Yet, while this vision may be true for some, it is just as often untrue for others. The "mother tongue" can be a site of alienation and disjuncture, as German was for Kafka; it can be the medium of chauvinist expulsion from, and endogamous self-enclosure into, identity (Adorno); the "mother tongue" can be experienced as enforcing a limiting, suffocating inclusion (Tawada) as well as being a carrier of state violence (Özdamar) and social abjection (Zaimoğlu). These dimensions are part of the less told story of the "mother tongue."

More importantly, however, this concept blocks from view the possibility of multiple, and even contradictory, attachments, of desire for something unfamiliar and unrelated as well as the plea- sure derived from new childhoods and new connections. Reading multilingual forms against the backdrop of the monolingual par- adigm reveals that languages not considered "mother tongues" can be the site of joy and significant reconfiguration, as French and Yiddish were for Kafka. It may be the "foreign" elements of a language that enable attachment to it in the first place, as in the case of Adorno. For him, as we have seen, foreign-derived words secure nonidentity and retain the memory of historical failures rather than smoothing them over. They also carry the utopian promise of a "language without soil." Such detachment from the mother tongue is also a desired outcome of Tawada's bilin- gualism, where a foreign language is a gateway to liberation and pleasure and provides new perspectives on the world and new experiences of it. Against the violence of the mother tongue, a new language can be the means of working through trauma and recovering liveliness (Özdamar). Additional languages can help project new locations on transnational maps, as English does in Zaimoğlu's *Kanak Sprak*, or they can locate subjects in relation- ship to national histories from which they are excluded, as Yid- dish and Hebrew fragments do in the same text.

But what about those for whom the "mother tongue" does in- deed fulfill its promise and to whom it gives a sense of wholeness, belonging, and affective attachment, one might rightly ask at this moment? What if the loss of a "mother tongue" is a painful experience rather than a liberating one? Eva Hoffman's memoir of being "lost in translation" provides such an account of leaving behind her beloved Polish to become a new person in English. The readings in this book lead me to argue that while the "mother tongue" may indeed be experienced as a wholesome unity by some, the problem lies in the monolingual paradigm's insistence that this is always and exclusively the case.

The distinct aspects of the monolingual paradigm that are tackled by each of the writers discussed in this book ultimately indicate that, rather than being a seamless whole, the "mother tongue" is an aggregate of differential elements, all of which are subject to historical and social configuration. They reveal that what is called the "mother tongue" combines within it a number of ways of relating to and through language, be it familial inheritance, social embeddedness, emotional attachment, personal identification, or linguistic competence. Contrary to the monolingual paradigm, it is possible for all these different dimensions to be distributed across *multiple* languages, a possibility that becomes visible only in multilingual formations or when the monolingual paradigm is held in abeyance. Multiple origins, relations, and emotional investments are possible and occur daily—something to which the texts analyzed in this book variously testify. This means that we need to reimagine subjects as open to crisscrossing linguistic identifications, if not woven from the fabric of numerous linguistic sources. Such multiplicity breaks with the monolingual premise so often hidden in the notion that language correlates to identity. Languages do indeed relate to identities, but not in any predetermined, predictable way, as this book demonstrates.

POLITICAL STAKES: MULTILINGUAL SUBJECTS AND MONOLINGUAL CONTAINMENT STRATEGIES

Recognizing the monolingual paradigm and its workings can be a step towards denaturalizing monolingualism as an unquestioned norm and standard according to which other linguistic configurations and practices are measured. Given the political investments in language as a boundary marker, such an undertaking necessarily has political implications. For a look at how the postmonolingual condition plays out in current public discourse in Germany and how it could be refigured, it is worth considering a recent media campaign sponsored by major corporations and endorsed by the German state.

In spring 2010, the *Deutschlandstiftung Integration* (Germany Integration Foundation), a foundation sponsored by major media corporations in Germany, started its first public campaign under the title "Raus mit der Sprache. Rein ins Leben." Its ostensible goal was to encourage immigrants living in Germany to learn German. To this end, the foundation produced publicity materials that were carried in newspapers and magazines, and on websites and public billboards. In all these formats, the campaign slogan was superimposed on a series of photographs, each showing a more or less prominent minority figure in his or her twenties, thirties, or forties. Ranging from sports stars and politicians to hip-hop musicians and other entertainers, the depicted subjects appear as lively, excited, and happy, or hipster cool. The focal point of each of these largely grey-hued pictures, meanwhile, is the tongue: each subject sticks out a tongue that has been painted in bright stripes of the German national colors of black, red, and gold. In this manner, the campaign promises inclusion and enjoyment to those who allow their bodies to be painted in the national colors exclusively.

The campaign's slogan underscores this exclusivist agenda: *Raus mit der Sprache* is an idiomatic expression that can be best translated as "spit it out." This demand to speak is usually addressed to a person reluctant to provide information. The campaign's message of "speak already" thus construes an addressee who is willfully silent and who needs to be playfully challenged to give up that position. The second part of the slogan, *rein ins Leben*, (throw yourself into life) promises the gain from following this challenge, while it likewise suggests that the addressees are not yet "in" life. As the English equivalent "spit it out" implies, this entry "into" life first requires the abjection of (another) language, for the literal meaning of *Raus mit der Sprache* is "out with the language." In order to enter life, you have to eject language. The economy of "in" and "out" follows a substitutional logic, in which there is no room for the coexistence and interplay of languages.[1] Instead, one language has to make room for the other. The images illustrating the campaign assert this monolingualizing assumption visually: this tongue can only have one national coloring; no blurring of the colors, no blurring of the lines is visible.

This campaign represents in some ways the opposite of the artwork *Wordsearch*, with which I began this book. As I have shown there, in *Wordsearch* the individual becomes the scale at which the mother tongue concept is preserved, while the global city on which it draws—New York—is imagined as multilingual via the side-by-side coexistence of undisturbed "mother tongues." In this way, *Wordsearch* may be multilingual but it does not go "beyond the mother tongue." The media campaign, on the other hand, responds to potential multilingualism in the national space by wanting to paint all tongues in the same colors. Here, the question of the "mother tongue" of the depicted individuals remains secondary to the desire to represent the nation as a linguistically homogeneous place.[2] As the campaign slogan suggests: out with the (other) language. Even the campaign's design underscores this attitude, as it advertises German language courses primarily in German rather than in languages that beginning learners might know. That is, the campaign refuses even to acknowledge the multilingualism of the very public it is allegedly addressing and instead insists on reproducing the vision of a purely monolingual national space.

With the recuperation of the notion of a "national tongue" and its inscription onto the very bodies of minorities, this campaign is symptomatic of recent political and social developments in contemporary Germany that once again stress homogeneity as an ideal.[3] Despite the deep-seated demographic changes in the

postwar period due to migration, elaborated in chapter 5, political elites admitted only in the late 1990s that such migration was
not a temporary or marginal issue. Yet this admission and some
accompanying legal changes—such as modifications of the citizenship law—provoked a defensive response that sought to assert
the continued primacy of German culture. The term *Leitkultur*
(guiding or lead culture), coined by political scientist Bassam Tibi
and popularized by Christian Democratic politician Friedrich
Merz in the late 1990s, articulated this desire for continued cultural hegemony. The German language was from the beginning
the sine qua non of this *Leitkultur.* Rather than simply see German as a necessary language for navigating in the country, this
debate increasingly cast other languages as damaging and counter to "integration."[4]

This stress on homogeneity, I would argue, constitutes an
inadvertent admission of the reality of heterogeneity. In postmonolingual terms, it constitutes an attempted reassertion of the
monolingual paradigm vis-à-vis the realization of multilingual
realities. Coloring the tongue is a response to recognizing that
not all tongues are German, that the country is multilingually inhabited. This particular vision does not want to admit the nature
of multilingual practices, the ability to live multiple belongings,
but neither does it want to admit the reality that many minorities
are already German speakers, even if the dominant society does
not yet believe that.

This move to homogeneity does not target all languages in the
same way, however. Recent debates about bilingual schools demonstrate differential treatment of multilingualisms in the German context.[5] While bilingual English-German schools are rapidly gaining in popularity and are welcome, the call for opening
Turkish-German bilingual schools has been met with a strong
negative reaction by the public.[6] Green Party head Cem Özdemir
noted in this context that the responses to a proposal for a bilingual Turkish-German school almost gave the impression that
"Turkish was a language of lepers" (quoted in Wierth, "Zweisprachige Gymnasien"), expressing the abjection of Turkish in

contemporary Germany. Multilingualism thus takes on a different status depending on the languages involved. This is even true
when the individuals involved are not themselves working-class
immigrants. The experiences of a Turkish-American academic
couple residing in Germany for research purposes illustrate this
differential treatment across levels of class and education.[7] Raising their children bilingually at home, with Turkish and English,
the couple also facilitated their German-learning in daycare during their temporary stay in the country. Despite this fact, daycare
workers reprimanded one parent for speaking in Turkish to the
children. No such situation arose for the parent speaking in English to the same children, however.

The differential attitude towards Turkish in the contemporary
German linguascape is closely connected to what anthropologist
Ruth Mandel helpfully calls "selective cosmopolitanism" (*Cosmopolitan Anxieties* 14). With this term, Mandel describes the
fact that Turkishness and forms of Turkish culture pose a challenge to German self-conceptions of cosmopolitanism. While
seeing themselves as cosmopolitan—as consumers of Italian or
Chinese food, Brazilian or African dancing, and so on—many
majority Germans cannot accept Turkishness as part of this cosmopolitanism. This means that, on the one hand, Turkish-Germans are not considered cosmopolitan themselves and, on the
other hand, that Turkish-German cultural expressions are not
considered part of a cosmopolitan spectrum, but rather are stigmatized and viewed as abject. Using Mandel's term, we could
therefore speak of a "selective multilingualism" reigning in contemporary Germany. Not all multilingual practices are rejected;
instead, some, involving particular languages, are more heavily
policed than others.

Given the selective multilingualism of the present vis-à-vis
Turkish (and Arabic), a historical memory of how various minority subjects have grappled with inclusion into and exclusion from
the German language could be a helpful corrective to the pathol-
ogizing attitudes towards Turkish and the position of Turkish-
German speakers in the contemporary political scene. The design

of my book, which combines pre- and post-Holocaust German-Jewish writing with postunification Turkish-German writing, as well as a Japanese-German writer, evokes that historical memory. There is a continuity of grappling with linguistic difference that affects primarily those deemed internal others, even if the specific linguistic practices, languages, and styles, as well as the larger historical dynamics, differ.

EMBRACING A DEETHNICIZED GERMAN, OR, GERMAN BEYOND THE MOTHER TONGUE

Especially in light of the selective multilingualism of the public sphere and although they relate stories of loss and exclusion, what is remarkable in the chapters of this book focusing on Turkish-German constellations is the turn towards German, accompanied by a—postmonolingual—twist. In fact, contrary to expectations, *Beyond the Mother Tongue* does not document multilingual moves *against* German. Rather, the writings discussed here all *embrace* German, but as something other than the public discourse would have it. The German that emerges here in postmonolingual perspective has been and continues to be a home for many—a home that is itself undergoing transformation, a home that is not exclusionary, that it is impure, marked, tainted, "enriched," and charged. The use of German by those not deemed legitimate speakers, whether Kafka or Zaimoğlu, indicates that German is already a lingua franca—with all the de/formations that happen to such a language, as the different forms of "Englishes" in the world demonstrate. This view of German as a lingua franca rather than as a purely national language could be a curative to the proprietary, exclusionary claims made on the language today. Instead of coloring the tongues of minorities in national colors, it would mean bringing out the new colors the language takes on through its multitude of new speakers.

How else to understand what German is doing in the periphery of Mongolia today? This question is raised by the German-language writings of Galsan Tschinag, a member of the Tuvan minority in Mongolia who learned German in the socialist "brother republic" of the GDR. After his return home, he transformed the heretofore solely oral traditions of his Tuvan people into literature in German. Tschinag continues to live in Mongolia and write in German. His use of the language radically delinks it from ethnicity and territory and turns German into a "nomadic" language and *trans*national cultural archive to inscribe a minority history in another national context. But Tschinag is not alone.

Let me end with a brief glance at another easily overlooked route through the contemporary linguascape. In the 1999 Turkish film *Güneşe Yolculuk* (Journey to the Sun) by director Yeşim Ustaoğlu, the German language makes an unexpected appearance. The film takes place in Turkey and combines a story about the repression of Kurds with a story about Turkish-Kurdish friendship and love. In the midst of this film, which moves from Istanbul to rural eastern Turkey and at first sight has nothing to do with Germany or Germans, a shy teenager, who does not speak any German, confesses his love to his girlfriend—in German. Through this shy, secretly learned *Ich liebe Dich*—or, as it is pronounced in the film "Ih libbe dih"—German becomes, for a short, moving moment, the language of a love in Anatolia. This German is not tied to nationality or ethnicity, but rather constitutes a moment in which the oppressive ethnic ascriptions that set the story into motion are held at bay in utopian fashion. This confession of love does not refer back to ethnicity but comes out of new linguascapes enabled by migration. The teenager addresses his girlfriend in German because she is one of the "re-migrants," a return immigrant from Germany. Through this return migration, the German language has also migrated into new spaces, and just as, despite all animosity towards them, Turkish and Kurdish have found a new home in Europe, German has also become a "Turkish" and "Kurdish" language. Like the German-language writings discussed in this book, this deterritorialized German confession of love is also an expression of the postmonolingual condition.

NOTES

INTRODUCTION

1. *Wordsearch* was realized under the auspices of the Deutsche Bank art series *Moment*, which began in 2001 and solicited original conceptual art works (Deutsche Bank Art). It can be partially viewed on the accompanying website: moment-art.com/moment/wordsearch/e/index.php.

The cover image of the present book is drawn from a photograph of another multilingual artwork, the mural *Le mur des je t'aime* (Wall of I Love Yous) conceived by Frédéric Baron and produced with the help of calligrapher Claire Kito in 2000. Printed on glazed tile, it features the handwritten phrase "I love you" in numerous languages in a small park adjacent to the Abbesses metro station in Paris. Visitors have added their own writings to the wall, thereby changing and expanding the original pattern. Much of the following analysis of *Wordsearch* also applies to *Le mur des je t'aime*. For an alternate multilingual employment of "I love you," see the example I discuss in my conclusion.

2. Throughout this book, I use "multilingualism" as an umbrella term that can refer to different linguistic phenomena involving two or more languages. Each of these phenomena will be separately described and defined when first mentioned. Such definitions are necessary since there is no coherent, agreed-upon terminology, either within or across specific disciplines (or languages). Anglophone linguists, for example, tend to use the term "multilingualism" when referring to language issues at the macro level (i.e., processes of language change and language death) and "bilingualism" when referring to language issues involving individual speakers at the micro level (i.e., the study of code-switching), although they sometimes also employ these terms to distinguish the number of languages concerned (Clyne, "Multilingualism"). Literary and cultural studies terminology is even less settled. It includes the

traditional "polyglot," which has usually been reserved for the linguistic abilities of intellectual elites—think Renaissance humanists—and is closely associated with elite cosmopolitanism. The more frequent contemporary umbrella terms are "bilingual" (see Sommer, *Bilingual Aesthetics;* Courtivron, *Lives in Translation*) and "multilingual" (see Sollors, *Multilingual America;* Schmeling and Schmitz-Emans, *Multilinguale Literatur*). Of these, "bilingual" may carry a greater political connotation, at least in the United States, as it is associated with the linguistic situation of immigrants and minorities—think "bilingual education." Further coinages with widely varying definitions include but are not limited to "polylingual," "interlingual," "plurilingual," or "translingual" (sometimes also featuring the suffix "-istic," such as in the "translinguistic sculpture"). This diversity testifies to the evolving state of the field and the great variety of phenomena that it includes. Because my study touches on a range of linguistic practices and conditions, I have chosen "multilingual" as an umbrella term. For my purposes, "bilingual" appears too tied to the individual level and to the numerical notion of two languages.

3. With roughly six thousand languages spoken in about two hundred countries currently in existence, it is obvious that language contact situations abound in the world, as linguist Li Wei notes ("Dimensions of Bilingualism" 3). Wei adds that "one in three of the world's population routinely uses two or more languages for work, family life, and leisure," especially in "many countries in Africa and Asia, [where] several languages co-exist and large sections of the population speak three or more languages" (4, 7). Michael Clyne, another linguist, concludes that "there are probably more bilinguals in the world than monolinguals" ("Multilingualism" 300). For documentations of multilingualism in literary history, see Forster, *The Poet's Tongues*, and Kellman, *The Translingual Imagination*.

4. For references to the belated nature of monolingualism, see translation scholar Lefevere, *Translation*; linguists Braunmüller and Ferraresi, *Aspects of Multilingualism*; education scholar Hu, *Schulischer Fremdsprachenunterricht*; literary critics Feldman, *Modernism and Cultural Transfer*; Forster, *The Poet's Tongues*; Kremnitz, *Mehrsprachigkeit in der Literatur*; and Steiner, *Extraterritorial*.

5. On a "monolingual bias" in the fields of linguistics, linguistic anthropology, and psychology, see Aneta Pavlenko (*Emotions and Multilingualism*). Mary Catherine Davidson likewise refers to a "monolingual bias" in the study of medieval multilingualism (*Medievalism, Multilingualism, and Chaucer*), while Ingrid Gogolin refers to a "monolingual habitus" built into the German educational system

(*Der monolinguale Habitus*). I use the term "paradigm" to indicate the way in which presumptions of monolingualism thoroughly structure both modern modes of thinking and the makeup of institutions.

6. Besides Gogolin, *Der monolinguale Habitus,* see Hu's remarkable case study, *Schulischer Fremdsprachenunterricht*, for two examples from contemporary Germany.

7. On widespread linguistic diversity in France at the time of the revolution, see David A. Bell, who notes that this multilingualism was not seen as an issue prior to 1790 ("Lingua Populi" 1409–10).

8. On the significance of language for the nation as imagined community, see the classic study by Benedict Anderson, *Imagined Communities*. His attention to print-capitalism indicates crucial historical preconditions for the monolingual paradigm. At the same time, Anderson's own assumptions about language(s) reveal that he, too, is caught up in this paradigm, falsely declaring, for instance, that "the bulk of mankind is monoglot" throughout history (*Imagined Communities* 38).

9. To this end, the EU has formulated specific language policies, such as in its New Framework Strategy for Multilingualism, although it has been slow to implement them. For a critical view of these policies, see Gal, "Migration, Minorities, and Multilingualism."

10. For an exemplary reading of mono- and multilingualism in transnational cinema, see David Gramling's essay on Fatih Akın's films, "On the Other Side of Monolingualism."

11. See, for example, Hoffman, *Lost in Translation*; Kaplan, *French Lessons*; Isabelle de Courtivron's collection of bilingual writers reflecting on their languages, *Lives in Translation*; Ogulnick's collection of testimonies from bilingual subjects speaking about their everyday experiences, *Language Crossings*. On the language memoir as a genre, see Kramsch, *The Multilingual Subject*, who productively draws on it for rethinking second-language acquisition from a multilingual perspective, as well as Brian Lennon's more critical take in his study *In Babel's Shadow*, where he points to the paradoxically monolingual form that most of these narratives take under the influence of trade publishing industry pressures.

12. Besides Forster, *The Poet's Tongues*, and Kellman, *The Translingual Imagination*, see Sollors, *Multilingual America*; Sommer's attention to multilingualism across the humanities, law, and education in her book *Bilingual Aesthetics* and her edited volume *Bilingual Games*; and Seyhan's exploration of multilingualism in U.S. and German minority literature, *Writing outside the Nation*. The edited volumes *Multilinguale Literatur im 20. Jahrhundert* (Manfred

Schmeling and Monika Schmitz-Emans) and *Exophonie: Anders-Sprachigkeit (in) der Literatur* (Susan Arndt et al.) are two significant German-language contributions to this field, focusing on literature.

13. On the cultural dynamics of globalization, albeit without attention to language, see Appadurai, *Modernity at Large*.

14. See, for instance, Kellman's list of what he calls "translingual" writers—meaning both those who write works in more than one language and those who write primarily in a belatedly acquired language—which usefully underscores the prevalence of multilingualism from antiquity to the present, yet does not provide historicized distinctions (*Translingual Imagination* 117–18).

15. For instance, literary critics Johann Strutz and Peter V. Zima note how amazed the French poet Mallarmé was that Englishman William Beckford wrote his 1782 novel *Vathek* in French; Mallarmé could only imagine a "mystérieuse influence" behind this choice (cit. in *Literarische Polyphonie* 7). This perspective—which Strutz and Zima share—presumes a vantage point where such writing is considered rare and out of the ordinary—that is, a vantage point informed by the monolingual paradigm. Beckford's writing, in contrast, belongs to a moment before the paradigm had become dominant.

16. Pieter Judson's study of so-called language frontiers in Imperial Austria demonstrates powerfully the persistence of multilingual practices and self-conceptions in early twentieth-century rural Bohemia and the concerted effort required by monolingually minded nationalist activists to displace these. Thus, even within Europe, the monolingual paradigm did not immediately take hold. In other contexts, especially colonial and postcolonial ones, monolingualism and multilingualism played out differently, in ways that require further study. For an illuminating contrast between multilingual practices in India and monolingual conceptions in Europe, for example, see Indian Germanist Anil Bhatti, "Mehrsprachigkeit und kulturelle Diversität." Bhatti suggests that in environments where multilingualism is the norm, other languages appear as merely "different," whereas normatively monolingual environments treat them as "foreign."

17. See, for instance, my discussion of the workings of the monolingual paradigm in Japan (chapter 3) and in Turkey (chapter 4). The latter is, of course, ambivalently situated at the margin of Europe.

18. A note on pronunciation: the Turkish letter ğ is a lengthening vowel and not a consonant. Zaimoğlu is thus roughly pronounced as Zime-OH-lou.

19. This is not to say that pre-monolingual writing did not follow any rules, but rather that those rules were not based on—anach-

ronistic—ethno-national identitarian categories. For an elucidation of multilingualism in medieval Britain, see Davidson, *Medievalism, Multilingualism, Chaucer*; for a discussion of language choice in early modern European literatures, see Kremnitz, *Mehrsprachigkeit in der Literatur.*

20. See also literary critic Emily Apter, who demonstrates that this "linguistic nominalism" (that is, the conjunction of language names with alleged characteristics) continues to be a crucial site in the struggles over language today (*Translation Zone* 5).

21. In contrast to this view of languages as objects, Gal proposes rethinking language as linguistic practice. Gal's field work in contemporary Eastern Europe demonstrates the impact of the dominant conception by showing how some linguistic practices are made invisible or marginal in numerous institutional frameworks, including the language policies of the European Union.

22. For an overview of Herder's thinking on language, see also Trabant, "Herder and Language."

23. See also Niekerk, "The Romantics and Other Cultures," on Herder's "theory of territoriality" that accompanied his view of cultural pluralism and has had a substantial impact on later conceptions of cultural difference.

24. The history of translation offers an important correlate to the study of multilingualism since the field of translation, too, deals with the conjunction of multiple languages, though it emphasizes the process of moving from one language to another, whereas multilingualism focuses on their forms of simultaneous presence. For the standard introduction to the growing field of translation studies, see Susan Bassnett, *Translation Studies.* For a short overview of the history of translation as well as important contributions to the conceptualization of translation, see Rainer Schulte and John Biguenet, *Theories of Translation.* However, Brian Lennon cautions against the impact of translation studies on multilingualism, since a focus on translation obscures the fact that translations take the place of the encounter with other languages and therefore in some sense lessen multilingualism (*In Babel's Shadow*).

25. For the terms "universalist" and "relativist," see, for example, George Steiner, *After Babel.*

26. See Steiner's discussion in *After Babel* (here 85).

27. See Cheah, *Spectral Nationality*, for an elaboration of the move from the mechanic to the organic paradigms and its implications.

28. See also Anderson on the importance of the conception of "natural ties" and their "unchosen" nature for the attachment to the

nation (*Imagined Communities* 143). He suggests that it is the notion that these ties are natural, and not chosen, that gives them a "halo of disinterestedness," thereby preparing patriotic passions.

29. Although Schleiermacher asserts that the question of writing in multiple languages cannot even be raised, his own essay is haunted by this thought, as he returns to that possibility again and again, in order to declare it impossible (see "Über die verschiedenen Methoden" 86–89). On this disavowal of other languages and their insistent return as central to Schleiermacher's hermeneutics, see Weidner, "Frevelhafter Doppelgänger."

30. I discuss Wagner's statement and its specifically antisemitic context more fully in chapter 1. For a range of other writers from the late eighteenth to the twentieth century who express similar sentiments that writing in anything but one's mother tongue is impossible see Kellman, *Translingual Imagination* (ix–x).

31. In the discourses at hand, "mother" operates abstractly, by merely alluding to the affective and psychic complexity of mothers, motherhood, and mother-child relations, without allowing this complexity to fully unfold and impact the discourse. In the following analyses, I therefore treat "mother" in a relatively abstract way that does not account either for mothers in the social world, or for motherhood as a complex experience and condition. See the volume edited by Garner et al., *The (M)other Tongue*, for feminist psychoanalytic explorations reflecting on these issues.

32. For the following account I draw on Ahlzweig's history of the term in his book *Muttersprache—Vaterland*.

33. For a summary of the historical scholarship on the changing affective quality of familial relationships, see Gestrich, *Geschichte der Familie*, especially 5–6, 35, 38, 73, 106.

34. Mary Gossy's intriguing readings of gender and language in Freudian psychoanalysis develop along this path; see *Freudian Slips*.

35. In his book *Discourse Networks 1800/1900*, Kittler charts the material conditions for the production of discourse. His attention to the "materialities of communication" leads him to posit distinct discursive constellations for the periods he names in shorthand "1800" and "1900." The turn to phonetics is one of the characteristic changes in the "discourse network 1800."

36. The section "Lesenlernen um 1800" (Learning to Read around 1800), in which Kittler lays out this development, is situated in the chapter entitled "Der Muttermund." By using a word that usually refers to the cervix, though it literally means "the mother's mouth,"

Kittler relates even more strongly the image of the birth of language to the mother's body (*Aufschreibesysteme*, 37–68).

37. See Robert, *Origins of the Novel*, who considers the family romance as the very source of the novel. I have learnt much about reading family romances from Biddy Martin. See her own stimulating readings in *Femininity Played Straight*.

38. Jacqueline Amati-Mehler, Simona Argentieri, and Jorge Canestri, *The Babel of the Unconscious: Mother Tongue and Foreign Languages in the Analytic Dimension*, 72. This jointly written book constitutes a landmark study about multilingualism and psychoanalysis. As they show in great detail, multilingualism has been integral to psychoanalysis from the beginning, both in its history and institutional forms, and in its praxis. Freud treated many of his patients in multiple languages or in a language that was not "native" to analyst and/or analysand. From Anna O. to the Wolf Man, many of the cases themselves involved multilingual dimensions.

39. This characterization is Pavlenko's summary of the dominant view of multilingualism in American psychoanalytic discourse in the later part of the twentieth century (*Emotions and Multilingualism* 30). Claire Kramsch similarly argues against ignoring the "affective resonances in the bodies of speakers and hearers," including those in the foreign language classroom (*The Multilingual Subject* 2).

40. See, for instance, its operation in the current German school system, as described by Gogolin, *Der monolinguale Habitus*, or Hu, *Schulischer Fremdsprachenunterricht*, in their respective studies.

41. See Sommer's extended discussion (*Bilingual Aesthetics* 157–75).

42. Forster's 1970 book *The Poet's Tongues: Multilingualism in Literature* was the first monograph on literary multilingualism. A New Zealand comparatist with a specialization in the late Middle Ages and the Early Modern period—that is, pre-monolingual periods—Forster compiled a wide range of examples of multilingualism from antiquity to the twentieth century during his career, and published individual articles on some of them, before he collected them in his book. At the time of publication, his book was welcomed, yet it did not have a lasting impact on the study of literature in general or on the specific study of literary multilingualism. Yet, because of its status as the only book-length documentation of multilingualism as a significant, albeit widely varying phenomenon in literature, *The Poet's Tongues* has been much more referenced in recent years. The fate of the book thus tells us something about the development of the field.

43. This important work has been done both in monographs (Kell-

man, *Translingual Imagination*; Seyhan, *Writing*), edited volumes (Sommer, *Bilingual Games*; Sollors, *Multilingual America*; Arndt et al., *Exophonie*; Schmeling and Schmitz-Emans, *Multilinguale Literatur*), and in collections gathering the reflections of authors on their multilingualism (Kellman, *Switching Languages*; Courtivron, *Lives in Translation*).

44. In the "Germanic" context alone, see, for example, experimentation with Swedish (Lacatus, *The (In)Visibility Complex*) and Dutch (Minnaard, *New Germans, New Dutch*).

45. Postcolonial studies of multilingualism offer important impulses for this book, such as Chantal Zabus's work on West African literature in chapter 4 (*The African Palimpsest*), yet it remains important to mark differences between historical contexts and cultural constellations as well, as I show in the course of that discussion. Although not specifically focused on language, the question posed by Hito Steyerl and Encarnación Gutiérrez Rodríguez's edited volume *Spricht die Subalterne deutsch?* (Does the Subaltern Speak German?) signals productive engagements with postcolonial legacies in German studies.

46. See also Sommer's criticism of Derrida as not recognizing multilingual specificity and glossing over it too much, as in his response to French-Algerian writer Abdelkebir Khatibi, the presumptive addressee of his essay (*Bilingual Aesthetics* 42–45).

47. Specifically, Arendt is speaking about the importance of having a large archive of German poems at the ready, when she suddenly cannot fully remember the expression "im Hinterkopf" and instead says, in English, "in the back of my mind." The slip is thus directly related to a mapping of the location of languages and their position in the foreground or in the back, as superficially present or deeply anchored. The published German version retains the English phrase, though it also completes the German expression she only partially remembers (Gaus, "Hannah Arendt: Was bleibt?" 24), while the English translation simply lists the English phrase without explanation (Arendt, "What Remains?" 13). The particular passage of the interview is also available on the Internet at www.youtube.com/watch?v=Qn3deYMRllk. An extended discussion of Arendt could show how much her thinking about language is indebted to the monolingual paradigm, while her decades-long bilingual writing practice—in German and English—contradicts her beliefs in concrete ways. In short, she acts out the tensions of the postmonolingual condition in exemplary ways.

48. I specifically take issue with Lennon's reading of Özdamar (see chapter 5), since her use of literal translation is inadequately captured by a focus on plurilingualism.

49. For debates and anxieties around the German language in an age of globalization, see the volume edited by Gardt and Hüppauf, *Globalization and The Future of the German*.

50. On Jewish literary multilingualism, see for instance Wirth-Nesher, *Call It English*; Feldman, *Modernism and Cultural Transfer*; Wittbrodt, *Mehrsprachige jüdische Exilliteratur*.

51. Michael Brenner's edited volume on Jewish languages in German contexts is a valuable contribution to this direction (*Jüdische Sprachen in deutscher Umwelt*).

52. Besides Adelson's pioneering conceptual work, see also Konuk's study of German-Jewish exiles in Turkey, *East West Mimesis*.

53. Some authors, such as Doğan Akhanlı and Kemal Yalçın, write in Turkish only, even as they live in Germany (on these authors see Konuk, "Taking on German and Turkish History"). Others, such as Aras Ören and Güney Dal, write in Turkish but do so in order to publish in German translation. Some generally write in German, but occasionally also compose in Turkish, such as Zafer Şenocak, who published his first Turkish-language novel, *Köşk*, in 2008. Yet others, such as Renan Demirkan and Zaimoğlu, write in German only. This brief sketch does not yet account for multilingual practices *within* the texts. Chapter 4 and 5 discuss such practices and also demonstrate how varied they are in form and in relation to the monolingual paradigm. For an extensive account of this literature, albeit exclusively focusing on prose, see Cheesman, *Novels of Turkish-German Settlement*. In his study *Cosmopolitical Claims*, Mani further expands the definition of "Turkish-German" by incorporating a chapter on Turkish writer Orhan Pamuk into his discussion. For the most extensive conceptual reflection, with emphasis on works since the 1990s, see Adelson, *The Turkish Turn*.

54. The labels have changed from "guest worker literature" in the 1970s to "foreigner's literature" (*Ausländerliteratur*) and "migrants' literature" in the 1980s, to "literature of migration," "minority literature," and "intercultural literature" in the 1990s, to "Turkish-German literature" and "German literature of Turkish migration" (the latter coined by Adelson), to name some of the most prominent designations. The terms have often overlapped and have been used in competing ways. On these labels, see, for example, Adelson, (*The Turkish Turn* 23–24) and Mani (*Cosmopolitical Claims* 14–15).

55. My formulation draws on Ruth Mandel, who speaks of "Turkish challenges to citizenship and belonging in Germany." Mandel is among a growing number of scholars in the field exploring versions of "cosmopolitanism" as an alternative framework for approaching the Turkish-

German context. See also Cheesman, *Novels of Turkish German Settlement* and Mani, *Cosmopolitical Claims*. Because of its primary emphasis on the functioning of the monolingual paradigm the present study does not pursue this framework, although given the close association of cosmopolitanism with multilingualism such a pursuit may be productive.

56. The "Turkish turn" has also had unforeseen multilingual effects for German studies: it has made Turkish a desirable research language and has led a number of (U.S.-based) German studies scholars to expand their linguistic repertoire by learning the language, thus multilingualizing the field itself in novel ways.

57. See moment-art.com/moment/wordsearch/e/son.htm.

58. See Freud, "Fetishism."

59. All translations are my own unless otherwise noted. I have retained Sander's gendered language in this passage.

60. Several assistants did the actual work of collecting words around New York City. See Lamprecht, "How many living languages."

61. On Frankfurt, see Römhild, "Global Heimat Germany."

62. For perspectives on "Americanization" discourse in the twentieth century, see Mueller, *German Pop Culture*.

63. For his theory of heteroglossia, see Bakhtin, "Discourse in the Novel," on whose dynamic and socially imbricated notion of language this book draws.

64. In keeping with the book's focus on particular practices rather than multilingual identities more generally, this definition of "bilingual writing" therefore excludes authors such as Joseph Conrad or Assia Djebar who are fluent in multiple languages but only write in one, even if it is considered a "nonnative" language.

I. THE UNCANNY MOTHER TONGUE

1. Rindler Schjerve and Vetter, for instance, argue for the relevance of understanding Austro-Hungarian multilingualism for the treatment of languages in the process of European integration ("Historical Sociolinguistics and Multilingualism" 36).

2. I identify a similar configuration in the 2002 *Wordsearch* art project in the introduction to this book. *Wordsearch* also posits a multilingual context, yet casts individuals as primarily monolingual, indicating the continued force of the monolingual paradigm.

3. On the language situation of early twentieth-century Prague, see Spector, *Prague Territories*. On the making of "language frontiers" in Austro-Hungary more generally, see Judson, *Guardians of the Nation*.

4. Nationalist movements sought to curtail, for instance, parents' willingness to send their children to schools of the other language group. For further examples of a more complex lived multilingualism in Bohemian lands at that time, see Judson, *Guardians of the Nation*.

5. The turn-of-the-century *Sprachskepsis* (linguistic skepticism) and *Sprachkrise* (linguistic crisis) that was prepared by Friedrich Nietzsche and prominently articulated by (Jewish-)Austrian thinkers and writers such as Fritz Mauthner and Hugo von Hofmannsthal adds another, philosophical, dimension to this conjunction. Spector points out the central paradox of the situation: While languages were enlisted as solid indicators of nationality, as in the official Austro-Hungarian census, and used as means for demarcating political territories, philosophy and literature underwent a loss of trust in the solidity and referential stability of language as such. (69).

6. Spector notes the disproportionately high number of writers from Prague publishing in literary journals and in books throughout Germany and Austria during that period, compared to other German-speaking cities (*Prague Territories* 5). There was also a burgeoning Czech literary scene.

7. For a comparison of the different strategies of these writers, see Spector, *Prague Territories*.

8. See Trost, who discusses and rejects this assertion by disproving critics' claims about the supposed characteristics of Prague German ("Franz Kafka und das Prager Deutsch").

9. "Minor" does not mean (ethnic) "minority," though it has been understood by many critics in this manner. For a particularly enlightening discussion of this controversial concept, see Spector, who marks the problems in Deleuze and Guattari's book but at the same time provides a sympathetic reading, a perspective I largely share (*Prague Territories* 27–30).

10. Kafka was raised in German by his parents and learned Czech from the family's employees and at school. There, he also studied French, Latin, and Greek. He continued to improve his French beyond school and could read literary texts in the original. In addition, he independently learned Italian, Yiddish, and Hebrew at later (and different) periods of his life. For the most extensive study of Kafka's linguistic situation, see Nekula, *Franz Kafkas Sprachen*. Nekula establishes Kafka's linguistic background, such as the languages spoken by his family and its employees, as well as Kafka's own linguistic skills in great detail. The home language of both of Kafka's parents, for example, was German rather than Czech, though both were fluent in the latter and used it extensively at work. While there is evidence that

especially Kafka's father knew at least a number of Yiddish expressions, neither of the parents spoke Yiddish in childhood or later, the language having been abandoned already by the previous generation (see 45–80). While Nekula discusses all languages relevant to Kafka, he focuses in particular on the relationship to Czech. In this context, Nekula's analysis also shows how some scholars have distorted Kafka's language abilities (5–13). An edition of Kafka's letters in Czech, prepared by German scholars, for instance, includes so many mistakes that it appears as if Kafka only had a poor command of the language. The Czech edition of the same writings, on the other hand, corrects a number of mistakes in the manuscripts, so that it seems that Kafka mastered the language perfectly. In his own examination of the manuscripts, Nekula comes to the conclusion that Kafka spoke Czech very well, though not flawlessly and that he was well acquainted with Czech literature in the original.

11. Czech, for example, enters Kafka's fictional texts primarily in the form of names, a tendency that points to his own name, which means "jackdaw" in Czech. For the multilingual dimension of names in Kafka's writing, see Rajec, *Namen und ihre Bedeutung.* His correspondence with Milena Jesenská, who wrote to him in Czech and to whom he responded in German, is an exception to this rule, as Kafka unhesitatingly intersperses numerous short expressions in Czech into his letters.

12. On the importance of the encounter with the Yiddish theater for the development of Kafka's mature style, see Beck's landmark study of 1971, *Kafka and the Yiddish Theater.*

13. See Preece ("Letters and Diaries") and Corngold (*Lambent Traces* 18–24) on letters and diaries as important sites of Kafka's writing in their own right.

14. For the German original, see Fischer's critical edition of the expanded and more widely circulated 1869 version, *Richard Wagners "Das Judentum in der Musik."*

15. Mark Anderson discusses Kafka's last story, "Josephine die Sängerin, oder das Volk der Mäuse," as a response to antisemitic tropes of Jewish amusicality and specifically relates Kafka's story to Wagner's essay, as well as to Otto Weininger's writings (Anderson, "'Jewish' Music?")

16. For a discussion of Wagner's essay in the context of nineteenth-century anti-Judaism and antisemitism, see Fischer. Referring to scholarship on antisemitism, Fischer points out that the more explicitly racial form of anti-Jewish agitation fully entered discourse in German together with the word "antisemitism" coined by Wilhelm Marr

around 1879. Wagner's text predates this definition, yet as Fischer also demonstrates, Wagner's essay is among those texts that prepare the shift towards the more explicitly racial antisemitism.

17. In the case of Hebrew, non-Jewish Arab writers of modern Hebrew literature, such as Anton Shammas, have put this equation into question, even if they have not yet succeeded in destabilizing it.

18. In its structure, this view is similar to the conception of separate "worlds" in the contemporary discourse on migrants and minorities in Germany. For a critical evaluation of that discourse, see Adelson's introduction to *The Turkish Turn*. Adelson's critique of the static notion underlying the conception of separate worlds also holds here.

19. In the introduction to the important volume *Jüdische Sprachen in deutscher Umwelt* that contains Gotzmann's essay, historian Michael Brenner notes the very recent turn away from "a conception of history [. . .] that is determined by the coordinates of assimilation and emancipation, antisemitism and 'contributions' to German culture" in German-Jewish scholarship (Introduction 8). Brenner links the scholarly blind spots that have prevented the recognition of a lively Jewish culture beyond assimilation, both in German and in Yiddish and Hebrew, to a more pervasive blind spot: "the refusal to imagine a multifaceted, one may even say multicultural, society in Germany—whether in retrospect or in the present" (9). For the present argument, it is significant that this reimagination of German culture, society, and history proceeds through accounts of the way languages were complexly mobilized and resignified.

20. On key Prague Jewish authors, see Spector, *Prague Territories*.

21. Kafka seems to have seen another Yiddish theater group already a year earlier, but it did not leave an impression in the way that Yitzhak Löwy and his troupe did. See *Tagebücher 1* (55) and editor's commentary (294).

22. In his study of East and West, Steven Ascheim observes that the turn to Yiddish was frequently an occasion to articulate the simmering controversy between Western Jewish fathers and sons (*Brothers and Strangers*). Hermann Kafka's extremely contemptuous attitude toward Eastern Jews in general, and Yitzchak Löwy in particular, which Kafka records in his diary, is a clear example of this behavior. Martin Buber aided the interest in Eastern Jewish culture with his translations of Hasidic tales in the first decade of the century. He also presented his cultural Zionist perspective in three famous lectures in Prague, starting in 1909, which Kafka attended.

23. After he meets the Yiddish theater group, Kafka's diary entries are dominated by issues of Jewish history, culture, and language. See

entries between October 1911 and March 1912 (*Tagebücher* volume
1, 48 to volume 2, passim). This writing amounts to almost a third of
his diaries.

24. Here and in the following, I draw on available translations but
modify them where necessary in order to convey the original phras-
ing as closely as possible since my own readings are based on specific
formulations.

25. Yiddish speakers refer to their language as *mame-loshn*
(mother language). I have not found any conclusive evidence about
whether Kafka was aware of this fact at this point or later, though it
seems likely that in his attempts to learn the language from the actors
he would have heard the name.

26. "Einleitungsvortrag über Jargon" (in *Reading Kafka*. 149–53).
For an English version, see the translation by Ernst Kaiser and Eithne
Wilkins, "An Introductory Talk on the Yiddish Language," published
in *Dearest Father* (New York: Schocken Books, 1954) and reprinted in
Anderson, *Reading Kafka* 263–66. Because of my attention to specific
turns of phrase in the original—starting from the difference between
"Jargon" and Yiddish—I provide my own translation of the speech,
even as I have consulted Kaiser and Wilkins's version. References to
the page numbers of the translation are therefore primarily for the
reader's convenience.

27. Binder, who describes the speech as documenting Kafka's Judaism, states in his 1979 Kafka handbook that the speech is an important document that scholars have wrongly ignored (*Kafka-Handbuch*).
For some recent commentary on the speech, see Natzmer Cooper,
Kafka and Language; Gilman, *Franz Kafka*; Isenberg, "In Search of
Language"; Liska, *When Kafka Says We*; Siegert, "Kartographien
der Zerstreuung"; Eshel, "Von Kafka bis Celan"; and Pareigis, "Wie
man in der eigenen Sprache fremd wird." What distinguishes my reading from these scholars' is my focus on what Kafka does to and with
German, rather than on how he positions Yiddish.

28. See Eshel on the different—allegorical—functions of Yiddish
and Hebrew for Kafka ("Von Kafka bis Celan").

29. The poems are printed in their entirety in Binder's *Kafka-Kommentar*, 400–403. They are: Rosenfeld's "Di historische peklach" (also
known as "Die Grine"); Frug's "Samd un schtern," and Frischmann's
"Sommernacht." All three writers were established writers in Yiddish-
speaking circles, though Frischmann tended to write in Hebrew more
often than in Yiddish. For further background information on the
event itself, see Binder's *Kafka-Handbuch*, 1:390–95 and 2:503–5 and
his *Kafka-Kommentar* 387–404.

30. In order to indicate this word choice, I retain the word in English as "Jargon" when I am discussing Kafka's use of it.

31. In his diary, Kafka refers to the speech as "Einleitungsvortrag über Jargon" (*Tagebücher* 2:35). Kafka had originally enlisted his friend Oskar Baum for the task of introducing the recital but after Baum reneged, he was forced to do it himself.

32. This and the following information on the development of the Yiddish language are taken from the classic account by Max Weinreich. On the names for the language, see Weinreich, *History of the Yiddish Language*, 315–27.

33. Israel Bartal, a leading historian of Jewish multilingualism, reminds us that Mendelssohn advocated language purism but not monolingualism ("From Traditional Bilingualism to National Monolingualism"). Mendelssohn and other *Maskilim* called on the Jewish community to embrace German rather than *Judendeutsch*, and Hebrew rather than the traditional *loshn-koydesh* (holy tongue), the language of the Bible that included Aramaic as well as various historical layers of Hebrew. In contrast to late nineteenth- and early twentieth-century linguistic nationalists, the *Maskilim* continued to hold on to Jewish bilingualism.

34. Kafka read Graetz as part of his study of Jewish history in the fall of 1911. See his diary entry for November 1, 1911 (*Tagebücher* 1:168).

35. Berkowitz reminds us, though, of the important role of German for early Zionist discourse, not just because it was the language of the movement's founder, Theodor Herzl, but also because it provided the only acceptable common ground for the so-called Hebraists and Yiddishists ("February 1896").

36. Weinreich dates the turn from *zhargon* to *Jiddisch* to the historically important 1908 conference in Czernowitz (*History of the Yiddish Language* 322).

37. It should be noted that what appears so self-evident to both scholars of Yiddish and to scholars of German-Jewish cultural discourse (see, for example, Gilman *Jewish Self-Hatred* 237, 261)—namely, that *Jargon* is another word, albeit of a pejorative nature, for Yiddish—is barely recorded in German language dictionaries. Grimm's German dictionary does not list the word *Jargon* at all. Kluge and Duden do refer to *Jargon* as a specialized language, but neither of them lists the meaning of *Jargon* as Yiddish. Among the numerous dictionaries that I have consulted, only the 1913 *Deutsches Fremdwörterbuch* prepared by Hans Schulz gestures towards that meaning when it lists the term *Judenjargon*, though without further discussion

and not as a primary meaning. This history is thus not part of the official linguistic archive of German.

38. Meyer Isser Pinès's history of Yiddish, Kafka's main source for his speech, gives a full account of the negative connotation of *Jargon* as well as its origin in the Jewish enlightenment. In his diaries, Kafka uses the word "Yiddish" as when he writes about his "desire to see a big Yiddish [*jiddisches*] theater [. . .]. Also the desire to get to know Yiddish [*jiddische*] literature" (*Tagebücher 1* 56).

39. On *Fremdwörter* and the monolingual paradigm, see the next chapter.

40. According to his own diary entry, he completed the speech the night before (*Tagebücher 2, 35*).

41. Kafka's undermining of the distance between the audience and that with which they are confronted resembles what Adorno says about the structure of Kafka's fictional works. In Kafka's prose, Adorno writes, "the contemplative relation between text and reader is shaken to its very roots. His texts are designed [. . .] to agitate [the reader's] feelings to a point where he must fear that the narrative will shoot towards him like a locomotive shoots towards the audience in recent three-dimensional film technology" ("Aufzeichnungen zu Kafka" 304; "Notes on Kafka" 246, trans. modified). The fact that we find this effect in the speech as well is a further indication that the speech should not merely be read as an interesting historical or biographical document, but as part of Kafka's literary writing and poetics.

42. The association of Kafka's writings with the uncanny is well established. Vidler, for example, lists Kafka as one of the major modernist artists who elucidate the uncanny and unhomely (*The Architectural Uncanny*).

43. Other scholars tend to identify Yiddish with the uncanny. See, for example, Siegert, "Kartographien der Zerstreuung"; Liska, *When Kafka Says We*, 32.

44. Kafka appears to have adapted this example from Andler's preface to Pinès ("Préface" iii). Andler also uses characterizations such as "plus régulière" (more regular), "naturelles" (natural), and "très logique" (very logical) for the various other such cases he cites (iii–iv). However, the Yiddish phrase should read "seinen" (or in the YIVO transliteration "zaynen"), a form which Kafka lists elsewhere in his diary (see *Tagebücher* 2:24 and discussion below). He thus either makes a mistake here or else deliberately moves Yiddish closer to German for his audience. Thanks to Harriet Murav for information regarding the Yiddish forms.

45. Again, see Liska, *When Kafka Says We*, on the significance of Kafka's use of the plural pronoun.

46. Kafka probably learned about this brand new publication in the Zionist-oriented Prague Jewish weekly *Selbstwehr*, to which he had a subscription (*Tagebücher* 2, 249).

47. See, for example, Pinès's characterization in *Histoire De La Littérature Judéo-Allemande* of the multiple linguistic sources for Yiddish and Kafka's rendition of the same issue in his speech.

48. The reference to the length of the book as five hundred pages is quite literal; the main text is 508 pages long.

49. See his prose rendition of a poem by Frug, introduced by Pinès as "la fille de schamesch" (*Tagebücher* 2, 26). As noted, Kafka selected one of Frug's other poems for the recital.

50. It is on the basis of this and similar statements by Kafka that Gilman diagnoses his "Jewish self-hatred" (see his *Kafka: The Jewish Patient*).

51. It might be an intentional irony or a revealing Freudian slip that in the very claim that no grammatical mistake is necessary to be dispossessed of the language, Kafka actually performs a grammatical inaccuracy by using the false superlative "einzigste" [the most unique].

52. Kafka explains to Milena Jesenská in a letter a few months earlier that he does not even possess his present, future, or past. Describing this condition as the fate of the assimilated German Jews, and referring to himself as the "westjüdischste" [most Western Jewish] of all "Western" Jews, he elaborates "that no one calm second is granted me, nothing is granted me, everything has to be *earned*, not only the present and the future, but the past too—something after all which perhaps every human being has inherited, this too must be *earned*, it is perhaps the hardest work" (letter of November 1920, *Briefe an Milena* 294; tr. *Letters to Milena* 219; emphases added).

53. We may want to recall that the circus and the sideshow, which are invoked in this passage through the image of walking the tightrope, provide numerous settings and motifs in Kafka's writing, as in the stories "Auf der Galerie," "Erstes Leid," and "Der Hungerkünstler." Even if the passage on *Zigeunerliteratur* [gypsy literature] sounds dismissive, Kafka's own writing explores artistic performances as sites linking art and life time and again.

2. THE FOREIGN IN THE MOTHER TONGUE

1. The alleged purity of German in contrast to French and other languages is at the core of Fichte's 1808 Berlin lectures, *Reden an die deutsche Nation*, given in defiance of French occupation.

2. For a general account, see Thomas, *Linguistic Purism*.

3. The language purist movements in Germany were not only especially forceful and effective, but even stimulated and modeled purism for a number of other language communities, particularly in Eastern Europe (Thomas, *Linguistic Purism* 214).

4. Peter von Polenz, one of the leading German language historians, polemically refers to Germany as the "land of *Fremdwörter* dictionaries" ("Fremdwort" 18). Slavic languages have a similarly extensive tradition of such dictionaries, while others such as English, French, or Spanish do not (see Kirkness, "Zur Lexikologie" 88n4; Thomas, *Linguistic Purism*).

5. The undated typescript of "Über den Gebrauch von Fremdwörtern" was probably composed in the late 1920s to early 1930s according to Tiedemann ("Editorische Nachbemerkung," *Noten zur Literatur*, 705–6) and Nicholsen (in Adorno, *Notes to Literature*, 236n20).

6. See, for instance, Buck-Morss, *Origin of Negative Dialectics*; Israel, *Outlandish*; Gandesha, "Leaving Home"; Garloff, "Essay, Exile, Efficacy."

7. In order to avoid this potential conflation, I refer to *Fremdwörter* either as "words of foreign derivation" or more succinctly as "foreign-derived words." Because the aspect of foreignness is so central to the category, the alternative English terms "loan word" or "borrowed word" with their divergent connotations are less appropriate. As a result of this terminological difference, I have modified all passages in the translations from *Notes to Literature* that involve "foreign words."

8. Most scholarship on Adorno's writing on the *Fremdwort* tends to treat Adorno's two main essays as if they were interchangeable (see, for example, Levin "Nationalities of Language"; Cheng "Fremdwörter"; Nicholsen, "Language").

9. These assumptions were not always philologically correct.

10. Gerhard Härle's in-depth discussion of the rhetorical concept of *puritas* and its elaboration in German discourses from the sixteenth to the eighteenth century demonstrates the growing rhetorical conjunction of "impure" and "foreign" in detail (*Reinheit der Sprache*).

11. Härle points to the aesthetic and the moral as the two realms

that the rhetorical concept of purity partakes in, yet the invocation of the foreign also implies a political dimension (*Reinheit der Sprache* 6).

12. On Jahn as a significant figure of German nationalism and antisemitism in the nineteenth century, see Langewiesche, *Nation, Nationalismus, Nationalstaat*.

13. See also the striking parallels to Richard Wagner's 1850 essay "Das Judentum in der Musik," where Wagner denies that Jews could ever be native speakers of European languages, as discussed in the previous chapter.

14. On the linguistic situation in the Austro-Hungarian empire and its form of multilingualism, see the previous chapter.

15. For a selection of Kraus's writings on language, see *Die Sprache*, which includes the relevant essays "An die Anschrift der Sprachreiniger" (16–20) and "Hier wird deutsch gespuckt" (13–15). See also Hofmannsthal, "Unsere Fremdwörter" and Spitzer, *Fremdwörterhatz*.

16. That this attitude might be counterintuitive is attested to by Levin's and Cheng's false assumptions that the National Socialists were *against* foreign-derived words (Levin, "Nationalities of Language" 118; Cheng, "Fremdwörter" 78). At the same time, their assumption is somewhat puzzling, since Adorno actually mentions the Nazis' tolerance towards *Fremdwörter* explicitly ("Wörter" 222–23).

17. Adorno makes reference to this change in nomenclature in *Minima Moralia*, where he rhetorically asks about the Nazis: "Schafften sie nicht die deutsche Literatur ab und ersetzten sie durch ihr Schrifttum?" (366).

18. Polenz suggests that this changed rhetoric was merely a way to legitimate the more pragmatic attitude among Nazi leaders towards *Fremdwörter* ("Fremdwort" 14). Other scholars have argued that the elimination of a relatively independent organization with its own following was at the heart of the neutralization of the *Sprachverein* (Hutton, *Linguistics and the Third Reich* 43).

19. Language was of course still an important aspect of Nazi ideology. It simply was not centered on the *Fremdwort*–native vocabulary dichotomy. Viktor Klemperer's first-hand account of language usage in the Third Reich, *LTI* (short for *Lingua Tertii Imperii*), provides a gripping picture of the entanglement of language in Nazi ideology. For a more recent account of the insights of linguistic scholarship on Nazi language, see Michael Townson's chapter "Regulation by and of Language: The Discourse of German Fascism 1933–1945" (*Mother-Tongue and Fatherland*, 120–62).

20. See also the extensive study of linguistics in the Third Reich

by Christopher Hutton who concludes: "It was not the confusion of linguistic and racial categories that defined Nazi linguistics; it was the perception that language and race were drifting ever further apart." (*Linguistics and the Third Reich* 304).

21. On race and language in the *völkisch* movement, as well as tensions and rivalry between them and National Socialists, see Puschner, *Die völkische Bewegung*. The Nazis ridiculed the backwards-oriented nature of the *Völkischen* and in contrast to them combined both modern and antimodern elements in their ideology. On the Nazis' relationship to modernity, see Jeffrey Herf, *Reactionary Modernism*.

22. For postwar debates on *Fremdwörter*, see Braun, *Fremdwort-Diskussion*.

23. The critic Rainer Hoffmann lists, for example: "Abdikation [abdication], Suavität [suaveness], Convenu, Penchant [penchant], imputieren [to impugn], expurgiert [expunged], girieren [to endorse], advozieren [to advocate], affichieren [to post something in public]" (*Figuren des Scheins* 18). All of these words are indeed very unusual in German, even as many of them are easily recognizable to educated English speakers because of the proximity of these Latinate words to their English versions.

24. Adorno's conception of language is an arena that has been relatively neglected in comparison to other aspects of his thought. Hohendahl (*Prismatic Thought*) and Shierry Weber Nicholsen ("Language") are two scholars who have more closely analyzed this dimension of his work. Both scholars point out that Adorno does not develop an explicit philosophy of language and that his implicit theory therefore has to be deduced from various places in his work.

25. Adorno owes this peculiar conception to Walter Benjamin and his theologically inflected philosophy of language, as developed in his early writing (see, for example, "Über die Sprache"). Benjamin's influence on Adorno with regard to language has been documented by a number of scholars, such as Buck-Morss, *Origin of Negative Dialectics*; Hohendahl, *Prismatic Thought*; and Nicholsen, "Language." On Benjamin's writings on language, see Richard Wolin, *Walter Benjamin*.

26. The translation in this case is mine, since this entire sentence is missing in *Notes to Literature*.

27. Contrast this perspective with Spitzer's analysis of anti-*Fremdwort* discourse as a chauvinist undertaking. Spitzer draws out the parallels and overlaps between attitudes towards foreign languages and foreign language elements in German, on the one hand, and those towards foreign peoples, on the other hand, as in-

dicated in the title of his pamphlet, *Fremdwörterhatz und Fremd-völkerhaß* (Witch Hunt for Foreign-Derived Words and Hatred of Foreign Peoples).

28. When Adorno comments on writers, he frequently and approvingly notes their use of foreign-derived words. See, for example, his comments on Stefan George's coinage of new *Fremdwörter* in the process of translating French poetry ("George" 531–32; tr. 187–88). Adorno considers these acts among George's most valuable contributions to German lyric and language. On Adorno's literary criticism more generally, see Plass, *Language and History*.

29. *Minima Moralia* consists of 153 titled entries, grouped into three sections, that vary in length between long aphorisms and short essays. Critics have remarked on the arrangement and development of the entries akin to musical composition, in which multiple themes are taken up, developed, and abandoned in overlapping fashion (see Raulff, "Die *Minima Moralia* nach fünfzig Jahren" 129–30; Israel, "Adorno" 79). "Zweite Lese" is among those entries that mirror the overall composition in their own form. It consists of a series of interspersed one-sentence aphoristic statements and paragraph-long aphorisms through which different themes move. In this compositional structure, no statement stands just for itself but rather unfolds its meaning through the configuration with the passages around it.

30. For a succinct account, see Martin Jay, "The Jews and the Frankfurt School." Based on Adorno's and Horkheimer's letters and discussion notes, Detlev Claussen pinpoints this change to the period between 1938 and 1940 (*Theodor W. Adorno* 282).

31. It should be noted, however, that despite the formulation in this letter, the proletariat as a class did not play a privileged role in Adorno's thinking (Buck-Morss, *Origin of Negative Dialectics*, 24–25).

32. See also Hohendahl's reading of Adorno's Heine essay ("Die Wunde Heine") on which I am drawing in this regard: "Reification, Jewish marginality, and antisemitic polemic are closely linked in Adorno's argument. Heine's poetry is singled out by German anti-Semites because it brings into the foreground the power of modernization that they fear but steadfastly deny. Instead of confronting the power of the modern state, they displace it onto the marginal group" (*Prismatic Thought* 108).

33. See also Nico Israel's comments on the "wavering specificity of the Jews" in Adorno's writing: "What is noteworthy in all of Adorno's approaches to questions concerning antisemitism is both the carefully calibrated specificity, and, alternately, the wide-ranging generality, of Jews themselves" ("Adorno" 114).

Related to this "wavering" are the slippages in Adorno's arguments about Jews and antisemitism that Hohendahl critically remarks. As he demonstrates, Adorno at times seems to assume an actually existing essential difference of Jews that contradicts the otherwise dominant emphasis on the centrality of projection in antisemitism. An example for such an essentializing assumption is Adorno's claim about the supposed linguistic difference of Heine to his non-Jewish German contemporaries (see *Prismatic Thought* 111–17 for the full argument).

34. Against those who portray Adorno as a detached elitist because of his critiques of mass media and popular culture, Pickford emphasizes Adorno's eagerness to work within all forms of mass media (radio, TV, and magazines) as a crucial means of critical intervention in postwar German discourse ("Critical Models"). On the degree of influence of the Frankfurt School in general and of Adorno in particular on shaping the democratization of the Federal Republic in the 1950s and 1960s, see Hohendahl, "The Frankfurt School Returns to Germany."

35. Adorno's lecture to an exile organization in the United States, to which he himself belonged, "met with precisely the same opposition I am now encountering in Germany" ("Wörter" 216). However, since he does not reveal which lecture he is referring to, it is not possible to investigate this case further.

36. The negative estrangement of this reaction should not be confused with *Verfremdung* (alienation effect). *Verfremdung* (alienation effect) describes a deliberate technique of making strange that, under the term "defamiliarization," was first formulated by the Russian formalists as an aesthetic principle (see especially Shklovsky) and then refunctioned by Brecht as a representational means of social critique. Adorno is not so much guided by a desire to alienate a concept deliberately in order to enable a new perception, but rather by the principle of representing thoughts as *getreu* ("Wörter" 216; loyally) as possible. In other words, not the addressee's reaction is the ultimate guide but rather the relationship between thought and presentation. See also Fredric Jameson on Russian formalism and the concepts of defamiliarization and alienation effect (*Prison-House*, chapter 2). Plass nevertheless describes Adorno's use of *Fremdwörter* in his literary criticism as a technique of defamiliarization (*Language and History*, XXV).

37. Garloff touches on *Fremdwörter* as an element of Adorno's essayistic strategies and their link to exile, the main focus of her inquiry ("Essay, Exile, Efficacy"). Among the critics, she is the only one to focus explicitly on the function of a specific foreign-derived word in Adorno's writing, in this case the word *Trauma*. She analyzes Ador-

no's use of the word *Trauma*, which means "wound" in Greek, in contrast to that of Germanic-derived *Wunde* [wound] in "Die Wunde Heine." Garloff argues that through *Trauma* Adorno invokes the psychoanalytic discourse that he saw as necessary for working through the Nazi past but that was met with great resistance in Germany. She concludes that the negative connotation of the *Fremdwort* character of *Trauma* expresses the resistance to the psychoanalytic discourse.

38. See Rothberg for a contextualization of this statement and Adorno's subsequent reformulations in other places, along with a discussion of the numerous ways in which it has been misrepresented and misunderstood ("After Adorno"). For a collection of a wide range of responses to the statement, see the volume edited by Kiedaisch, *Lyrik nach Auschwitz*.

39. The Latin term *pax romana* originally referred to the forced pacification of much of Europe in late antiquity due to overarching Roman power, and more generally denotes the peace imposed by a dominant imperial power.

40. For this reason, simply enumerating such words out of context, as Hoffmann does in his study of Adorno's language, reveals nothing about their actual function.

41. Hohendahl observes that Adorno shares with Heidegger "the belief that language is more than signification [. . .] and that facts (reality) and language (signs) are not independent of each other." (*Prismatic Thought* 230). See also Gandesha who provides an overview of the scholarship on Adorno and Heidegger ("Leaving Home"). Gandesha concludes that the two philosophers "approach the same constellations of problems"—such as the possibility of experience—"from opposite sides" (119).

42. See also Hohendahl: "Adorno treats ontology as a form of ideology that has a specific political and social function in postwar Germany" (*Prismatic Thought* 229). My account of the history of the word *Jargon* as a derogatory name for Yiddish in the previous chapter adds an additional, ironic dimension to Adorno's title, as it can be read as labeling Heidegger's language as somehow "Eastern Jewish."

43. Adorno's critical perspective on English, which admittedly slides into stereotyping at times (see Levin, "Nationalities of Language"; Cheng "Fremdwörter"), makes it easy to ignore the fact that he wrote some texts in the language. A consideration of this bilingual writing practice might render new insights into Adorno's thinking, as Claussen's comparison of Adorno's 1949 English-language essay "Toward a Reappraisal of Heine" with the much better-known 1956

German essay "Die Wunde Heine" suggests (Claussen, *Theodor W. Adorno*, 38–40).

44. On communication versus expression, see also Nicholsen, "Language" 66–67.

45. For a contrary perspective on the possibilities of writing in a foreign language, see the next chapter on the Japanese and German bilingual writer Yoko Tawada.

46. In his translator's preface to *Prisms*, in which he discusses the (un)translatability of Adorno's German into English, Samuel Weber largely agrees with Adorno's contention on the "metaphysical surplus" of the German language ("Translating the Untranslatable"). Weber argues that this dimension, based in part on the concreteness of German terms such as *Anschauung* or *Aufhebung* is lost in translation into Latinate forms. He thus suggests that the true German philosophical terminology is native-derived, to the exclusion of the significance of foreign-derived words. From Weber's remarks, one may get the impression that Adorno's philosophical terminology is purely made up of these Germanic, non-Latinate words. This characterization obscures the centrality of foreign-derived words in Adorno's writing.

But Weber's comments on the problems involved in translating Adorno into English nevertheless illuminate the function of the foreign-derived word in Adorno's writing. In English, translators are frequently forced to rely on Latinate words where Adorno chooses "Germanic" ones in the original. As a result, the English translation cannot render the constant interplay between *Fremdwort* and "Germanic" word that, as I argue, marks Adorno texts.

47. In contrast to the familiar nature of the word "zealotry" in English, *Zelotentum*—which originally referred to a Jewish party that attempted to overthrow Roman rule in the first century—is a little-used word in German. *Paränese* refers to a religious tract of caution.

48. As Hohendahl points out, however, Adorno's analysis of power relations in education is complicated. Teachers, for Adorno, are "a relatively powerless and therefore potentially resentful social group" (*Prismatic Thought* 62). Yet they are also "persons who enforce social discipline" and thereby "become the mediators of social violence" (63).

49. On the "mother tongue" as a stand-in for the law of the father, see also the introduction.

50. *Ressentiment* is a foreign-derived term that Adorno uses a few paragraphs earlier in the same essay and that is a significant term in postwar German discourse. For Nietzsche, who introduced the term to German discourses, *ressentiment* is a key element of slave moral-

ity that does not want others to enjoy what it cannot have for itself. Such a view of resentments came into play in the postwar years as a way to deflect German feelings of guilt and Jewish victimization. See also Jean Améry's important contribution to the debate in the 1960s in his essay "Ressentiments," where he defends the feeling as a necessary ethical reminder in the absence of a proper working through of the events of the Holocaust.

51. The significance of this combination of both sexualization and racialization for the specific valuation of the words in Adorno's discourse becomes even more evident if we consider these axes in his earlier essay. In "Über den Gebrauch von Fremdwörtern," Adorno distinguishes between "soft," assimilatory *Fremdwörter*, and "hard," disruptive ones. He characterizes words such as *Geste* (gesture) and *mondän* (of highly elegant style) as words "that adapt to the language or affirm it through charm and refinement while seeming to stand in its way" (642; tr. 288). The references to fashionable stylishness and charm code these words as feminine. The behavior that is ascribed to them in an anthropomorphic way—namely, passive integration or at best counterfeit resistance—also follows clichés of female behavior. Adorno dismisses these types of foreign-derived words as too easily appropriable by a purist discourse.

He juxtaposes them to words that are coded as masculine: "But what about the hard, artificial, unyielding foreign-derived words [. . .] that do not dissolve into language?" (642; tr. 288). Elsewhere in the same essay, Adorno likens these *Fremdwörter* to "wandering bullets" in the "language body" thus underscoring their metallic, inorganic, dangerous, solid, and, not the least, phallic nature that does not "melt away." The distinction between assimilatory and disruptive *Fremdwörter* that governs this essay occurs only alongside a gendered axis without additional racialized connotations. In this gendered but not racialized contrast, the qualities of the masculine coded words are the only ones to ensure continued nonidentity to the surrounding language, since they are disruptive and unyielding.

In "Words from Abroad" the dimension of racial difference that is implied in the "exotic girls" simile deflects the danger of assimilation that Adorno ascribes to the refined, European, feminine *Fremdwörter*. While the race-based difference of these "exotic girls" does not seem to run the risk of dissolving into the German language, their nonidentity is however not an adversarial, threatening one like that of the "wandering bullets" in the early essay.

No gender dimension is specified in the passage "Words of foreign derivation are the Jews of language." We can however speculate that the unmarked case most often refers to the dominant element in a binary pair, which in this case would be male. The "Jews" of the *Minima Moralia* passage could thus be read as implicitly male. In that way they would represent the position of *Fremdwörter* figured as racialized and male.

52. While the exotic girls are a simile for foreign-derived words, they are not figured as having or using any language themselves. They are mute figures who embody an attractive, tantalizing otherness, not a different language. This muteness sets them apart from the figure of the sirens who play such an important role in Adorno and Horkheimer's reading of the dialectic of enlightenment. See also Nancy Love on the sirens as figurations of the feminine ("Why do the Sirens Sing?").

53. Adorno writes of the *Stockung* (hesitation, here also: blockage) that the foreign-derived word causes (231; tr.198).

54. See Hoffmann, who categorizes Adorno's *Fremdwörter* into three groups: general educated language (*Bildungssprache*), disciplinary terminology from philosophy and related fields (*Fachsprache*), and finally rare and unusual words that are not part of either of the first groups, such as the ones listed earlier, which he describes as belonging to Adorno's idiolect (*Figuren des Scheins* 18).

55. Although *Minima Moralia* is rightly considered among Adorno's most autobiographical writings, it is not so in any conventional sense, not the least because Adorno rigorously problematizes the concept of subjectivity, as Israel reminds us ("Adorno" 77).

56. See *Adorno Bildmonographie* (175) for excerpts of his mother's 1948 account of their experiences during and after *Kristallnacht*.

57. The grammatical category of mood (in German: *Modus*) should not be confused with the nonlinguistic term "mood" (in German: *Stimmung*), referring to an atmosphere or a person's state of mind or temper, though in this case it is an intriguing coincidence that Adorno uses this grammatical category to express a mood in the latter sense.

58. This vocabulary choice represents yet another case where the English translation cannot render the difference between *Fremdwort* and Germanic word, as Weber laments, that is significant in the unfolding of the passage.

59. On the connection of melancholia and spatialization as characteristic of the figurations of this affect, see Schwarz, *Melancholie*.

60. The Greek-derived *Echo* might be added to this list, though it might also be considered a *Lehnwort*.

61. *Konjunktiv* is the central term of this passage, describing

the linguistic form that causes the emotional upheaval in greatest proximity.

62. Both the lure of the seductive (racial) other and shock are part of the inventory of modernism, albeit testifying to its different facets and emphases. The provenance of both these models underscores that Adorno's approach to the *Fremdwort* is embedded in a modernist sensibility, with his arguments, images, and figurations specifically connected to high modernist aesthetics. It is this sensibility that sets his take apart from other defenses of the foreign-derived word in the twentieth century.

63. *Erde* in the phrase *Sprache ohne Erde* can be translated as "soil," "earth," or "ground."

64. For essays engaging with this figure, see Gerhard Richter, *Language without Soil*. Numerous essays in this excellent collection touch on "Wörter aus der Fremde" and *Fremdwörter* more generally, but none discuss them in depth.

65. See the rhetoric of the "Verein Deutsche Sprache e.V." (VDS), the leading contemporary purist organization, which focuses almost entirely on English words in current German usage. For a critique of the VDS see linguist Anja Stukenbrock, "Aus Liebe zur Muttersprache?"

66. For a range of perspectives on this issue, see Gardt and Hüppauf, *Globalization and the Future of German*.

3. DETACHING FROM THE MOTHER TONGUE

1. This chapter's definition of literary bilingualism as *writing* in two or more languages would thus include authors such as Vladimir Nabokov and Samuel Beckett but not Joseph Conrad, who wrote in one language only, albeit not in the "mother tongue."

2. See the "Synchronopse," an annotated bibliography of Tawada's publications in Germany and Japan in two parallel columns, compiled by Yumiko Saitô, which visually illustrates her bilingual publication history from 1987 to 2010. Tawada is the only significant author to write in both Japanese and German. On other "Asian authors writing in German," see Ulrike Reeg. To date, a small selection of Tawada's books are available in English translation. The collection *Where Europe Begins* contains primarily texts first published in German (the short novels *The Bath* and *A Guest*, as well as short prose pieces from *Talisman*). The novel *The Naked Eye* is also translated from German, although it exists in a Japanese version as well. Translations from her Japanese oeuvre include the novels *Facing the Bridge* and *The Bridegroom was a Dog*. The latter novel gained Tawada Japan's highest lit-

erary prize, the Akutagawa-Sho, in 1993. For translations of Tawada's shorter essays into English as well as translations of various texts into French, see the primary bibliography in Ivanonic, *Yoko Tawada: Poetik der Transformation*.

3. Translations of her works have generally been prepared by others (see Kloepfer and Matsunaga). When Tawada decided to translate one of her own texts from German into Japanese for the first time in 1995, the attempt resulted in an expansion and complete rewriting of the source text rather than its translation (see the comments in her essay "Zukunft ohne Herkunft" 69–71).

4. On surrealism as a context for reading Tawada, see Brandt "The Unknown Character." The collection in which Brandt's essay appears, *Yoko Tawada: Voices from Everywhere*, edited by Slaymaker, is the first scholarly volume dedicated to the author and contains contributions by scholars in Japanese studies, German studies, and comparative literature, who provide insights into her styles in Japanese and German.

5. On language choice in the early modern period, see Kremnitz, *Mehrsprachigkeit in der Literatur*.

6. For more examples see the list of writers compiled in Kellman, *The Translingual Imagination*.

7. On Nabokov, Elsa Triolet, and other bilingual Russian writers, see Elizabeth Klosty Beaujour, *Alien Tongues*. Beaujour's book is an important landmark in the study of bilingual writing in general.

8. For the multilingual turns of German-Jewish exiles from Nazi Germany, see the excellent annotated bio-bibliography by Andreas Wittbrodt. The best-known case of a canonical bilingual writer in postwar but preunification German literature is probably Peter Weiss, who first wrote in Swedish while in exile in Sweden.

9. For a discussion of the numerous commonalities as well as the differences between postwar Germany and Japan, see Schlant and Rimer, *Legacies and Ambiguities*.

10. The following account draws primarily on Noguchi and Fotos, *Studies in Japanese Bilingualism*. In addition, Reiko Tachibana stresses the importance of Prussia and the Prussian-led unified German *Kaiserreich* for the language ideology of Japan (154–55).

11. Based on available scholarship on Tawada's Japanese language writing, (see, for example, Tachibana, "Tawada Yoko's Quest for Exophony"), it would seem that the political dimension of her work is more readily visible in her Japanese oeuvre than in her German publications.

12. Tawada's 1996 prose text "Rothenburg ob der Tauber: Ein

deutsches Rätsel" [Rothenburg on the Tauber: A German Mystery], written solely in German, contains many of the elements that return in the later play. In that text, the Japanese first-person narrator, who is on a guided tour of the well-preserved German tourist town, likens the remnants of the Middle Ages to a "stage set" and a "theater play" ("Rothenburg" 28). Spatial continuity and temporal difference are at the center of the narrator's musings.

13. See anthropologist Johannes Fabian's landmark study of this trope, *Time and the Other*. On Tawada's frequent ironic rewriting of "Western" ethnographic poses, see Breger, "Meine Herren"; Krauß, "Talisman."

14. In the published version of the play (by Tawada's longtime German publisher Konkursbuchverlag), the Japanese dialogue is printed in the original script in the main text. German translations are provided in an appendix. Having to move back and forth between different sections of the book retains some sense of the distance between the languages for the non-bilingual German-language reader.

15. Tawada's refusal to be a guide to intercultural communication for her audience defies the expectation of those critics in German studies who read all writing by non-German authors as a site of potential intercultural dialogue. Beate Laudenberg, for instance, discusses Tawada's short novel *Ein Gast* (1993) in those terms ("Aspekte der deutschsprachigen Migrantenliteratur."). Recent German scholarship, however, is increasingly moving away from the "intercultural" model and its focus on self/other dichotomies and towards a consideration of transcultural dynamics.

16. On audience reaction, see Terry Albrecht's interview with Tawada ("Kultur und Bildersprache"). The staging was a collaboration between German and Japanese acting companies. One of them, the Berlin-based experimental theater group Lasenkan, has been dedicated to staging all of Tawada's plays and touring with them internationally since 1997. See lasenkan.com.

17. Leslie A. Adelson draws attention to the fact that today, "conjuring a world [. . .] seems indispensable to a wide range of critical and descriptive projects" (*Turkish Turn* 2). As she further suggests, it is therefore useful to ask how "a world" is imagined in a specific case.

18. For more recent neurolinguistic studies that reaffirm these findings see Li Wei, "Dimensions of Bilingualism"; Aneta Pavlenko, *Emotions and Multilingualism*.

19. Beaujour cites Adler's 1977 book *Collective and Individual Bilingualism: A Sociolinguistic Study* on bilingualism. While this sentiment was the norm in the first half of the twentieth century, most

linguists, however, came to rethink bilingualism already in the 1960s. That decade saw Wallace Lambert and Elizabeth Peal's studies of French-English bilinguals in Canada, which for the first time provided evidence of the benefits of bilingualism, marking a key turning point. The more positive view of bilingualism among linguists has not, however, fully translated into a similar attitude among the general public, especially with regard to minority and immigrant bilingualism. See, for example, Yamamoto Masayo for the continuing negative attitudes towards bilingualism in Japan ("Japanese Attitudes"), and Adelheid Hu's observations about Germany (*Schulischer Fremdsprachenunterricht.*)

20. The emphasis on the productivity of bilingualism is Beaujour's, who thereby rewrites Grayson's original argument that it is Nabokov's "foreignness" that leads him to see language differently.

21. See also Tawada's 2003 Japanese-language essay collection *Exusphoni: bogo no soto e deru tabi* (Exophony: Traveling Outward from One's Mother Tongue), as discussed by Keijiro Suga, "Translation, Exophony, Omniphony."

22. For an excellent reading of the parallels and differences between Kafka and Tawada, which gestures towards but does not spell out the fundamental difference in their linguistic vantage points, see Hansjörg Bay ("A und O").

23. See Steiner's memoirs, *Errata*, on growing up in English, French, and German simultaneously and equally. On Zaimoğlu, see chapter 5.

24. By 1990, twice as many Japanese women as Japanese men traveled abroad, while the number of study abroad students was 80 percent female (Kelsky, *Women on the Verge* 2, 5). Kelsky also argues for the significance of this phenomenon beyond the number of the women who actually traveled, since an entire discourse emerged from it and around it. This discourse circulated widely within Japan—and one may assume transnationally—among the women abroad. Although the economic crisis of recent years has forced more men to follow the women, their relationship to "the foreign" is markedly different, according to Kelsky (7–8).

25. Though associated with America and Europe, the "West" is primarily a "trope" and "fantasy" (Kelsky, *Women on the Verge* 7). See also Naoki Sakai on the imaginary status of both "Japan" and the "West" ("You Asians"). Sakai argues that both terms emerged in relation to each other, in what he calls a "schema of configuration," and can therefore not be considered separately.

26. Matsunaga traces the frequent appearance of interpret-

ers both in Tawada's German and Japanese writing ("Schreiben als Übersetzung"). Discussing Tawada's German oeuvre, Breger focuses on Tawada's staging of her figures as "tourists" ("Meine Herren"), while Laudenberg focuses on them as "migrants" ("Aspekte der deutschsprachigen Migrantenliteratur"). None of these scholars relates these facets to the phenomenon of Japanese women's internationalism.

27. Tawada, who studied Russian at Waseda University in Tokyo in the early 1980s, had originally wanted to move to Moscow, but due to cold war divisions was not able to obtain a visa. Germany was in some ways an accidental destination.

28. On the conflictual relationship between Tawada's female Asian protagonists and their European white male companions, see also Miho Matsunaga, who identifies this recurring schema especially in her early German-language work ("Ausländerin, einheimischer Mann, Confidente").

29. Susan Anderson, discussing some of Tawada's other texts, characterizes her work overall through its "hyperattentiveness to form and literality," what Anderson usefully calls the "hyperliteral" attention to the surface of language ("Surface Translations" 50).

30. Since the English translation lacks the gendered dimension that is crucial to the passage, I have inserted the German article into my rendition. The original reads: "Das kleine Reich auf dem Schreibtisch wurde nach und nach sexualisiert: der Bleistift, der Kugelschreiber, der Füller—die männlichen Gestalten lagen männlich da und standen männlich auf, wenn ich sie in die Hand nahm" (12).

31. The neuter status of "girl" in German (*das Mädchen*) can be explained by its primary grammatical feature—namely, its status as a diminutive, as indicated by its ending (*-chen*), so that *Mädchen* is literally "little maid/woman." In German, all diminutives become neuter, a logic that in itself invites interrogation.

32. The prize is named for Adelbert von Chamisso (1781–1838), who was born a French aristocrat and, following the French Revolution, fled to Germany as a teenager. There he learned German and ultimately became a significant German Romantic writer. His lifetime coincided with the shift to the monolingual paradigm.

33. For purposes of analysis I have rendered this passage quite literally and made use of brackets. Monika Totten's more fluid and explanatory translation reads as follows: "A certain kind of noodle soup, for example, is called 'ramen,' just like the German word 'Rahmen,' which means 'frame' in English. A shop where these noodles can be bought could be called a 'Rahmenhandlung.' Literally translated, this would mean 'frame shop.' The pun here is—I am sorry to have to ex-

plain it—that it also refers to a frame in a story or a framework. Historically, these two words have, of course, nothing to do with each
other. That is why such a phenomenon is not taken seriously and is
dismissed as a chance occurrence" ("Writing in the Web" 152).

34. Tawada, whose German-language poem "O Adana o Istanbul" relies on Japanese-Turkish homophones, also remarks on this dimension of her name.

35. See also Tawada's reflection on the "gate" in her reading of
Paul Celan's poetry in Japanese ("Das Tor des Übersetzers" [The Gate
of the Translator]). That essay pursues the reappearance of the sign 門
for "gate" (or opening) in the ideograms of the Japanese translation of
Celan's poems. There, the sign for gate is the opening through which
Tawada approaches Celan and the space between languages. In subsequent essays on Celan, Tawada develops this bilingual reading practice further (see "Rabbi Löw" and "Die Krone aus Gras").

36. It should be added that the East-West axis itself takes on multiple connotations in Tawada's writing of the 1980s and 1990s. She
engages both with a colonial, Orientalist map where Japan is "East"
and a capitalist, cold-war map where the same country is "West." The
German division into East and West is a further reference point for
her writing, as in her 1991 spy story "Das Leipzig des Lichts und der
Gelatine" (Leipzig, City of Light and of Gelatin) that takes a female
Japanese narrator to the borderland between these states.

37. As even a perfunctory look at psychoanalysis reveals, however,
the unconscious does not make a distinction between national languages or limit itself to just one, but uses all available material. For
the overlooked importance of multilingualism in psychoanalysis, both
in its practical and institutional development (with a large number
of Freud's analyses taking place in a language that was not "native"
to analyst, analysand, or both) and in its insights (with many of the
analyses hinging on revealing the multilingual encodings of the unconscious, as in the case of the Wolf Man), see the landmark study of
Amati-Mehler et al.

38. This question is frequently posed to individuals with more than
one language. See, for instance, a newspaper interview with Maria
Cecilia Barbetta, an Argentinean immigrant in Germany who writes
in German and achieved instant recognition with her first novel *Ände-
rungsschneiderei Los Milagros* [Alteration Shop Los Milagros, 2008]
(Schiller, "Verliebt in die deutsche Sprache").

39. *Bioscoop* is also Dutch, the language from which Afrikaans developed and with which it shares most of its vocabulary and grammar.
As a result of Dutch colonial history, *bioscoop* is also used for "movie

theater" in Indonesia. For an extensive discussion of the relationship between Dutch, Afrikaans, and other languages in "Bioskoop," see the illuminating essay by Bettina Brandt and Désirée Schyns who also discuss the challenges that Tawada's text posed for their own translation of the "Bioskoop" text into Dutch ("Neu vernetzt").

40. Tawada's novel *Das nackte Auge* (2004) manifests this tendency clearly. The novel's protagonist is a young Vietnamese woman who comes to France via Germany and lives illegally in Paris for several years. As in the turn to South Africa in "Bioskoop," the Vietnamese-French constellation in the new novel functions as both a displacement and an expansion of the Japanese-German pairing. In the 2007 essay "Metamorphosen der Personennamen," Tawada even explicitly states that she seeks out new locations for her writing, "when the readers begin to believe that they can find the Japanese gaze in my texts" because it makes her feel "repelled and locked up in a cell named origin" (101).

On *Das nackte Auge*, see Brandt, "The Post-Communist Eye." Brandt focuses on the fact that the novel is set at the end of the cold war and the fall of communism—an event that the protagonist, a convinced communist youth leader, entirely misses while she is held quasi-hostage by a West-German man. Brandt argues that together with "Bioskoop," *Das nackte Auge* constitutes a new turn to the political in Tawada's writing.

4. SURVIVING THE MOTHER TONGUE

1. To retain the difference, I will translate "Mutterzunge" as "mothertongue."

2. *Çevirmek* means both "to translate" and "to twist, to turn around, to turn inside out" in Turkish. See also Kader Konuk (*Identitäten im Prozess*) and Azade Seyhan (*Writing*), who have both discussed these as well as other examples in Özdamar's writing.

3. Because literal translation does not involve the actual presence of words in other languages, it may not look "plurilingual," to use Brian Lennon's useful term for forms of multilingualism featuring distinct other languages in a text. However, Lennon's criticism of Özdamar's "weak plurilingualism" overlooks and in turn "domesticates" the significance of this other form, by reading it only from a monolingual reader's perspective for its "foreignizing" titillation rather than exploring it from a multilingual perspective, as the present chapter sets out to do (*In Babel's Shadow* 82–83).

4. A substantial number of these speakers were also bilingual in

Turkish and Kurdish. Migrants from Turkey have constituted the largest minority in Germany since the early 1970s. For a social and cultural history of Turkish migration to Germany, see Rita Chin, *The Guest Worker Question in Postwar Germany*. For an extensive anthropological study of Turkish-German life since the 1980s, see Ruth Mandel, *Cosmopolitan Anxieties*. For a theorization of the impact of Turkish migration on German literature, see Leslie Adelson, *The Turkish Turn*.

5. As noted in the previous chapter, Tawada also employs forms of "literal translation" in her writing, yet to use Susan Anderson's useful term, these are instances of "hyperliteral" translation, which in any case do not presume a potential bilingual audience.

6. Among other prizes, Özdamar received the Ingeborg Bachmann Preis (1991) and the Kleistpreis (2004). Tom Cheesman notes that there is "far more critical literature on [Özdamar's] work than on that of all other Turkish German writers combined" (*Novels of Turkish-German Settlement* 13). Eva Kolinsky and David Horrocks's 1996 volume, *Turkish Culture in German Society Today,* is primarily devoted to Özdamar and her work.

7. Özdamar's reception has proceeded in an uneven manner. Vera Viehöver rightly characterizes Özdamar's status in Germany as "bekannt und unbekannt zugleich" (343; simultaneously known and unknown). While close to canonical in German studies in Anglophone academia, she is still somewhat marginal to *Germanistik* in Germany.

8. Özdamar's Turkish-language book is a memoir of her friendship with the important but controversial Turkish poet Ece Ayhan (1931–2002) and includes a diary she kept while caring for him in Zurich in 1974 as well as his letters to her from the 1990s.

9. For a productive reading of literature and migration by female writers of Turkish descent, which includes Turkish-language author Latife Tekin and English-language author Güneli Gün, besides German-language author Özdamar, see Konuk, *Identitäten im Prozess*.

10. This stress on the transnational dimension, which draws out both Turkish *and* German national specificity and their mutual interaction in Özdamar's writing, also distinguishes my reading from other approaches to "German literature of Turkish migration," to use Leslie Adelson's apt term. Seyhan privileges the Turkish context almost to the exclusion of the German one, which does not figure prominently in her analyses of Özdamar (*Writing*), while Adelson primarily emphasizes "reconfigurations of the German national archive" (*The Turkish Turn* 12), which I see as an important, but only partial aspect at least of Özdamar's early work. As I seek to demonstrate in the following

reading, it is possible to draw out the specificity of Turkish references in Özdamar's text as a way of accounting for the transnational transformation of the Turkish and the German archive in the process. That is, "Turkish" references may emerge out of and function to reimagine German and Germany, as well as referring to Turkish history or memory.

11. See Ahlzweig, *Muttersprache—Vaterland*.

12. Okara's approach represents one end of the spectrum of postcolonial responses to the dominance of the colonial language. At the other end, one finds Ngugi wa Thiong'o, who famously advocated the turn away from the colonial language towards the reclamation and revalorization of colonized languages for literature (see *Decolonising the Mind*). He himself began to write in Gikuyu, thus becoming a bilingual author in the sense employed in this book. Okara and Ngùgì thus practice two different modes of multilingualism: literal translation versus bilingual writing.

13. Özdamar has articulated this idea in a number of places. See, for example, her interview in Horrocks and Kolinsky (52–53).

14. Because the English translation of *Mutterzunge*, *Mother Tongue* by Craig Thomas, smooths out much of the style of the text, and "corrects" such aspects as tense, I present my own translations in the following. Although it is a pity that Thomas chose to proceed in this manner, the appearance of his translation was still valuable, as it introduced Anglophone readers to Özdamar for the first time. *Publisher's Weekly* named *Mother Tongue* one of the best books of fiction published in 1994, while the *London Times Literary Supplement* chose it as International Book of the Year.

15. It should be added, though, that the passage contains a slight historical mistake, since the script reform was introduced in 1928, not 1927 (for the correct date see Lewis, *Turkish Language Reform* 34).

16. See Seyhan, who extensively demonstrates this key constellation (*Writing outside the Nation*).

17. Diglossia describes a linguistic situation in which a given population routinely uses distinct languages or language forms in different contexts. The German-speaking part of Switzerland, for instance, features a diglossic situation where everyday informal interaction takes place in highly differentiated dialects, whereas official communication—TV news, bureaucracy, etc. use High German, a linguistic form that Swiss speakers learn in school. Swiss German dialects in turn are unintelligible to speakers of High German.

18. The following account draws on Lewis, *Turkish Language Reform*. On the use of calques—that is, neologisms developed through literal translation—in the creation of modern Turkish, see 110–111.

19. The calendar itself was of course also changed from the Muslim lunar year to the Gregorian calendar in 1927, quite literally introducing a new era. To add a personal note to this language history: although generally aware of the linguistic changes that the state had introduced, in part because my own grandparents, born in the 1910s and '20s, used a number of "outdated" words that were no longer common (such as *tayyare* instead of *uçak* for airplane), I was astounded by the reform's reach and the fact that utterly common words, such as *ekim* (October) had been invented and introduced only so recently.

20. In Özdamar's second novel, *Brücke vom Goldenen Horn*, arguments between the narrator and her mother about the daughter's wish to become a theater actress provide the impetus for the narrator's decision to become a temporary guest worker in Germany.

21. Seyhan also reads the mother as a representative of the new secular, republican Turkey, trying to negotiate different traditions and translating them for her daughter (*Writing* 145). She does not, however, consider the tension between mother and daughter in the text, nor the daughter's alliance with the grandmother, who is time and again the narrator's refuge.

22. Although the gender and national markers are implicit in the text, the narrator ultimately is not a "figural person" but remains an abstract site of enunciation, in an important distinction highlighted by Adelson for readings of the literature of Turkish migration (see especially 16–20).

23. On "Alamania," see Haines and Littler (123n11).

24. The three words are *Görmek, Kaza gecirmek, ISCI* (*Mutterzunge* 10; to see, to have an accident, WORKER). The text itself translates *Kaza gecirmek* poetically as *Lebensunfälle erleben* (10), though generally the expression simply means "to have an accident." See also Brandt, who convincingly argues that the narrator's collection of words serves to replace kinship as a mode of affiliation in "Großvaterzunge."

25. On Özdamar's preference for this mode of writing in vignettes, see Bay, Bird, Brandt, and Cheesman.

26. On the political history of Turkey in the 1960s and 1970s, see, for instance, Feroz Ahmad (121–80). Jane Cousins's 1973 publication *Turkey: Torture and Political Persecution* vividly documents the extent of political oppression, by collecting testimonials and witness accounts of tortured and killed leftists.

27. Other scholars, such as Konuk (*Identitäten* 85), Haines and Littler (123–24), Brandt (296), and Cheesman (71), have also highlighted the importance of this historical context, though they have

not related this particular historical experience to Özdamar's translational form.

28. See also the last section of *Brücke*, in which the fate of "der Studentenführer Deniz" and his comrades is recounted and interspersed with the protagonist's own experiences (302–25).

29. On Çayan, see, for instance, Cousins (32–37) and Wikipedia.

30. The same expression reappears in the section "Stimmen der Mütter" (Voices of the Mothers) in *Brücke*, right after the death sentence for Deniz Gezmiş and his comrades. An anonymous mother says "The milk, which they drank from our breasts, came out of their noses" (326).

31. The Turkish expressions are "anasından emdiği süt burnundan geldi" (literally: the milk which he/she drank from his/her mother came out of his/her nose) or just "burnundan getirdiler" (literally: they brought it out of his/her nose). See *Türkçe Deyimler Sözlüğü* [Dictionary of Turkish sayings].

32. To refer back to the earlier discussion, these "mothers" find themselves in an oppositional position to the state, and are not its allies.

33. Seyhan briefly alludes to this sentence as invoking torture (*Writing* 123). The "bizarre imagery" of some of these literally translated expressions, Sohelia Ghaussy observes, may be "disconcerting for many native German speakers" ("Das Vaterland verlassen" 7).

34. It is at this point where I disagree with the otherwise insightful reading of Seyhan, who also stresses the importance of the Turkish context for understanding Özdamar's project. Seyhan writes: "although Özdamar writes in German, her idiom retains its unmistakably Turkish memory, embodying both its rhetorical outbursts and its silences. [...] The memory of the (m)other tongue will not be erased and transfigures the new medium" (*Writing* 148). As I have argued, the memory of the mother tongue is erased by the violence in the mother tongue itself. German is necessary for the retrieval of these memories; it is not the medium that blocks them.

35. See Brandt on the "calming anesthesia" of the cut, which she relates to the technique of montage (299).

36. On the relationship between acting out and working through, see also Dominick LaCapra. For an excellent elaboration of the relationship between translation and survival, see Bella Brodzki, *Can These Bones Live?* In her readings of postcolonial and post-Holocaust texts, Brodzki productively builds on Walter Benjamin and his notion of translation as the "afterlife" of the original. Benjamin's point that translation can bring out a dimension inherent but not

immediately visible in the original applies also to Özdamar's mode of literal translation, which summons in German what remains occluded in Turkish (Benjamin, "Aufgabe des Übersetzers"; tr. "Task of the Translator").

37. This context once again contrasts with the one most often assumed by critics—namely, splitting into two due to migration and cultural difference. The notion of being split between two cultures is closely related to the dominant trope of *dazwischen* (betweenness) that Adelson has most forcefully criticized (*Turkish Turn* 3–7). In her reading of "Großvaterzunge," Adelson demonstrates concretely how "halving, dividing, coupling, and re-membering" function as "abstract patterns and literary conceits" that "demarcate a hyperactive relay where national remainders circulate in newly intelligible and interactive frames of reference" (155).

38. The difference between the functioning of sentences, on the one hand, and literally rendered words, on the other, recalls Benjamin's comment in his translation essay that "if the sentence is the wall before the language of the original, literalness is the arcade" ("Task of the Translator" 79). Although Benjamin's emphasis on literalness in translation aims at revealing "pure language" rather than reworking a historically specific trauma, his thinking and Özdamar's poetics meet in seeing literalness as a promising opening.

39. See Adelson (*Turkish Turn* 20–21) for an elaboration of this concept.

40. This is not to say that the Nazi past is absent in Özdamar's writing, though. For a reading tracing the encoding of this past in "Großvaterzunge," see Adelson (*Turkish Turn* 150–58, especially 154). See also Konuk ("Taking on German and Turkish History") for a somewhat critical take on *Vergangenheitsbewältigung* in *Seltsame Sterne*.

41. Özdamar of course does not reference only German writers. Besides anonymous Turkish folk poetry and song and the Koran, her texts regularly feature writers as diverse as Shakespeare, Baudelaire, Nazım Hikmet, Konstantinos Kavafis, and Can Yücel. Overall, there is a greater concentration of modernist writers among those whom she cites. Sometimes writers and texts are present in more implicit ways, such as the echo of Hölderlin in the phrase *klirrende Fahnen* in "Grossvaterzunge," to which Adelson draws attention (*Turkish Turn* 153–54). In the current context, I am primarily interested in the shape that the German literary tradition as a form of genealogy takes in her writing on the most explicit level.

42. Kermani presented this essay, which was also discussed in *Die Zeit*, printed in *Wespennest*, and reprinted in a shorter version in the

Süddeutsche Zeitung, initially at the Konrad-Adenauer Stiftung in Berlin in December 2006. The full text is available on the author's website.

43. On code-switching in Özdamar, see Seyhan (*Writing* 109, 112).

5. INVENTING A MOTHERLESS TONGUE

1. Edited by Irmgard Ackermann for the Munich-based Institut Deutsch als Fremdsprache (Institute for German as a Foreign Language), the volume *Türken deutscher Sprache* [Turks of German language] presents submissions to a literary competition initiated by the Institute.

2. Among the sources for the term "postmigrant" is the Berlin-based cultural curator Shermin Langhoff, who used it in the context of the annual Beyond Belonging festival (started in 2007). Langhoff has also made "postmigrant" the central category for the innovative performance space Ballhaus Naunynstraße, located in the immigrant district of Berlin-Kreuzberg, whose first director she is. See ballhausnaunynstrasse.de. Tom Cheesman has been one of the first German Studies scholars to adopt this term (see *Novels of Turkish-German Settlement*).

3. Even after the change of German citizenship law in 2000 from a "blood-based" (*ius sanguinis*) to a partially birthplace-based (*ius soli*) principle, German public discourse continues to struggle with the extended notion of belonging, as evidenced in the use of such paradoxical formulations as *eingebürgerte Ausländer* (naturalized foreigners), where the notion of foreignness persists even after naturalization.

4. Azade Seyhan has done the most to articulate the similarities and differences between these groups and their writings. See *Writing outside the Nation*.

5. The pervasive nature of dismissive attitudes towards multilingual mixing—by casting it as a result of deficiency—can be found in arenas far afield from postmigrants as well. Davidson describes how only a new perspective derived from sociolinguistics led scholars of medieval sermons to conclude that "mixed-language sermons were evidence not of improficiency in two languages" as had been presumed before, "but normative forms of bilingual literacy" (*Medievalism* 82). That these changes in medieval scholarship date to the 1990s is further evidence of that decade's function as a historical watershed with regard to perceptions of multilingualism.

6. Only a small portion of Zaimoğlu's writing has been translated into English at this point. See Kristin Dickinson, Robin Ellis, and Pris-

cilla D. Layne's award-winning translation of selected monologues from *Koppstoff* [Head Stuff], and Darren Illet's translation of "The Father Story" from *Abschaum* [Scum]. While those earlier works are written in a style similar to *Kanak Sprak*, Zaimoğlu's move to a different literary voice is apparent in his 2004 story collection *Zwölf Gramm Glück* [Twelve Grams Happiness], two stories from which are available in English translation (by Margot Bettauer Dembo) on the Web (see Zaimoğlu, *Twelve Grams of Happiness*, trans. Margot Bettauer Dembo).

7. Several subsequent novels, story collections, theater plays and highly publicized media appearances have firmly established Zaimoğlu as a leading figure in contemporary German literature. For an overview of his career and discussions of his other works, see Tom Cheesman and Karin Yeşilada's forthcoming edited volume *Feridun Zaimoğlu*.

8. On the fit and function of the male-to-female transsexual in the array of male *Kanak* monologists, as well as the treatment of masculinity in Zaimoğlu's early work more generally, see Yildiz, "Wordforce."

9. On the reception of the book, see Cheesman, *Novels of Turkish German Settlement*; on the spread of the label "Kanak Sprak," see Yildiz "Critically '*Kanak*.'"

10. The word *Kanake* itself has made a curious journey from the South Seas to postwar Germany. The Canaques of New Caledonia in the South Pacific are an indigenous people, colonized by the French, who have struggled for self-rule throughout the twentieth century and into the twenty-first. In Hawai'ian, the word simply means "human being" (see Adelson "Touching" 116n63). Under colonialism, the word traveled from the Pacific to Europe and France, where it took on the connotation of cannibal, before becoming a standard slur hurled at labor migrants in Germany after the 1960s.

11. For a detailed comparison between actual linguistic practices of Turkish-German youth and the linguistic style presented by Zaimoğlu, see Carol Pfaff, "Kanaken in Alemannistan."

12. Matthew Hart, *Nations of Nothing but Poetry*. Hart's primary focus is on synthetic vernaculars in Anglophone poetry from high modernism to the 1990s, yet his concept also refers to similar techniques in prose, such as in the writings of James Joyce.

13. The fact that Zaimoğlu does include Turkish words and passages on occasion in his subsequent works (such as the volumes *Abschaum* and *Koppstoff*) makes this absence in *Kanak Sprak* even more remarkable.

14. See political scientist Nevim Çil's *Topographie des Außenseiters*, a study of Turkish-German experiences of the fall of the Berlin

Wall and its aftermath, which provides a generationally differentiated picture of perceptions of and responses to this period.

15. In German public discourses, Turkish-German women have primarily been depicted as victims of their culture and religion, while young men have been represented as potential victimizers. On stereotypes about young women and their function in German discourses, see Yildiz, "Turkish Girls."

16. In a remark that underscores the artificial quality of *Kanak Sprak*, sociolinguists Inci Dirim and Peter Auer, referring to their extensive data collection, note that they have not encountered any young Turkish-Germans actually referring to themselves as *Kanake* in the way employed by Zaimoğlu (*Türkisch sprechen nicht nur die Türken* 8n11).

17. Like "queer," *Kanak* has become the umbrella name of an antinormative cultural and political movement, *Kanak Attak* (see their "Kanak Attak und Basta!"). Antke Engel discusses the parallels and overlaps between the queer and *Kanak* movements in Germany in some detail. See Engel, "Queer-feministische und kanakische Angriffe auf die Nation."

18. As Hart notes, about synthetic vernacular writings more generally, "they trouble the border between vernacular self-ownership and the willful appropriation of languages that will be forever foreign. They are the authentic text of an inauthentic world" (*Nations of Nothing But Poetry* 7).

19. It is in part this ethnographic dimension that leads Petra Fachinger to read *Kanak Sprak* as a parodic take on muckraking journalist Günter Wallraff's 1984 book *Ganz Unten* (At the Very Bottom), which contributed greatly to the view of Turkish-Germans as helpless, speechless victims destined to be forever on the bottom rungs of society. See Fachinger, *Rewriting Germany from the Margins*. For his book, Wallraff put on "ethnic drag" and pretended to be a Turkish guest worker named "Ali"—see Sieg, *Ethnic Drag*, for the many problematic dimensions of this undertaking. Venkat Mani, meanwhile, is dubious about Zaimoğlu's claims to authenticity and criticizes their ambivalent function in his reception and establishment as prime voice of the *Kanak* figure (see chapter 3, *Cosmopolitical Claims*).

20. No monologue in *Kanak Sprak* capitalizes nouns as would be orthographically required. The text thus visually announces its transgression of rules governing the German language. To render this dimension of the text in translation, I also avoid capitalization of the "I" and proper nouns in the English version.

21. For a critical discussion of the trope of betweenness, see Adelson, "Against Between."

22. On *Fremdwörter*—that is, German words of foreign derivation—see chapter 2.

23. Through this category, we could situate *Kanak Sprak* in a longer twentieth-century tradition of noticeably mixing and melding different levels of language, and put it alongside canonical works such as Joyce's *Finnegans Wake*.

24. See Chantal Zabus, *The African Palimpsest*, for further examples from West African literature.

25. As noted, *Kanak Sprak* contains a monologue by a male-to-female transsexual, but it does not include voices of gay Turkish-German men. In general, Turkish-German gay culture is currently more visibly represented in film (see, for example, Kutluğ Ataman, *Lola und Bilidikid*) and performance (see Nurkan Erpulat and Tuncay Kulaoğlu's play *Jenseits—Bist du schwul oder bist du Türke*) than in literature. My thanks to Koray Yılmaz-Günay of the Turkish-German gay and lesbian organization GLADT e.V. for additional information on this point.

26. Some of the monologues present outright homophobic attitudes. Venkat Mani, focusing on *Abschaum*, critically remarks on the seemingly constitutive role of misogyny and homophobia for *Kanak* figures (*Cosmopolitical Claims* 121). I am more inclined to read the narrative voices that the author creates for his male figures as "ethnic straight male drag," and therefore as ironically staged (Schmidt, "Feridun Zaimoğlu's Performance of Gender and Authorship" 200).

27. See Zaimoğlu, "Gastarbeiterliteratur: Ali macht Männchen."

28. On the recurrent figure of "Ali" in German literature of Turkish migration, see Chessman's chapter "Ali Alias Alien: Mutations of the UnCosmopolitan" in *Novels of Turkish German Settlement*.

29. Güney Dal's 1975 book, *Wenn Ali die Glocken läuten hört* [When Ali hears the bells toll] literalizes this alignment of labor victimization and feminization. There, Kadir Derya, a Turkish guest worker at a chemical lab inexplicably begins to grow breasts. Unable to deal with the situation, ashamed, and with no one to turn to, he tries to mutilate himself. In the end, the text reveals that he was the victim of the cruel joke of German lab workers who gave him estrogen when he complained about stomach ache. On this specific novel, see also Adelson, "Migrants and Muses."

30. See the jointly authored essay by Jamal Tuschick and Feridun Zaimoğlu. "Ihr habt Angst vor unserem Sperma."

31. See texts such as Irvine Welsh's novel *Trainspotting*. Ahmad adds that this gendered dimension has changed since the 1980s, when female authors such as Alice Walker and Sapphire also began to write vernacular literature for explicitly feminist purposes (*Rotten English* 23). In *Koppstoff*, the female pendant to *Kanak Sprak*, Zaimoğlu creates a number of analogous female *Kanaka* figures speaking in his stylized vernacular, although, as I argue elsewhere, they at times appear to be merely ventriloquizing male *Kanak* voices (see Yildiz, "Wordforce"). With the appearance of the sexually aggressive Turkish-German rapper and media personality Lady Bitch Ray (pseudonym of Reyhan Şahin) in the 2000s, the German public has also encountered a provocative female performer enacting a version of *Kanak* aesthetics in person.

32. Mennel derives the term "ghetto aesthetic" from critic Jacquie Jones.

33. Linguist Braj Kachru pioneered the notion of "World Englishes" to describe the manifold variants of the language and especially to point to the important role of nonnative speakers in the development of their diverse forms.

34. For the German discourse, in which a critical view of English as Americanization dominates, see the volume edited by Gardt and Hüppauf, *Globalization and the Future of German*.

35. Hip-hop is the overarching term that refers to such practices as rap, graffiti, and break-dancing. Rap, on the other hand, refers specifically to the characteristic textual and musical style (Menrath, *Represent What* 51).

36. As Adelson points out, rap marks the text beyond the specific monologues attributed to rappers, since "most of the interviews read like rapid-fire, rap-like bursts of transgressive linguistic material" ("Touching" 115).

37. This anti-pop rant comes at a time of the emergent wave of *Popliteratur* in 1990s German literature, which is associated with a glorification of consumption and brand commodities, emphasizing distinction based on consumption, particularly in musical taste (Ernst, "Jenseits von MTV"). Cheesman suggests that despite Zaimoğlu's polemical stance against this literary trend (see *Kopf und Kragen*, 2001), *Popliteratur* is in fact his "proper cultural context" rather than "'migrant literature' or 'multicultural literature'" ("Talking 'Kanak'" 92).

38. *Breaker* belongs to the larger category of pseudo-English words in German, such as *der Barkeeper* (bartender) and *das Handy* (cell phone). See Jürgen Schiewe, "Sprachpurismus als Aufklärung" on this category of words.

39. On this characteristic of the perception of rap music as "minoritarian," despite its commercial success and dominance, see, for example, Menrath (*Represent What* 57).

40. Cheesman identifies the rapper as Ali Aksoy, who was part of the collaborative hip-hop project Cartel, which had a short-lived but significant success in the mid-1990s. On Cartel, see also Levent Soysal, "Rap, Hip-Hop, Kreuzberg."

41. The protagonist in Zaimoğlu's novel *Leinwand* (2003) has made this step and is a Turkish-German police officer. The language of that novel starkly signals the association of a *Kanak Sprak* code with the abject in society's margins by rendering only the speech of minority youth and that of a homeless man in a manner reminiscent of the early books, while the narrative voice and the majority of the figures—many of them police—are in standard High German. The policing of language finds its expression in this form.

42. The association between Turkish-German minority culture and hip-hop appears to exist outside Germany as well, as indicated by the first-ever *New York Times* feature to use the term "Turkish-German." The 2003 article presents Turkish-German youth via a portrait of filmmaker Neco Çelik and the focus on his hip-hop, graffiti, and gang member experience (Bernstein, "A Bold New View of Turkish-German Youth"). Mennel's essay is a critical assessment of this trend, whereas *Kanak Attak* activist and writer Imran Ayata regards it more positively as an "entry ticket to the broader public" ("Kanak-Rap in Almanya" 275).

43. What this linkage also obscures is the presence of Afro-Germans. For a groundbreaking history and self-representation of Afro-Germans, see the volume *Farbe bekennen*, edited by Katharina Oguntoye, May Opitz, and Dagmar Schultz (translated as *Showing Our Colors*).

44. See also Dirim and Auer, who stress this equation in 1990s German cultural discourse (*Türkisch sprechen nicht nur die Türken*).

45. See also the projection of multilingualism to New York instead of a German city in the artwork *Wordsearch* that I discussed in the introduction.

46. On the function of the thieves' cant *Rotwelsch* in *Kanak Sprak*, as well as its complex history with Yiddish, see Yildiz, "Critically 'Kanak.'"

47. In their essay "Germany—Home for Turks?" writer Zafer Şenocak and his sometime collaborator Bülent Tulay ask: "Doesn't immigrating to Germany also mean immigrating to, entering into, the arena of Germany's recent past?" (Şenocak, *Atlas* 6). Şenocak's own

literary work constitutes the most sophisticated exploration of this question to date, as in his novel *Gefährliche Verwandtschaft* (1998). For an extended discussion of that novel, see Adelson, *Turkish Turn* (104–22).

48. For a detailed discussion see Adelson, *Turkish Turn*.

49. In other works by Zaimoğlu, Jews also appear as part of contemporary Germany, not just as part of the past. See the character "Dina" in *Liebesmale, scharlachrot* (Love Marks, Scarlet Red, 2000).

50. For an excellent study of voice in *Kanak Sprak*, see Julia Abel, "Konstruktionen 'authentischer' Stimmen."

51. Zaimoğlu links abjection to postmigrant masculinity in other works as well. In his first fictional work, the epistolary novel *Liebesmale, scharlachrot*, for instance, the masculine sufferings of his two male protagonists propel the plot. One is the hypersexual lower-class figure Hakan, who is mostly unsuccessful in his sexual pursuits. He undergoes grotesque procedures to gain the (sexual) attention of his neighbor, yet ends up repeatedly hurting or disfiguring himself or being abused by the woman. The other, Serdar, is a poet on vacation in a Turkish beach resort whose struggle with creative and sexual impotence is at the center of the book. Between thwarted hypersexuality and impotence, the drama of postmigrant masculinity in this case unfolds as a tragicomic narrative.

52. See also Rey Chow, *The Protestant Ethnic*, for a critique of the celebration of difference in theoretical discourse versus the expression of difference as abjection in literary and autobiographical writings by ethnic minorities. Chow develops her argument through a reading of Asian and Asian-American texts. For a critique of hybridity in the German minority context, see Erel, "Grenzüberschreitungen" and Gutiérrez Rodríguez, "Auf der Suche," who both point to hybridity as an easily consumable and therefore politically limited category.

53. Drawing on Bakhtin, Petra Fachinger emphasizes the subversive aspect of Zaimoğlu's "grotesque realism" and its function in "writing back" to previous discourses on Turkish-Germans (*Rewriting Germany from the Margins* 106).

54. See Androutsopoulos ("Ideologizing Ethnolectal German") for an excellent summary of the characteristics of the ethnolect and its media versions.

CONCLUSION

1. See also Uli Linke on the crucial role of the corporeal logic of *raus* in the German discourse on "foreigners" ("Murderous Fantasies").

2. Because the depicted individuals advertise the idea of success through language learning, they are not "mother tongue" speakers of German in the logic of the campaign. Yet a number of them have learned German at home as their first (and possibly only) language. See, for example, Afro-German soccer player Jerome Boateng, who grew up with a white German mother in his native Berlin. Noticeably, no white German native speakers are included in the campaign.

3. The immense positive response to the racist anti-immigrant and anti-Muslim theses put forth by Social Democratic politician and board member of the German Central Bank Thilo Sarrazin in the fall of 2010 has dramatically accelerated and discursively radicalized this development further. For a very succinct account of the troubling public mood on the twentieth anniversary of German unification, see the *New York Times* op-ed by Jürgen Habermas.

4. The rise of the term "integration," which replaced even weak notions of "multiculturalism," further underscored this development towards greater homogeneity as an ideal. Multiculturalism, in any case, had never taken the form of actual policies in Germany, but rather remained a slogan propagated by some Green Party followers, without much support from minorities themselves. For a critical take on multiculturalism among immigrant activists, see, for instance, the manifesto of Kanak Attak, who reject its culturalist dimension in favor of greater social and political equality ("Kanak Attak und Basta!").

5. In this regard it is useful to distinguish between attitudes towards "elite bilingualism" and "migrant bilingualism," as Doris Sommer suggests for the U.S. context. As Sommer observes, majority society differentiates strongly between the bilingualism of elites, which is appreciated as constituting additional capital, and the bilingualism of immigrants and minorities, which is stigmatized and discouraged (*Bilingual Aesthetics*).

6. The biggest difference between the status of Spanish in the United States and Turkish in Germany lies in the fact that Spanish is the most-taught "foreign" language in the States, whereas Turkish is only offered in exceptional cases in German schools and universities.

7. I would like to thank the couple for sharing their experiences with me.

Abel, Julia. "Konstruktionen 'authentischer' Stimmen. Zum Verhältnis von 'Stimme' und Identität in Feridun Zaimoglus Kanak Sprak." In *Stimme(n) im Text: Narratologische Positionsbestimmungen*, edited by Andreas Blödorn, Daniela Langer, and Michael Scheffel. Berlin: de Gruyter, 2006. 297–320.

Ackermann, Irmgard, ed. *Türken Deutscher Sprache*. Munich: dtv, 1984.

Adelson, Leslie A. *The Turkish Turn in Contemporary German Literature: Towards a New Critical Grammar of Migration*. New York: Palgrave Macmillan, 2005.

———. "Against Between: A Manifesto." In *Unpacking Europe: Towards a Critical Reading*, edited by Salah Hassan and Iftikhar Dadi, 244–55. Rotterdam: NAi Publishers, 2001.

———. "Migrants and Muses." In *A New History of German Literature*, edited by David E. Wellbery, 912–17. Cambridge, Mass.: Belknap Press of Harvard University Press, 2004.

———. "Touching Tales of Turks, Germans, and Jews: Cultural Alterity, Historical Narrative, and Literary Riddles for the 1990s." *New German Critique*. 80 (2000): 1–32.

Adorno, Theodor W. "Aufzeichnungen zu Kafka." In *Prismen*, 302–42.

———. "Cultural Criticism and Society." In *Prisms*, 17–34.

———. "George." In *Noten zur Literatur*, 523–35.

———. *Jargon der Eigentlichkeit: zur deutschen Ideologie*. Frankfurt am Main: Suhrkamp, 1964.

———. "Kleine Proust-Kommentare." In *Noten zur Literatur*, 203–15.

———. "Kulturkritik und Gesellschaft." In *Prismen*, 7–31.

———. *Minima Moralia: Reflexionen aus dem beschädigten Leben.* Frankfurt am Main: Suhrkamp, 1951.

———. *Minima Moralia: Reflections from Damaged Life.* Trans. E. F. N. Jephcott. London: Verso, 1974.

———. *Noten zur Literatur,* edited by Rolf Tiedemann. Frankfurt am Main: Suhrkamp, 1998.

———. *Notes to Literature.* Trans. Shierry Weber Nicholsen. Vol. 1. New York: Columbia University Press, 1991.

———. *Notes to Literature.* Trans. Shierry Weber Nicholsen. Vol. 2. New York: Columbia University Press, 1992.

———. "Notes on Kafka." In *Prisms,* 243–71.

———. "On the Question: 'What is German?'" In *Critical Models: Interventions and Catchwords.* Trans. Henry W. Pickford, 205–14. New York: Columbia University Press, 1998.

———. "On the Use of Foreign Words." In *Notes to Literature,* 2:286–91.

———. *Prismen: Kulturkritik und Gesellschaft.* Frankfurt am Main: Suhrkamp, 1955.

———. *Prisms.* Trans. Samuel Weber and Shierry Weber. Cambridge, Mass.: MIT Press, 1981.

———. "Stefan George." In *Notes to Literature,* 2:178–92.

———. "Über den Gebrauch von Fremdwörtern." In *Noten zur Literatur,* 640–46.

———. "Wörter aus der Fremde." In *Noten zur Literatur,* 216–32.

———. "Words from Abroad." In *Notes to Literature,* 1:185–99.

Adorno: Eine Bildmonographie, edited by Theodor W. Adorno Archiv. Frankfurt am Main: Suhrkamp, 2003.

Ahlzweig, Claus. *Muttersprache—Vaterland: Die deutsche Nation und ihre Sprache.* Opladen: Westdeutscher Verlag, 1994.

Ahmad, Dohra. *Rotten English: A Literary Anthology.* New York: Norton, 2007.

Ahmad, Feroz. *The Making of Modern Turkey.* London: Routledge, 1993.

Albrecht, Terry. Interview. "Kultur und Bildersprache. Yoko Tawada im Gespräch mit Terry Albrecht." In *Theater Kultur Vision: Arbeitsbuch Theater der Zeit,* edited by Therese Hörnigk, Bettina Masuch, and Frank M. Raddatz, 135–37. Berlin: Gemeinschaftsprojekt mit dem Literaturforum im Brecht-Haus Berlin, 1998.

Amati-Mehler, Jacqueline, et al. *Babel of the Unconscious: Mother Tongue and Foreign Tongues in the Analytic Dimension*. Madison, Conn.: International Universities Press, 1993.

Améry, Jean. "Ressentiments." In *Jenseits von Schuld und Sühne: Bewältigungsversuche eines Überwältigten*, 102–29. 2 ed. Stuttgart: Klett-Cotta, 1977 [1966].

Anderson, Benedict. *Imagined Communities: Reflections on the Origin and the Spread of Nationalism*. London: Verso, 1983.

Anderson, Mark. "'Jewish' Music? Otto Weininger and 'Josephine the Singer'" In *Kafka's Clothes: Ornament and Aestheticism in the Habsburg Fin de Siècle*, 194–216. Oxford: Clarendon Press, 1992.

———, ed. *Reading Kafka: Prague, Politics, and the Fin de Siècle*. New York: Schocken, 1989.

Anderson, Susan C. "Surface Translations: Meaning and Difference in Yoko Tawada's German Prose." *Seminar* 46.1 (2010): 50–70.

Andler, Charles. "Préface." In Pinès, *Histoire*, i–xviii.

Androutsopoulos, Jannis. *From the Streets to the Screens and Back Again: On the Mediated Diffusion of Ethnolectal Patterns in Contemporary German*. 2000. Available at: jannisandroutsopoulos. files.wordpress.com/2009/09/iclave_2001_laud.pdf. Accessed 15 June 2011.

———. "Ideologizing Ethnolectal German." In *Language Ideologies and Media Discourse*, edited by Sally Johnson and Tommaso M. Milani. London: Continuum, 2010. Available at: jannisandroutsopoulos.files.wordpress.com/2009/12/sjohnson_10_fpp.pdf. Accessed 15 June 2011.

Anzaldúa, Gloria. *Borderlands/La Frontera: The New Mestiza*. San Francisco: Spinsters/aunt lute, 1987.

Appadurai, Arjun. *Modernity at Large: Cultural Dimensions of Globalization*. Minneapolis: University of Minnesota Press, 1996.

Apter, Emily. *The Translation Zone. A New Comparative Literature*. Princeton, N.J.: Princeton University Press, 2006.

Arendt, Hannah. "'What Remains? The Language Remains': A Conversation with Günter Gaus." Trans. Joan Stambaugh. In *Essays in Understanding 1930–1954*, edited by Jerome Kohn, 1–23. New York: Harcourt, Brace and Company, 1994.

Arndt, Susan, Dirk Naguschewski, and Robert Stockhammer, eds. *Exophonie: Anders-Sprachigkeit (in) der Literatur*. Berlin; Kulturverlag Kadmos, 2007.

Aschheim, Steven E. *Brothers and Strangers: The East European Jew in German and Jewish Consciousness, 1800–1923*. Madison: University of Wisconsin Press, 1982.

Ayata, Imran. "Kanak-Rap in Almanya—Über die schweren Folgen Deutschlands." In *Angeworben, eingewandert, abgeschoben: Ein anderer Blick auf die Einwanderungsgesellschaft Bundesrepublik Deutschland*, edited by Katja Dominik, Marc Jünemann, und Jan Motte, 273–87. Münster: Westfälisches Dampfboot, 1999.

Aydemir, Murat, and Alex Rotas, eds. *Migratory Settings*. Amsterdam: Rodopi, 2008.

Aytaç, Gürsel. "Sprache als Spiegel der Kultur: Zu Emine Sevgi Özdamars Roman *Das Leben ist eine Karawanserei*." In Howard, ed. *Interkulturelle Konfigurationen*, 171–77.

Bakhtin, M. M. "Discourse in the Novel." Trans. Caryl Emerson and Michael Holquist. In *The Dialogic Imagination: Four Essays*, edited by Michael Holquist, 259–422. Austin: University of Texas Press, 1981.

Baioni, Giuliano. *Kafka: Literatur und Judentum*. Stuttgart: J. B. Metzler, 1994.

Balibar, Etienne. "The Nation Form: History and Ideology." In *Race, Nation, Class: Ambiguous Identities*, edited by Etienne Balibar and Immanuel Wallerstein, 86–106. London: Verso, 1991.

Bartal, Israel. "From Traditional Bilingualism to National Monolingualism." In *Hebrew in Ashkenaz: A Language in Exile*, edited by Lewis Glinert, 141–50. New York: Oxford University Press, 1993.

Bassnett, Susan. *Translation Studies*. 3rd ed. New York: Routledge, 2002.

Bay, Hansjörg. "A und O. Kafka—Tawada." In Ivanonic, ed. *Yoko Tawada*, 149–69.

———. "Der verrückte Blick. Schreibweisen der Migration in Özdamars Karawanserei-Roman." *Sprache und Literatur in der Wissenschaft* 83 (1999): 29–45.

Beaujour, Elizabeth Klosty. *Alien Tongues: Bilingual Russian Writers of the "First" Emigration*. Studies of the Harriman Institute. Ithaca, N.Y.: Cornell University Press, 1989.

Beck, Evelyn Torton, *Kafka and the Yiddish Theater: Its Impact on His Work*. Madison: University of Wisconsin Press, 1971.

Benjamin, Walter. *Sprache und Geschichte: Philosophische Essays*, edited by Rolf Tiedemann. Stuttgart: Reclam, 1992.

————. "Die Aufgabe des Übersetzers." In *Sprache und Geschichte*, 50–64.

————. "The Task of the Translator." Trans. Harry Zohn. In *Illuminations*, edited by and with an introduction by Hannah Arendt, 69–82. New York: Schocken, 1968.

————. "Über die Sprache überhaupt und über die Sprache des Menschen." In *Sprache und Geschichte*, 30–49.

Bell, David A. "Lingua Populi, Lingua Dei: Language, Religion, and the Origins of French Revolutionary Nationalism." *American Historical Review* 100.5 (1995): 1403–37.

Berkowitz, Michael "February 1896." In Gilman and Zipes, eds., *Yale Companion*, 227–31.

Berman, Sandra, and Michael Wood, eds. *Nation, Language, and the Ethics of Translation*. Princeton, N.J.: Princeton University Press, 2005.

Bernstein, Richard. "A Bold New View of Turkish-German Youth." *New York Times* 12 April 2003.

Bhatti, Anil. "Mehrsprachigkeit und kulturelle Diversität. Europa und Indien als Beispiel." Available at: www.goethe.de/ges/phi/prj/ffs /the/spr/de4980085.htm. Accessed 15 June 2011.

Binder, Hartmut, ed. *Kafka-Handbuch in 2 Bänden*. Stuttgart: Kröner, 1979.

————. *Kafka-Kommentar zu den Romanen, Rezensionen, Aphorismen und zum Brief an den Vater*. Munich: Winkler, 1976.

Bird, Stephanie. *Women Writers and National Identity: Bachmann, Duden, Özdamar*. Cambridge: Cambridge University Press, 2003.

Braese, Stephan. *Eine europäische Sprache: Deutsche Sprachkultur von Juden 1760–1930*. Göttingen: Wallstein, 2010.

————. "Introduction." In Braese, *In der Sprache der Täter: Neue Lektüren deutschsprachiger Nachkriegs- und Gegenwartsliteratur*, 7–12. Opladen: Westdeutscher Verlag, 1998.

Braidotti, Rosi. *Nomadic Subjects: Embodiment and Sexual Difference in Contemporary Feminist Theory*. New York: Columbia University Press, 1994.

Braun, Peter, ed. *Fremdwort-Diskussion*. Munich: W. Fink, 1979.

Braunmüller, Kurt, and Gisella Ferraresi. *Aspects of Multilingualism in European Language History*. Amsterdam: J. Benjamins, 2003.

Brandt, Bettina. "Collecting Childhood Memories of the Future: Ara-

bic as Mediator between Turkish and German in Emine Sevgi Özdamar's *Mutterzunge*." *Germanic Review* 79.4 (2004): 295–315.

———. "The Post-Communist Eye. An Interview with Yoko Tawada."
World Literature Today. January-February (2006): 43–45.

———. "The Unknown Character: Traces of the Surreal in Yoko
Tawada's Writing." In Slaymaker, ed., *Yoko Tawada*, 111–24.

Brandt, Bettina, and Désirée Schyns. "Neu vernetzt: Yoko Tawada
'Bioskoop der Nacht' auf Niederländisch." *Études Germaniques*
65.3 (2010): 535–49.

Braun, Peter, ed. *Fremdwort-Diskussion*. Munich: W. Fink, 1979.

Breger, Claudia. "'Meine Herren, spielt in meinem Gesicht ein Affe?'
Strategien der Mimikry in Texten von Emine S. Özdamar und Yoko
Tawada." In Gelbin, Konuk, and Piesche, eds., *Aufbrüche*, 30–59.

Brenner, Michael, ed. *Jüdische Sprachen in deutscher Umwelt: He-
bräisch und Jiddisch von der Aufklärung bis ins 20. Jahrhundert*.
Göttingen: Vandenhoeck und Ruprecht, 2002.

———. Introduction. Brenner, *Jüdische Sprachen*, 7–10.

Brodzki, Bella. *Can These Bones Live? Translation, Survival, and
Cultural Memory*. Stanford: Stanford University Press, 2007.

Buck-Morss, Susan. *The Origin of Negative Dialectics: Theodor W.
Adorno, Walter Benjamin and the Frankfurt Institute*. New York:
Free Press, 1977.

Businesswire. "Deutsche Bank Places 68-Page Advertising Insert with
the *New York Times Magazine*; Preamble to Oct. 4th Art Project
Shows Support for the Arts." 28 September 2002. Available: busi-
nesswire.com. Accessed: 16 February 2006.

Burger, Hanna. "Die Vertreibung der Mehrsprachigkeit am Beispiel
Österreichs 1867–1918." In *Über Muttersprachen und Vaterlän-
der: Zur Entwicklung von Standardsprachen und Nationen in Europa*, edited by Gerd Hentschel, 35–49. Frankfurt am Main: Peter
Lang, 1997.

Butler, Judith. *Bodies That Matter: On the Discursive Limits of
"Sex."* New York: Routledge, 1993.

Çağlar, Ayşe. "Management kultureller Vielfalt. Deutsch-Türkischer
Hip-Hop, Rap und Türkpop in Berlin." In Hess and Lenz, eds., *Geschlecht und Globalisierung*, 221–41.

Caruth, Cathy, ed. *Trauma: Explorations in Memory*. Baltimore:
Johns Hopkins University Press, 1995.

———. "Trauma and Experience: Introduction." In *Trauma*, 3–12.

———. "Recapturing the Past: Introduction." In *Trauma*, 151–57.

Casanova, Pascale. *The World Republic of Letters*. Trans. M. B. De-Bevoise. Cambridge, Mass.: Harvard University Press, 2004.

Celan, Paul. "Ansprache anlässlich der Entgegennahme des Literaturpreises der Freien Hansestadt Bremen." In *Gesammelte Werke*, 3:185–86.

———. "Antwort auf eine Umfrage der Librairie Flinker, Paris (1961)." In *Gesammelte Werke*, 3:175.

———. *Gesammelte Werke in fünf Bänden*, edited by Beda Allemann and Stefan Reichert, with Rolf Bücher. Frankfurt am Main: Suhrkamp, 1983.

Cheah, Pheng. *Spectral Nationality. Passages of Freedom from Kant to Postcolonial Literatures of Liberation*. New York: Columbia University Press, 2003.

Cheesman, Tom. *Novels of Turkish German Settlement: Cosmopolite Fictions*. Rochester, N.Y.: Camden House, 2007.

———. "Akçam—Zaimoğlu—'Kanak Attak': Turkish Lives and Letters in German." *German Life and Letters* 55.2 (2002): 180–95.

———. "Talking 'Kanak': Zaimoğlu contra *Leitkultur*." *New German Critique* 92 (Spring/Summer 2004): 82–99.

Cheesman, Tom, and Karin Yeşilada, eds. *Feridun Zaimoğlu*. Cardiff, UK: University of Wales Press (forthcoming).

Cheng, Sinkwan. "Fremdwörter as the 'Jews of Language' and Adorno's Politics of Exile." In *Adorno, Culture, and Feminism*, edited by Maggie O'Neill, 75–103. London; Thousand Oaks, Calif.: SAGE Publications, 1999.

Chiellino, Carmine. *Interkulturelle Literatur in Deutschland: Ein Handbuch*. Stuttgart: J.B. Metzler, 2000.

Ch'ien, Evelyn Nien-Ming. *Weird English*. Cambridge, Mass.: Harvard University Press, 2004.

Chin, Rita. *The Guest Worker Question in Postwar Germany*. Cambridge: Cambridge University Press, 2007.

Chow, Rey. *The Protestant Ethnic and the Spirit of Capitalism*. New York: Columbia University Press, 2002.

Çil, Nevim. *Topographie des Außenseiters*. Berlin: Hans Schiler Verlag, 2007.

Claussen, Detlev. *Theodor W. Adorno: Ein letztes Genie*. Frankfurt am Main: Fischer, 2003.

Clyne, Michael. "Multilingualism." In *The Handbook of Sociolin-

guistics, edited by Florian Coulmas. Oxford: Blackwell Publishing, 1997.

Corngold, Stanley. *Lambent Traces: Franz Kafka.* Princeton, N.J.: Princeton University Press, 2004.

Courtivron, Isabelle de, ed. *Lives in Translation: Bilingual Writers on Identity and Creativity.* New York: Palgrave Macmillan, 2003.

Cousins, Jane. *Turkey: Torture and Political Persecution.* London: Pluto Press, 1973.

Dal, Güney. *Wenn Ali die Glocken läuten hört.* Trans. Brigitte Schreiber-Grabitz. Berlin: Edition der 2, 1979.

Daniel, Jamie Owen. "Temporary Shelter: Adorno's Exile and the Language of Home." *New Formations* 17 (Summer 1992): 26–35.

Davidson, Mary Catherine. *Medievalism, Multilingualism, and Chaucer.* New York: Palgrave Macmillan, 2010.

Deleuze, Gilles, and Félix Guattari. *Kafka: Toward a Minor Literature.* 1975. Trans. Dana Polan. Minneapolis: University of Minnesota Press, 1986.

Derrida, Jacques. *Monolingualism of the Other, or, the Prosthesis of Origin.* Trans. Patrick Mensah. Stanford: Stanford University Press, 1998.

Deutsche Bank Art. *Wordsearch: A Translinguistic Sculpture by Karin Sander.* Frankfurt am Main, 2002. 68-page advertising insert in *New York Times*, 29 September 2002. See also: moment-art.com/moment/wordsearch/e/index.php. Accessed 15 June 2011.

Dickinson, Kristin, Robin Ellis, and Priscilla D. Layne. "Translating Communities: Rethinking the Collective in Feridun Zaimoğlu's *Koppstoff.*" *TRANSIT* 4.1 (2008). Available at: www.escholarship.org/uc/item/8z027orh. Accessed 15 June 2011.

Dirim, Inci, and Peter Auer. "Socio-Cultural Orientation, Urban Youth Styles and the Spontaneous Acquisition of Turkish by Non-Turkish Adolescents in Germany." In *Discourse Construction of Youth Identities*, edited by Jannis Androutsopoulos and Alexandra Georgakopoulou. Amsterdam: John Benjamins Pub., 2003. 223–246.

———. *Türkisch sprechen nicht nur die Türken: Über die Unschärfebeziehung zwischen Sprache und Ethnie in Deutschland.* Berlin: de Gruyter, 2004.

Engel, Antke. "Queer-Feministische und kanakische Angriffe auf die Nation." *Vor der Information* (1999/2000): 2–5.

Erel, Umut. "Grenzüberschreitungen und kulturelle Mischformen als antirassistischer Widerstand?" Gelbin, Konuk, and Piesche, eds., *Aufbrüche*, 172–94.

Ernst, Thomas. "Jenseits von MTV und Musikantenstadl. Popkulturelle Positionierungen in Wladimir Kaminers 'Russendisko' und Feridun Zaimoglus 'Kanak Sprak.'" *Literatur und Migration*, edited by Heinz Ludwig Arnold. Text + Kritik. Sonderband IX. Munich, 2006.

Erpulat, Nurkan, and Tuncay Kulaoğlu. *Jenseits—Bist du schwul oder bist du Türke*. Directed by Nurkan Erpulat. Hebbel am Ufer. Berlin, Germany. 6 May 2008.

Eshel, Amir. "Von Kafka bis Celan: Deutsch-Jüdische Schriftsteller und ihr Verhältnis zum Hebräischen und Jiddischen." In Brenner, ed., *Jüdische Sprachen* 96–108.

Fabian, Johannes. *Time and the Other: How Anthropology Makes Its Object*. New York: Columbia University Press, 1983.

Fachinger, Petra. *Rewriting Germany from the Margins: "Other" German Literature of the 1980s and 1990s*. Montreal: McGill-Queen's University Press, 2001.

Feldman, Yael S. *Modernism and Cultural Transfer: Gabriel Preil and the Tradition of Jewish Literary Bilingualism*. Hoboken, N.J.: Hebrew Union College Press, 1986.

Fichte, Johann Gottlieb. *Reden an die deutsche Nation*. Hamburg: Felix Meiner, 1955.

Fischer, Jens Malte. *Richard Wagners "Das Judentum in der Musik."* Frankfurt am Main: Insel, 2000.

Fischer, Sabine, and Moray McGowan, eds. *Denn du tanzt auf einem Seil: Positionen deutschsprachiger MigrantInnenliteratur*. Tübingen: Stauffenburg, 1997.

Forster, Leonard Wilson. *The Poet's Tongues: Multilingualism in Literature*. London: Cambridge University Press, 1970.

Freud, Sigmund. "The 'Uncanny.'" Trans. Alix Strachey. *Collected Papers*. Vol. 4, 368–407. London: Hogarth and Institute of Psycho-Analysis, 1924–1950.

———. "Das Unheimliche." In *Gesammelte Werke*, edited by Anna Freud, 12:227–68. London: Imago, 1941.

———. "Der Familienroman der Neurotiker." In *Gesammelte Werke*, 7:227–31. London: Imago, 1941.

———. "Fetishism." In *Collected Papers*. Vol. 5, 198–204. London: Hogarth and Institute of Psycho-Analysis, 1924–1950.

Gal, Susan. "Migration, Minorities and Multilingualism: Language Ideologies in Europe." In *Language Ideologies, Policies, and Practices: Language and the Future of Europe*, edited by Clare Mar-Molinero and Patrick Stevenson, 13–27. Basingstoke: Palgrave, 2006.

Gandesha, Samir. "Leaving Home: On Adorno and Heidegger." In *The Cambridge Companion to Adorno*, edited by Tom Huhn, 101–28. Cambridge: Cambridge University Press, 2004.

Gardt, Andreas, and Bernd Hüppauf, eds. *Globalization and the Future of German*. Berlin: Mouton de Gruyter, 2004.

Garloff, Katja. "Essay, Exile, Efficacy: Adorno's Literary Criticism." *Monatshefte* 94.1 (2002): 80–95.

Garner, Shirley Nelson, Claire Kahane, and Madelon Sprengnether, eds. *The (M)other Tongue: Essays in Feminist Psychoanalytic Interpretation*. Ithaca, N.Y.: Cornell University Press, 1985.

Gaus, Günter. Interview. "Hannah Arendt: Was bleibt? Es bleibt die Muttersprache." In *Zur Person: Porträts in Frage und Antwort*, 15–32. Munich: Feder, 1964.

Gelbin, Cathy, Kader Konuk, and Peggy Piesche, eds. *Aufbrüche: Kulturelle Produktionen von Migrantinnen, Schwarzen und jüdischen Frauen in Deutschland*. Königstein: Ulrike Helmer, 1999.

FAZ.net. "Gerichtsurteil: Kein Monopol auf 'Türkdeutsch.'" 2 January 2007. www.faz.net/artikel/C31013/gerichtsurteil-kein-monopol-auf-tuerkdeutsch-30274596.html. Accessed 15 June 2011.

Gestrich, Andreas. *Geschichte der Familie im 19. und 20. Jahrhundert*. Munich: R. Oldenbourg, 1999.

Ghaussy, Sohelia. "Das Vaterland verlassen: Nomadic Language and 'Feminine Writing' in Emine Sevgi Özdamar's *Das Leben ist eine Karawanserei*." *German Quarterly* 72.1 (1999): 1–16.

Gilman, Sander. *Franz Kafka: The Jewish Patient*. New York: Routledge, 1995.

———. *Jewish Self-Hatred: Anti-Semitism and the Hidden Language of the Jews*. Baltimore: Johns Hopkins University Press, 1986.

Gilman, Sander, and Jack David Zipes, eds. *Yale Companion to Jewish Writing and Thought in German Culture, 1096–1996*. New Haven: Yale University Press, 1997

Gogolin, Ingrid. *Der monolinguale Habitus der multilingualen Schule*. Münster: Waxmann, 1994.

———. "Sprachen rein halten—eine Obsession." In Gogolin, Graap, and List, eds., *Über Mehrsprachigkeit*, 71–96.

Gogolin, Ingrid, Sabine Graap, and Günther List, eds. *Über Mehrsprachigkeit*. Tübingen: Stauffenburg Verlag, 1998.

Gossy, Mary S. *Freudian Slips. Women, Writing, the Foreign Tongue*. Ann Arbor: University of Michigan Press, 1995.

Gotzmann, Andreas. "Vatersprache und Mutterland: Sprache als nationaler Einheitsdiskurs im 19. Jahrhundert." In Brenner, ed., *Jüdische Sprachen*, 28–42.

Gramling, David. "On the Other Side of Monolingualism: Fatih Akın's Linguistic Turn(s)." *German Quarterly* 83.3 (2010): 353–72.

Gutiérrez Rodríguez, Encarnación. "Auf der Suche nach dem Identischen in einer "hybriden" Welt—Über Subjektivität, postkoloniale Kritik, Grenzregime und Metaphern des Seins." In Hess and Lenz, eds., *Geschlecht und Globalisierung*, 36–55.

Habermas, Jürgen. "Leadership and Leitkultur." *New York Times*, 29 October 2010.

Haines, Brigid, and Margaret Littler. "Emine Sevgi Özdamar, 'Mutter Zunge' and 'Großvater Zunge' (1990)." In *Contemporary Women's Writing in German: Changing the Subject*, 118–38. Oxford: Oxford University Press, 2004.

Haraway, Donna. "Cyborg Manifesto." In *Simians, Cyborgs, and Women: The Reinvention of Nature*. New York: Routledge, 1991.

Harris, Roxy. *New Ethnicities and Language Use*. New York: Palgrave MacMillan, 2006.

Härle, Gerhard. *Reinheit der Sprache, des Herzens und des Leibes: Zur Wirkungsgeschichte des rhetorischen Begriffs puritas in Deutschland von der Reformation bis zur Aufklärung*. Tübingen: Max Niemeyer, 1996.

Hart, Matthew. *Nations of Nothing But Poetry: Modernism, Transnationalism, and Synthetic Vernacular Writing*. New York: Oxford University Press, 2010.

Hassan, Waïl S. "Agency and Translational Literature: Ahdaf Soueif's *The Map of Love*." *PMLA* 121.3 (2006): 753–68.

Herf, Jeffrey. *Reactionary Modernism: Technology, Culture, and Politics in Weimar and the Third Reich*. Cambridge: Cambridge University Press, 1984.

Herder, Johann Gottfried. "Über die neuere deutsche Literatur." (Fragmente) In *Ausgewählte Werke. Schriften zur Literatur*, edited by Regine Otto. Berlin: Aufbau, 1985.

Hess, Sabine, and Ramona Lenz, eds. *Geschlecht und Globalisierung:*

ein kulturwissenschaftlicher Streifzug durch transnationale Räume. Königstein/Taunus: Ulrike Helmer, 2001.

Hirsch, Marianne. "The Generation of Postmemory." *Poetics Today* 29.1 (2008): 103–28.

Hoffman, Eva. *Lost in Translation: A Life in a New Language*. New York: Penguin, 1987.

Hoffmann, Rainer. *Figuren des Scheins: Studien zum Sprachbild und zur Denkform Theodor W. Adornos*. Bonn: Bouvier, 1984.

Hofmannsthal, Hugo von. "Unsere Fremdwörter." In *Reden und Aufsätze II: 1914–1924*, edited by Bernd and Rudolf Hirsch Schoeller, 360–66. Vol. 9 in *Gesammelte Werke*. Frankfurt am Main: Fischer, 1979.

Hohendahl, Peter Uwe. *Prismatic Thought: Theodor W. Adorno*. Lincoln: University of Nebraska Press, 1995.

———. "The Frankfurt School Returns to Germany." In Gilman and Zipes, eds., *Yale Companion*, 683–90.

Horrocks, David, and Eva Kolinsky, eds. *Turkish Culture in German Society Today*. Providence: Berghahn, 1996.

Howard, Mary, ed. *Interkulturelle Konfigurationen: Zur deutschsprachigen Erzählliteratur von Autoren nichtdeutscher Herkunft*. Munich: Iudicium, 1997.

Hu, Adelheid. *Schulischer Fremdsprachenunterricht und migrationsbedingte Mehrsprachigkeit*. Tübingen: Gunter Narr Verlag, 2003.

Hutton, Christopher M. *Linguistics and the Third Reich: Mother-Tongue Fascism, Race and the Science of Language*. New York: Routledge, 1999.

Isenberg, Noah. "In Search of Language: Kafka on Yiddish, Eastern Jewry, and Himself." In *Between Redemption and Doom: The Strains of German-Jewish Modernism*, 19–50. Lincoln: University of Nebraska Press, 1999.

Israel, Nico. "Adorno, Los Angeles, and the Dislocation of Culture." In *Outlandish: Writing between Exile and Diaspora*, 75–122. Stanford: Stanford University Press, 2000.

Ivanovic, Christine, ed. *Yoko Tawada: Poetik der Transformation. Beiträge zum Gesamtwerk. Mit dem Stück Sancho Pansa von Yoko Tawada*. Tübingen: Stauffenburg, 2010.

Ivy, Marilyn. *Discourses of the Vanishing: Modernity, Phantasm, Japan*. Chicago: University of Chicago Press, 1995.

Jahn, Friedrich. *Die Deutsche Turnkunst*. Berlin: Eiselen EWB, 1960.

Jakobson, Roman. "On Linguistic Aspects of Translation." In Schulte and Biguenet, ed., *Theories of Translation*, 144–51.

Jameson, Fredric. *The Prison-House of Language: A Critical Account of Structuralism and Russian Formalism*. Princeton, N.J.: Princeton University Press, 1972.

Jay, Martin. "Abjection Overruled." In *Cultural Semantics: Keywords of Our Time*, 144–56. Amherst: University of Massachusetts Press, 1998.

———. "The Jews and the Frankfurt School: Critical Theory's Analysis of Antisemitism." In *Permanent Exiles: Essays on the Intellectual Migration from Germany to America*, 90–100. New York: Columbia University Press, 1985.

Johnson, Barbara. *Mother Tongues: Sexuality, Trials, Motherhood, Translation*. Cambridge, Mass.: Harvard University Press, 2003.

Judson, Pieter M. *Guardians of the Nation: Activists on the Language Frontiers of Imperial Austria*. Cambridge, Mass.: Harvard University Press, 2006.

Kachru, Braj B. "World Englishes: Approaches, Issues and Resources." *Language Teaching* 25 (1992): 1–14.

Kafka, Franz. *Briefe 1902–1924*, edited by Max Brod. New York: Schocken Books, 1958.

———. *Briefe an Milena*. Erweiterte und neu geordnete Ausgabe, edited by Jürgen Born and Michael Müller. Frankfurt am Main: Fischer Taschenbuchverlag, 1986.

———. *Dearest Father*. Trans. Ernst Kaiser and Eithne Wilkins. New York: Schocken, 1954.

———. *The Diaries of Franz Kafka 1910–1913*, edited by Max Brod. Trans. Joseph Kresh. New York: Schocken Books, 1948. [Cited as *Diaries*]

———. *Gesammelte Werke in zwölf Bänden*. Nach der Kritischen Ausgabe, edited by Hans-Gerd Koch. 12 vols. Frankfurt am Main: Fischer, 1994.

———. *Letters to Friends, Family, and Editors*. Trans. Richard Winston and Clara Winston. New York: Schocken Books, 1977. [Cited as *Letters*]

———. *Letters to Milena*. Trans. Tania Stern and James Stern, edited by Willy Haas. New York: Schocken Books, 1953.

———. *Tagebücher 1909–1912*. Vol. 9, bk. 1 of *Gesammelte Werke*, edited by Koch. [Cited as *Tagebücher 1*]

———. *Tagebücher 1912–1914*. Vol. 9, bk. 2 of *Gesammelte Werke*, edited by Koch. [Cited as *Tagebücher 2*]

———. "Einleitungsvortrag über Jargon." In *Beschreibung eines Kampfes und andere Schriften aus dem Nachlaß*, 149–53. Vol. 5 of *Gesammelte Werke*, edited by Koch. Frankfurt am Main: Fischer, 1994.

———. "An Introductory Talk on the Yiddish Language." Trans. Ernst Kaiser and Eithne Wilkins. In Anderson, ed., *Reading Kafka*, 263–66.

Kanak Attak. "Kanak Attak und Basta! Manifest gegen Mültikültüralizm, gegen demokratische und hybride Deutsche sowie konformistische Migranten." *die tageszeitung*, 29 January 1999.

Kaplan, Alice. *French Lesson: A Memoir*. Chicago: University of Chicago Press, 1994.

Kellman, Steven G. *The Translingual Imagination*. Lincoln: University of Nebraska Press, 2000.

———. *Switching Languages: Translingual Writers Reflect on Their Craft*. Lincoln: University of Nebraska Press, 2003.

Kelsky, Karen. *Women on the Verge: Japanese Women, Western Dreams*. Durham, N.C.: Duke University Press, 2001.

Kermani, Navid. "Was ist deutsch an der deutschen Literatur?" www .navidkermani.de/media/raw/Kermani_Literatur.pdf. Accessed 15 June 2011.

Khalil, Iman Osman. *Das Fremdwort im Gesellschaftsroman Theodor Fontanes: Zur literarischen Untersuchung eines sprachlichen Phänomens*. Frankfurt am Main: Peter Lang, 1978.

Kiedaisch, Petra. *Lyrik nach Auschwitz? Adorno und die Dichter*. Stuttgart: Philipp Reclam, 1995.

Kirkness, Alan. "Zur Lexikologie und Lexikographie des Fremdworts." In Braun, ed., *Fremdwort-Diskussion*, 74–89.

Kittler, Friedrich A. *Aufschreibesysteme 1800/1900*. Munich: Fink, 1985.

———. *Discourse Networks, 1800/1900*. Trans. M. Metteer with C. Cullens, Foreword D. E. Wellbery. Stanford: Stanford University Press, 1990.

Klemperer, Victor. *LTI: Notizbuch eines Philologen*. Stuttgart: Reclam, 1968.

Konuk, Kader. *East West Mimesis: Auerbach in Turkey*. Stanford: Stanford University Press, 2010.

———. *Identitäten im Prozess: Literatur von Autorinnen aus und in der Türkei in deutscher, englischer und türkischer Sprache.* Essen: Blaue Eule, 2001.

———. "Das Leben ist eine Karawanserei: Heim-at bei Emine Sevgi Özdamar." In *Kein Land in Sicht: Heimat-Weiblich?* Ed. Gisela Ecker, 143–57. Munich: W. Fink, 1997.

———. "Taking on German and Turkish History: Emine Sevgi Özdamar's *Seltsame Sterne.*" *Gegenwartsliteratur* 6 (2007): 232–56.

Kramsch, Claire. *The Multilingual Subject: What Foreign Languages Learners Say about Their Experience and Why It Matters.* Oxford: Oxford University Press, 2009.

Krauß, Andrea. "'Talisman.' 'Tawadische Sprachtheorie.'" In *Migration und Interkulturalität in neueren literarischen Texten*, edited by Aglaia Blioumi, 55–77. Munich: Iudicium, 2002.

Kraus, Karl. *Die Sprache.* Vol. 2 of *Werke von Karl Kraus*, edited by Heinrich Fischer. Munich: Kösel, 1954.

Kremnitz, Georg. *Mehrsprachigkeit in der Literatur: Wie Autoren ihre Sprachen wählen; Aus der Sicht der Soziologie der Kommunikation.* Vienna: Edition Praesens Verlag für Literatur- und Sprachwissenschaft, 2004.

Kristeva, Julia. *Powers of Horror: An Essay on Abjection.* New York: Columbia University Press, 1982.

Kuruyazıcı, Nilüfer. "Emine Sevgi Özdamars *Das Leben ist eine Karawanserei* im Prozess der interkulturellen Kommunikation." In Howard, ed., *Interkulturelle Konfigurationen*, 179–88.

LaCapra, Dominick. "Trauma, Absence, Loss." In *Writing History, Writing Trauma.* Baltimore: Johns Hopkins University Press, 2001.

Lacatus, Corina. *The (In)visibility Complex. Negotiating Otherness in Contemporary Sweden.* Book Series of the Center for Research on International Migration and Ethnic Relations. Stockholm: Stockholm University Press, 2008.

Lamping, Dieter. "Zweisprachigkeit und Interkulturalität in der Jüdischen Literatur. Zum Problem des 'Literarischen Internationalismus.'" In *Literatur im Zeitalter der Globalisierung*, edited by Manfred Schmeling, 247–58. Würzburg: Königshausen und Neumann, 2000.

Lamprecht, Franziska. "How Many Living Languages Can You Find in New York? Wie viele gesprochene Sprachen könnt Ihr in New York finden?" In Deutsche Bank Art, 44–47.

Langewiesche, Dieter. *Nation, Nationalismus, Nationalstaat in Deutschland und Europa.* Munich: C. H. Beck, 2000.

"Lasenkan Theater Berlin." *Eine moderne Theaterform an den Grenzen von Sprachen und Kulturen.* www.lasenkan.com/Lasenkan .html. Accessed 15 June 2011.

Laudenberg, Beate. "Aspekte der deutschsprachigen Migrantenliteratur, dargestellt an Yoko Tawadas 'Ein Gast.'" *Literatur im interkulturellen Dialog: Festschrift zum 60. Geburtstag von Hans-Christoph Graf V. Nayhauss,* edited by Manfred Durzak and Beate Laudenberg, 130–43. Bern: P. Lang, 2000.

Lefevere, André. *Translation, Rewriting and the Manipulation of Literary Fame.* London: Routledge, 1992.

———. "Translated Literature: Towards an Integrated Theory." *Bulletin of the Midwest Modern Language Association.* 14.1 (Spring 1981): 68–78.

Lennon, Brian. *In Babel's Shadow: Multilingual Literatures, Monolingual States.* Minneapolis: University of Minnesota Press, 2010.

Levin, Thomas Y. "Nationalities of Language: Adorno's *Fremdwörter:* An Introduction to 'On the Question: What Is German?'" *New German Critique* 36 (1985): 111–19.

Linke, Uli. "Murderous Fantasies: Violence, Memory, and Selfhood in Germany." *New German Critique* 64 (Winter 1995): 37–59.

Liska, Vivian. *When Kafka Says We: Uncommon Communities in German-Jewish Literature.* Bloomington: Indiana University Press, 2009.

Littler, Margaret. "Diasporic Identity in Emine Sevgi Özdamar's *Mutterzunge.*" In *Recasting German Identity: Culture, Politics, and Literature in the Berlin Republic,* edited by Stuart Taberner and Frank Finley, 219–34. Rochester, N.Y.: Camden House, 2002.

Love, Nancy S. "Why Do the Sirens Sing?: Figuring the Feminine in Dialectic of Enlightenment." In *Rethinking the Frankfurt School: Alternative Legacies of Cultural Critique,* edited by Jeffrey T. Nealon and Caren Irr, 111–21. Albany: SUNY Press, 2002.

Mandel, Ruth. *Cosmopolitan Anxieties: Turkish Challenges to Citizenship and Belonging in Germany.* Durham: Duke University Press, 2008.

Mani, Venkat. *Cosmopolitical Claims: Turkish-German Literatures from Nadolny to Pamuk.* Iowa City: University of Iowa Press, 2007.

Martin, Biddy. *Femininity Played Straight: The Significance of Being Lesbian*. New York: Routledge, 1996.

Matsunaga, Miho. "Ausländerin, einheimischer Mann, Confidente. Ein Grundschema in Yoko Tawadas Frühwerk." In Ivanovic, ed., *Yoko Tawada*, 249–61.

———. "'Schreiben als Übersetzung': Die Dimension der Übersetzung in den Werken von Yoko Tawada." *Zeitschrift für Germanistik* 12.3 (2002): 532–46.

McGowan, Moray. "Multiple Masculinities in Turkish-German Men's Writing." In *Conceptions of Postwar German Masculinity*, edited by Roy Jerome, 289–312. Albany: SUNY Press, 2001.

Mennel, Barbara. "Bruce Lee in Kreuzberg and Scarface in Altona: Transnational Auterism and Ghettocentrism in Thomas Arslan's 'Brothers and Sisters' and Faith Akin's 'Short Sharp Shock.'" *New German Critique* 87 (2002): 133–56.

Menrath, Stefanie. *Represent What . . . Performativität von Identitäten im HipHop*. Hamburg: Argument-Verlag, 2001.

Minnaard, Liesbeth. *New Germans, New Dutch: Literary Interventions*. Amsterdam: Amsterdam University Press, 2008.

Mueller, Agnes C., ed. *German Pop Culture: How "American" Is It?* Ann Arbor: University of Michigan Press, 2004.

Müller, Regula. "'Ich war Mädchen, war ich Sultanin.' Weitgeöffnete Augen betrachten türkische Frauengeschichte(n)/ Zum *Karawanserei*-Roman von Emine Sevgi Özdamar." In Fischer and McGowan, eds., *Denn du tanzt*, 133–49.

Natzmer Cooper, Gabriele von. *Kafka and Language: In the Stream of Thoughts and Life*. Studies in Austrian Literature, Culture, and Thought. Riverside, CA: Ariadne Press, 1991.

Nekula, Marek. *Franz Kafkas Sprachen: " . . . in einem Stockwerk des innern Babylonischen Turmes . . . "* Tübingen: Niemeyer, 2003.

Neubert, Isolde. "Searching for Intercultural Communication: Emine Sevgi Özdamar—A Turkish Woman Writer in Germany." In *Post-War Women's Writing in German: Feminist Critical Approaches*, edited by Chris Weedon. Providence: Berghahn, 1997.

Ngugi wa Thiong'o. *Decolonising the Mind : The Politics of Language in African Literature*. London: Heinemann, 1986.

Nicholsen, Shierry Weber. "Language: Its Murmurings, Its Darkness, and Its Silver Rib." In *Exact Imagination, Late Work: On Adorno's Aesthetics*, 59–102. Cambridge, Mass.: MIT Press, 1997.

Niekerk, Carl. "The Romantics and Other Cultures." In *Cambridge Companion to German Romanticism*, edited by Nicholas Saul, 147–61. Cambridge: Cambridge University Press, 2009.

Noguchi, Mary Goebel, and Sandra Fotos, eds. *Studies in Japanese Bilingualism*. Clevedon, UK: Multilingual Matters, 2001.

North, Michael. *The Dialect of Modernism. Race, Language & Twentieth-Century Literature*. New York: Oxford University Press, 1994.

Ogulnick, Karen, ed. *Language Crossings: Negotiating the Self in a Multicultural World*. New York: Teachers College Press, 2000.

Oguntoye, Katharina, May Opitz, and Dagmar Schultz. *Farbe bekennen: Afro-Deutsche Frauen auf den Spuren ihrer Geschichte*. Frankfurt am Main: Fischer Taschenbuchverlag, 1992 [1986].

———. *Showing Our Colors: Afro-German Women Speak Out*. Trans. Anne V. Adams. Amherst: University of Massachusetts Press, 1992.

Okara, Gabriel. "African Speech . . . English Words." [1963]. In Kellman, ed., *The Translingual Imagination*, 185–87.

Özdamar, Emine Sevgi. *Bridge of the Golden Horn*. Trans. Martin Chalmers. London: Serpent's Tail, 2007.

———. *Die Brücke vom Goldenen Horn*. Cologne: Kiepenheuer und Witsch, 1999.

———. *Hayat Bir Kervansaray, Iki Kapısı Var, Birinden Girdim, Birinden Çıktım*. Trans. Ayça Sabuncuoğlu. Istanbul: Varlık Yayınları, 1993.

———. *Der Hof im Spiegel: Erzählungen*. Cologne: Kiepenheuer & Witsch, 2001.

———. *Kendi kendinin terzisi bir kambur*. Istanbul: Yapı Kredi Yayınları, 2007.

———. *Das Leben ist eine Karawanserei hat zwei Türen aus einer kam ich rein aus der anderen ging ich raus*. Cologne: Kiepenheuer & Witsch, 1992.

———. *Life Is a Caravanserai Has Two Doors I Came in One I Went out the Other*. Trans. Luise von Flotow. London: Middlesex University, 2000.

———. *Mother Tongue*. Trans. Craig Thomas. Toronto: Coach House Press, 1994.

———. *Mutterzunge: Erzählungen*. Berlin: Rotbuch, 1990.

———. *Seltsame Sterne starren zur Erde: Wedding—Pankow 1976/77.* Cologne: Kiepenheuer & Witsch, 2003.

———. "Meine deutschen Wörter haben keine Kindheit. Eine Dankrede." In *Der Hof im Spiegel*, 125–32.

———. "Schwarzauge in Deutschland." In *Hof im Spiegel*, 47–53.

Pareigis, Christina. "Wie man in der eigenen Sprache fremd wird. Franz Kafka, Shimon Frug, and Yitzhak Katznelson auf den Wegen der jiddischen Überlieferung." In Arndt, Naguschewski, and Stockhammer, eds., *Exophonie*, 35–47.

Pavlenko, Aneta. *Emotions and Multilingualism.* Cambridge: Cambridge University Press, 2005.

Pfaff, Carol. "'Kanaken in Alemannistan': Feridun Zaimoglu's Representation of Migrant Language." In *Sprachgrenzen überspringen. Sprachliche Hybridität und polykulturelles Selbstverständnis*, edited by Volker Hinnenkamp and Katharina Meng. Tübingen: Gunter Narr Verlag, 2005.

Pickford, Henry W. "Critical Models: Adorno's Theory and Practice of Cultural Criticism." *The Yale Journal of Criticism* 10.2 (1997): 247–70.

Pinès, M[eyer Isser]. *Histoire de la Littérature Judéo-Allemande.* Paris: Jouve, 1911.

Plass, Ulrich. *Language and History in Theodor W. Adorno's "Notes to Literature."* New York: Routledge, 2007.

Polenz, Peter von. *Deutsche Sprachgeschichte vom Spätmittelalter bis zur Gegenwart: 19. und 20. Jahrhundert.* Vol. 3. Berlin: Walter de Gruyter, 1999.

———. "Fremdwort und Lehnwort sprachwissenschaftlich betrachtet." In Braun, ed., *Fremdwort-Diskussion*, 9–31.

Preece, Julian. "The Letters and Diaries." In *The Cambridge Companion to Kafka*, edited by Julian Preece. Cambridge: Cambridge University Press, 2002, 111–30.

Puschner, Uwe. *Die völkische Bewegung im wilhelminischen Kaiserreich. Sprache—Rasse—Religion.* Darmstadt: Wissenschaftliche Buchgesellschaft, 2001.

Rajec, Elizabeth M. *Namen und ihre Bedeutungen im Werke Franz Kafkas: Ein interpretatorischer Versuch.* Bern: Peter Lang, 1977.

Raulff, Ulrich. "Die *Minima Moralia* nach fünfzig Jahren. Ein philosophisches Volksbuch im Spiegel seiner frühen Kritik." In *Theodor W. Adorno, "Minima Moralia" neu gelesen*, edited by Andreas

Bernard and Ulrich Raulff, 123–31. Frankfurt am Main: Suhrkamp, 2003.

Richter, Gerhard, ed. *Language without Soil: Adorno and Late Philosophical Modernity*. New York: Fordham University Press, 2010.

Rindler Schjerve, Rosita, and Eva Vetter. "Historical Sociolinguistics and Multilingualism: Theoretical and Methodological Issues in the Development of a Multifunctional Framework." In *Diglossia and Power: Language Policies and Practice in the 19th Century Habsburg Empire*, edited by Rosita Rindler Schjerve, 35–66. Berlin: Mouton de Gruyter, 2003.

Robert, Marthe. *Origins of the Novel*. Trans. Sacha Rabinovitch. Bloomington: Indiana University Press, 1980.

Römhild, Regina. "Global Heimat Germany. Migration and the Transnationalization of the Nation State." *TRANSIT* 1.1 (2004). Available at: escholarship.org/uc/item/57z2470p. Accessed 15 July 2011.

Rothberg, Michael. "After Adorno: Culture in the Wake of Catastrophe." In *Traumatic Realism: The Demands of Holocaust Representation*, 25–58. Minneapolis: University of Minnesota Press, 2000.

Saitô, Yumiko. "Synchronopse der Buchpublikationen von Yoko Tawada in Deutschland und Japan." In Ivanovic, ed., *Yoko Tawada*, 471–85.

Sakai, Naoki. *Translation and Subjectivity: On Japan and Cultural Nationalism*. Minneapolis: University of Minnesota Press, 1997.

———. "'You Asians': On the Historical Role of the West and Asia Binary." *SAQ: The South Atlantic Quarterly* 99.4 (2000): 789–817.

Sander, Karin. "Wordsearch, 2002." In Deutsche Bank Art, 17.

Sanders, Mark. *Complicities: The Intellectual and Apartheid*. Durham, N.C.: Duke University Press, 2002.

Schiewe, Jürgen. "Sprachpurismus als Aufklärung: Soll man Fremdwörter verdeutschen?" Ed. Volker Michael Strocka. *Die Deutschen und ihre Sprache*. Uwe Pörksen, Jürgen Schiewe, Georges-Arthur Goldschmidt, Bernhard Waldenfels, 35–68. Bremen: Hempen. 2000.

Schiller, Maike. "Verliebt in die deutsche Sprache. Gespräch mit María Cecilia Barbetta." *Hamburger Abendblatt*, 9. Juni 2009. www.abendblatt.de/kultur-live/article1045315/Verliebt-in-die-deutsche-Sprache.html. Accessed 15 June 2011.

Schlant, Ernestine, and Thomas J. Rimer, eds. *Legacies and Ambi-*

guities: Postwar Fiction and Culture in West Germany and Japan. Washington, D.C.: Woodrow Wilson Center Press and Baltimore: Johns Hopkins University Press, 1991.

Schleiermacher, Friedrich Daniel Ernst. "Über die verschiedenen Methoden des Übersetzens." In *Friedrich Daniel Ernst Schleiermacher Kritische Gesamtausgabe*, edited by Martin Rössler and Lars Emersleben. Vol. 11, 67–93. Berlin: Walter de Gruyter, 2002 [1813].

———. "*From* On the Different Methods of Translating." Trans. Waltraud Bartscht. In Schulte and Biguenet, eds., *Theories of Translation*, 36–54.

Schmeling, Manfred, and Monika Schmitz-Emans, eds. *Multilinguale Literatur im 20. Jahrhundert.* Würzburg: Könighausen & Neumann, 2002.

Schmidt, Gary. "Feridun Zaimoğlu's Performance of Gender and Authorship." In *German Literature in a New Century*, edited by Katharina Gerstenberger and Patricia Herminghouse, 196–213. New York: Berghahn, 2008.

Schulte, Rainer, and John Biguenet. *Theories of Translation: An Anthology of Essays from Dryden to Derrida.* Chicago: University of Chicago Press, 1992.

———. "Introduction." In Schulte and Biguenet, eds., *Theories of Translation*, 1–10.

Schwarz, Anette. *Melancholie: Figuren und Orte einer Stimmung.* Vienna: Passagen, 1996.

Şenocak, Zafer. *Atlas of a Tropical Germany: Essays on Politics and Culture, 1990–1998.* Trans. and ed. Leslie A. Adelson. Lincoln: University of Nebraska Press, 2000.

———. "Germany—Home for Turks? A Plea for Overcoming the Crisis between Orient and Occident." In *Atlas of a Tropical Germany*, 1–9.

Seyhan, Azade. *Writing outside the Nation.* Translation/Transnation. Princeton, N.J.: Princeton University Press, 2001.

Shklovsky, Victor. "Art as Technique." Trans. Lee T. Lemon and Marion J. Reis. In Shklovsky, Tomashevsky, and Eichenbaum, *Russian Formalist Criticism: Four Essays*, 3–24. Lincoln: University of Nebraska Press, 1965.

Sieg, Katrin. *Ethnic Drag: Performing Race, Nation, Sexuality in West Germany.* Ann Arbor: University of Michigan Press, 2002.

Siegert, Bernhard. "Kartographien der Zerstreuung: 'Jargon' und die Schrift der Jüdischen Tradierungsbewegung bei Kafka." In *Franz*

Kafka: Schriftverkehr, edited by Wolf Kittler and Gerhard Neumann, 222–47. Freiburg: Rombach, 1990.

Slaymaker, Douglas, ed. *Yoko Tawada: Voices from Everywhere*. Lanham, Md.: Lexington Books, 2007.

Şölçün, Sargut. "Gespielte Naivität und ernsthafte Sinnlichkeit der Selbstbegegnung: Inszenierungen des Unterwegsseins in Emine Sevgi Özdamars Roman *Die Brücke vom Goldenen Horn*." In *Migration und Interkulturalität*, edited by Aglaia Blioumi, 92–111. Munich: Iudicium, 2002.

Sollors, Werner, ed. *Multilingual America: Transnationalism, Ethnicity, and the Languages of American Literature*. New York: New York University Press, 1998.

Sommer, Doris. *Bilingual Games: Some Literary Investigations*. New York: Palgrave Macmillan, 2003.

———. *Bilingual Aesthetics: A New Sentimental Education*. Durham, N.C.: Duke University Press, 2004.

Soysal, Levent. "Rap, Hip-Hop, Kreuzberg: Scripts of/for Migrant Youth Culture in the World City Berlin." *New German Critique*. 92 (2004): 62–81.

Spector, Scott. *Prague Territories: National Conflict and Cultural Innovation in Franz Kafka's Fin De Siècle*. Weimar and Now 21. Berkeley: University of California Press, 2000.

Spitzer, Leo. *Fremdwörterhatz und Fremdvölkerhaß: Eine Streitschrift gegen die Sprachreinigung*. Vienna: Manzsche Hof-, Verlags- und Universitätsbuchhandlung, 1918.

Steiner, George. *After Babel. Aspects of Language and Translation*. New York: Oxford University Press, 1975.

———. *Errata: An Examined Life*. New Haven: Yale University Press, 1999.

———. *Extraterritorial: Papers on Literature and the Language Revolution*. New York: Atheneum, 1971.

———. "The Hollow Miracle." In *George Steiner: A Reader*. 207–20. New York: Oxford University Press, 1984 [1959].

Steyerl, Hito, and Encarnación Gutiérrez Rodríguez, eds. *Spricht die Subalterne deutsch? Migration und postkoloniale Kritik*. Münster: Unrast Verlag, 2003.

Strutz, Johann, and Peter V. Zima, eds. *Literarische Polyphonie: Übersetzung und Mehrsprachigkeit in der Literatur*. Tübingen: Narr, 1996.

Stukenbrock, Anja. "Aus Liebe zur Muttersprache? Der VDS und die fremdwortpuristische Diskurstradition." *Aptum: Zeitschrift für Sprachkritik und Sprachkultur* 3 (2005).

Suchoff, David. "Kafka's Canon: Hebrew and Yiddish in the Trial and Amerika." In Sommer, ed., *Bilingual Games*, 251–74.

Suga, Keijirō. "Translation, Exophony, Omniphony." In Slaymaker, ed., *Yoko Tawada*, 21–33.

Tachibana, Reiko. "Tawada Yoko's Quest for Exophony: Japan and Germany." In Slaymaker ed., *Yoko Tawada*, 153–68.

Tawada, Yoko. *Das Bad.* Tübingen: Konkursbuchverlag Claudia Gehrke, 1989.

———. "Till." In *Orpheus oder Izanagi: Hörspiel; Till: Theaterstück.* Tübingen: Konkursbuchverlag Claudia Gehrke, 1998.

———. *Das nackte Auge.* Tübingen: Konkursbuchverlag Claudia Gehrke, 2004.

———. *Sprachpolizei und Spielpolyglotte.* Tübingen: Konkursbuchverlag Claudia Gehrke, 2007.

———. *Talisman.* Tübingen: Konkursbuchverlag Claudia Gehrke, 1996.

———. *Überseezungen.* Tübingen: Konkursbuchverlag Claudia Gehrke, 2002.

———. "Absturz und Wiedergeburt." In *nur da wo du bist da ist nichts,* 118/11–119/10. Tübingen: Konkursbuchverlag Claudia Gehrke, 1987.

———. "Bioskoop der Nacht." In *Überseezungen,* 61–91.

———. "Die Krone aus Gras: Zu Paul Celans 'Die Niemandsrose.'" Tawada, *Sprachpolizei und Spielpolyglotte,* 63–84.

———. "Eine leere Flasche." In *Überseezungen,* 53–57.

———. "Das Leipzig des Lichts und der Gelatine. Erzählung." In *Wo Europa anfängt.* Tübingen: Konkursbuchverlag Claudia Gehrke, 1991. 7–26.

———. "Metamorphosen der Personennamen." In *Sprachpolizei und Spielpolyglotte* 91–102.

———. "Rabbi Löw und 27 Punkte: Physiognomie der Interpunktion bei Paul Celan." In *Sprachpolizei und Spielpolyglotte,* 38–44.

———. "Schreiben im Netz der Sprachen." In *Halbe Sachen: Dokumente der Wolfenbütteler Übersetzergespräche 1–3,* edited by Olaf Kutzmutz and Peter Waterhouse, 36–43. Wolfenbüttel: Bundesakademie für kulturelle Bildung, 2004.

———. "Sieben Geschichten der sieben Mütter." In *Talisman* 100–104.

———. "Das Tor des Übersetzers oder Celan liest Japanisch." In *Talisman*, 121–34.

———. "Von der Muttersprache zur Sprachmutter." In *Talisman*, 9–15.

———. "Writing in the Web of Words." In *Lives in Translation: Bilingual Writers on Identity and Creativity*, edited by Isabelle de Courtivron. Trans. Monika Totten, 147–57. New York: Palgrave Macmillan, 2003.

———. "Zu Else Lasker-Schülers 'Mein blaues Klavier.'" Tawada, *Sprachpolizei und Spielpolyglotte*, 45–47.

Thomas, George. *Linguistic Purism*. London: Longman, 1991.

Tiedemann, Rolf. "Editorische Nachbemerkung." In Adorno, *Noten zur Literatur*, 697–708.

Townson, Michael. *Mother-Tongue and Fatherland: Language and Politics in German*. Manchester, UK: Manchester University Press, 1992.

Trabant, Jürgen. "Herder and Language." In *A Companion to the Works of Johann Gottfried Herder*, edited by Hans Adler and Wulf Köpke, 117–39. Rochester, N.Y.: Camden House, 2009.

Trost, Pavel. "Franz Kafka und das Prager Deutsch." *Germanistica Pragensia* (1964): 29–37.

Tuschick, Jamal, and Feridun Zaimoğlu. "Ihr habt Angst vor unserem Sperma." In *Morgen Land: Neueste Deutsche Literatur*, edited by Jamal Tuschick, 9–20. Frankfurt am Main: Fischer Taschenbuch, 2000.

Vidler, Anthony. *The Architectural Uncanny: Essays in the Modern Unhomely*. Cambridge, Mass.: MIT Press, 1992.

Viehöver, Vera. "Materialität und Hermeneutik der Schrift in Emine S. Özdamars Romanen *Das Leben ist eine Karawaserei* und *Die Brücke vom Goldenen Horn*." In *Schriftgedächtnis—Schriftkulturen*, edited by Vera Viehöver, Vittoria Borsò, Gertrude Cepl-Kaufmann, Tanja Reichlein, 343–70. Stuttgart: Metzler, 2002.

Volk, Gregory. "Karin Sander in the *New York Times* and at D'Amelio Terras." *Art in America* 91.4 (2003): 139–40.

Wagner, Richard. "Das Judentum in der Musik." In Fischer, *Richard Wagners "Das Judentum in der Musik,"* 139–96.

———. "Judaism in Music." In *Richard Wagner's Prose Works* Trans. William Ashton Ellis, 1894, 77–122. New York: Broude Bros.

Wallraff, Günter. *Ganz unten*. Cologne: Kiepenheuer & Witsch, 1985.

Weber, Samuel. "Translating the Untranslatable." In Adorno, *Prisms*, 9–15.

Wei, Li, ed. *Bilingualism Reader*. London: Routledge, 2000.

———. "Dimensions of Bilingualism." In Wei, *Bilingualism Reader*, 3–22.

Weidner, Daniel. "Frevelhafter Doppelgänger und sprachbildende Kraft. Zur Wiederkehr der Anderssprachigkeit in Schleiermachers Hermeneutik." In Arndt, Naguschewski, and Stockhammer, eds., *Exophonie*, 229–47.

Weinreich, Max. *History of the Yiddish Language*. Trans. Shlomo Noble with Joshua A. Fishman. Chicago: University of Chicago Press, 1973.

Weinrich, Harald. "Chamisso, Chamisso Authors, and Globalization." Trans. Marshall Brown and Jane K. Brown. *PMLA* 119.5 (2004): 1336–46.

Wierschke, Annette. "Auf den Schnittstellen kultureller Grenzen tanzend: Aysel Özakin und Emine Sevgi Özdamar." In Fischer and McGowan, eds., *Denn du tanzt*, 179–94.

Wierth, Alke. "Zweisprachige Gymnasien: Französisch ja, Türkisch nein!" *die tageszeitung*, 29 March 2010.

Winnubst, Shannon. "Vampires, Anxieties, and Dreams: Race and Sex in the Contemporary United States." *Hypatia* 18.3 (2003): 1–20.

Wirth-Nesher, Hana. *Call It English: The Languages of Jewish American Literature*. Princeton, N.J.: Princeton University Press, 2006.

Wittbrodt, Andreas. *Mehrsprachige Jüdische Exilliteratur. Autoren des Deutschen Sprachraums: Problemaufriss und Auswahlbibliographie*. Aachen: Shaker, 2001.

Wolin, Richard. *Walter Benjamin: An Aesthetic of Redemption*. New York: Columbia University Press, 1982.

Yamamoto Masayo. "Japanese Attitudes towards Bilingualism. A Survey and Its Implications." In Noguchi and Fotos, eds., *Studies in Japanese Bilingualism*, 24–44.

Yildiz, Yasemin. "Critically 'Kanak': A Reimagination of German Culture." In Gardt and Hüppauf, eds., *Globalization*, 319–40.

———. "Turkish Girls, Allah's Daughters, and the Contemporary German Subject: Itinerary of a Figure." *German Life and Letters* 62.4 (2009): 465–81.

———. "Wordforce: Ethnicized Masculinity and Literary Style in *Kanak Sprak* and *Koppstoff*." In Cheesman and Yeşilada, eds., *Feridun Zaimoğlu* (forthcoming).

Zabus, Chantal. *The African Palimpsest: Indigenization of Language in the West African Europhone Novel*. Amsterdam: Rodopi, 2007.

Zaimoğlu, Feridun. *Abschaum: Die wahre Geschichte von Ertan Ongun*. Hamburg: Rotbuch, 1997.

———. "The Father Story." Trans. Darren Ilett. *Chicago Review*. 48: 2/3 (2002): 331–34.

———. "Gastarbeiterliteratur: Ali macht Männchen." In *Globalkolorit: Multikulturalismus und Populärkultur*, edited by Ruth Mayer and Mark Terkessidis, 85–97. St. Andrä/Wördern: Hannibal, 1998.

———. *Kanak Sprak: 24 Mißtöne vom Rande der Gesellschaft*. Hamburg: Rotbuch, 1995.

———. *Kopf und Kragen : Kanak-Kultur-Kompendium*. Frankfurt am Main: Fischer, 2001.

———. *Koppstoff : Kanaka Sprak vom Rande der Gesellschaft*. Hamburg: Rotbuch, 1998.

———. *Leinwand*. Hamburg: Rotbuch, 2003.

———. *Liebesmale, scharlachrot: Roman*. Hamburg: Rotbuch, 2000.

———. "Selections from *Koppstoff*." Trans. Kristin Dickinson, Robin Ellis, and Priscilla D. Layne. *TRANSIT* 4 (1). Available at: escholarship.org/uc/item/0cc704mx(2008). Accessed 15 June 2011.

———. *Twelve Grams of Happiness*. Trans. Margot Bettauer Dembo. Litrix.de. Available at: www.litrix.de/buecher/belletristik /jahr/2004/zwoelfgrammglueck/leseproben/enindex.htm. Accessed 15 June 2011.

———. *Zwölf Gramm Glück*. Cologne: Kiepenheuer & Witsch, 2004.

Zaptçıoğlu, Dilek. *Der Mond isst die Sterne auf*. Stuttgart: Thienemann, 1998.

Abel, Julia, 257n50
Ackermann, Irmgard, 251n1
Adelson, Leslie A., 20, 225n18, 241n17, 254n29; on betweenness, 250n37; on "German literature of Turkish migration," 221n53, 221n54, 246n4, 246n10, 248n22, 250n37; on Özdamar, 250n37, 250n40, 250n41; on Şenocak, 256–57n47; on "touching tales," 19, 167, 221n52; on Zaimoğlu, 192, 196–97, 252n10, 255n36
Adorno, Theodor W., "Auf die Frage: Was ist deutsch?," 91–93, 101; and Benjamin, 83, 104, 232n25; and conception of language, 70–71, 79–81, 83, 92–93, 232n23, 232n24; and dialect, 100–102; on George, 233n28; and Heidegger, 79–80, 91–92, 235n41, 235n42; on Kafka, 228n41; *Minima Moralia*, 27, 70, 84–86, 88, 94, 97, 100–102, 104, 234n29, 238n51, 238n55; and the monolingual paradigm, 92–94; and racialization of *Fremdwörter*, 85, 89, 97–98, 237n51; and sexualization of *Fremdwörter*, 98–99, 237n51; "Über den Gebrauch von Fremdwörtern," 70–71, 78–84, 94, 230n5, 237n51; "Wörter aus

der Fremde," 27, 69–71, 86–91, 94–99, 102–5, 237n51, 239n64. *See also Fremdwort*; linguistic family romance
Africa, 148, 214n3, 220n45; South Africa, 135–36, 138–39
African Americans, 190, 191; and English, 188, 189, 191; and hip-hop 187, 189
Afrikaans, 135–41, 224n39
Afro-Germans, 256n43, 258n2
Ahlzweig, Claus, 218n32, 247n11
Ahmad, Dohra, 180, 181, 185, 255n31
Amati-Mehler, Jacqueline, et al., 13, 219n38, 244n37
Améry, Jean, 236–37n50
Anderson, Benedict, 215n8, 217–18n28
Anderson, Mark, 224n15, 226n26
Anderson, Susan C., 243n29, 246n5
Andler, Charles, 229n44
Androutsopoulos, Jannis, 200, 257n54
Anzaldúa, Gloria, 16, 168, 180, 182
Appadurai, Arjun, 109, 216n13
Apter, Emily, 5, 180, 217n20
Arabic, 109, 149–51, 155
Arendt, Hannah, 16, 220n47
Arndt, Susan, et al., 216n12, 220n43
Aschheim, Steven E., 225n22
Austro-Hungarian empire, 30–32, 75–76, 105, 216n16, 222n1, 223n5,

Ayata, Imran, 190–91, 256n42
Aydemir, Murat and Alex Rotas, 19
Aytaç, Gürsel, 160

Baioni, Giuliano, 49
Bakhtin, M. M., 154, 222n63, 257n53
Balibar, Etienne, 170
Bassnett, Susan, 144, 217n24
Bay, Hansjörg, 242n22, 248n25
Beaujour, Elizabeth Klosty, 118–19, 120, 240n7, 241–42n19, 242n20
Beck, Evelyn Torton, 43, 224n12
Beckett, Samuel, 15, 104, 113, 120–21, 239n1
Bell, David A., 215n7
Benjamin, Walter, 167; and Adorno, 83, 104, 232n25; on translation, 249–50n36, 250n38
Berkowitz, Michael, 227n35
bilingualism, 245–46n4, 251n5; advantages of, 118; definitions of, 213n2, 239n1, 258n5; German attitudes towards, 208–9, 242n19; Japanese attitudes towards, 242n19; Jewish enlightenment (*Haskala*) attitudes towards, 51, 227n33; linguistic attitudes towards, 241–42n19; testimonials of, 215n11. See also bilingual writing; multilingualism
bilingual writing, 146, 221n53, 240n7, 247n12; and Adorno, 108, 235n43; and Celan, 18; definition of, 239n1; and displacement, 113–14, 240n8; in Wittgenstein, 14. See also Beckett; Nabokov; Tawada
Binder, Hartmut, 226n27, 227n29
Braese, Stephan, 18–19, 39–40, 167
Braidotti, Rosi, 11
Brandt, Bettina: on Özdamar, 146, 160, 248n24, 248n25, 249n35; on Tawada, 240n4, 245n39, 245n40
Braun, Peter, 106, 232n22
Braunmüller, Kurt and Gisella Ferraresi, 214n4

Breger, Claudia, 241n13, 242–43n26
Brenner, Michael, 221n51, 225n19
Brodzki, Bella, 249n36
Buck-Morss, Susan, 70, 232n25, 233n31
Burger, Hanna, 30–31
Butler, Judith, 175, 193, 196

Çağlar, Ayşe, 189–90
Caruth, Cathy, 161–64
Casanova, Pascale, 33, 61
Celan, Paul, 18, 167, 244n35
Ch'ien, Evelyn Nien-Ming, 15, 180
Chamisso, Adalbert von, 243n32
Chamisso Prize, 130
Cheah, Pheng, 217n27
Cheesman, Tom, 221n53, 222n55; on Özdamar, 246n6, 248n25; on postmigrant, 251n2; on Zaimoğlu, 198, 200, 252n7, 252n9, 255n37, 256n40
Cheng, Sinkwan, 70–71, 230n8, 231n16, 235n43
Chin, Rita, 246n4
Chow, Rey, 257n52
Çil, Nevim, 252–53n14
Claussen, Detlev, 233n30, 235–36n43
Clyne, Michael, 213n2, 214n3
code-mixing, 24, 198
code-switching: by Arendt, 16, 220n47; as everyday practice, 133, 173–74; in Özdamar, 168; in Zaimoğlu, 29, 176, 179, 198
Corngold, Stanley, 34, 224n13
Courtivron, Isabelle, de, 213–14n2, 215n11, 219–20n43
Cousins, Jane, 248n26, 249n29
Czech, 31–32, 61, 223n10, 224n11

Dal, Güney, 221n53, 254n29
Daniel, Jamie Owen, 101
Davidson, Mary Catherine, 6, 214n5, 216–17n19, 251n5
defamiliarization, 27, 48, 54, 119, 160, 234n36
Deleuze, Gilles and Félix Guattari, 33–34, 223n9

Derrida, Jacques, 16, 26, 40–42,
    171, 220n46
dialect: and Adorno, 100–102; and
    Jargon, 52; in Japan, 114; and
    Kafka, 33; and Özdamar, 152–
    54; in Switzerland, 247n18; and
    Zaimoğlu, 178, 200
diglossia, 247n17
Dirim, Inci and Peter Auer, 253n16,
    256n44
Dutch, 72, 137–38, 220n44, 244n39

English, 3, 15–16, 68, 70, 216n15,
    216n20, 235n43; and African
    Americans, 188–91; in
    Germany, 106, 208–9, 239n65,
    255n34; and globalization, 110,
    186–87, 199; as postcolonial
    language, 113, 187. *See also*
    Ahmad; Ch'ien
Erel, Umut, 257n52
Ernst, Thomas, 256n37
Eshel, Amir, 226n27, 226n28
Europe, 2–5, 6–10, 216n17, 242n25;
    and language migrations, 109,
    144, 211; multilingualism
    in, 112, 216n16, 217n19.
    See also monolingualism;
    multilingualism; Tawada;
    Wagner

Fachinger, Petra, 253n19, 257n53
family romance, 12–13, 219n37. *See
    also* linguistic family romance
Fichte, Johann Gottlieb, 230n1
Fischer, Jens Malte, 224n14,
    224–25n16
Fontane, Theodor, 75
Forster, Leonard, 15, 72, 214n3,
    219n42
Fremdwort (foreign-derived word),
    27, 148; American attitudes
    towards, 68; Austrian attitudes
    towards, 75–76; definition of,
    68; desire for, 96–99, 104–
    5; in German literature, 75,
    233n28; history of, 72–77, 106;
    and Jargon, 52, 66; National
    Socialist attitudes towards, 76–
    77, 231n17, 231n18, 231n19.

See also Adorno; linguistic
    purism
French, 3, 109, 151, 180, 230n4,
    242n19; and Adorno, 90, 106,
    233n28; and bilingual writing,
    72, 111, 112–13, 120, 216n15,
    242n23, 243n32; and Derrida,
    40–41; in Germany, 6, 72, 74,
    106, 230n1; in Kafka, 13, 35,
    55–59, 65–66, 204, 223n10;
    and Özdamar, 160
Freud, Sigmund, 12; on dreams,
    136, 138; and multilingualism,
    219n38, 244n37; on the
    uncanny, 53–54. *See also* family
    romance

Gal, Susan, 7, 216n9, 217n21
Gandesha, Samir, 235n41
Gardt, Andreas and Bernd Hüppauf,
    221n49, 255n34
Garloff, Katja, 88, 97, 234–35n37
Gastarbeiter. See guest worker
Gastarbeiterliteratur. See guest
    worker literature
German: current public discourse
    on, 205–10; as a Jewish
    language, 18–19, 39–49; in
    Mongolia, 210–11; as post-
    Holocaust language, 16, 17,
    27, 89, 94, 103–5, 166, 168; in
    Prague, 31–33, 43; in Turkey,
    211. *See also Fremdwort*;
    linguascape; linguistic purism;
    monolingual paradigm;
    multilingualism; postmigrant
Ghaussy, Sohelia, 164, 249n33
Gilman, Sander, 37–38, 227n37,
    229n50
Gogolin, Ingrid, 214–15n5, 219n40
Gossy, Mary, 218n34
Gotzmann, Andreas, 39, 225n19
Gramling, David, 215n10
Greek: 82, 91, 104, 223n10; words
    in German, 98, 99, 104, 234–
    35n37, 238n60
guest worker, 149, 245–46n4,
    253n19
guest worker literature, 185,
    221n54. *See also* Dal; Ören

Gürsel, Nedim, 160
Gutiérrez Rodríguez, Encarnación,
　　220n45, 257n52

Habermas, Jürgen, 258n3
Haines, Brigid, 248n23, 248–49n27
Haraway, Donna, 129
Härle, Gerhard, 230n10, 230–31n11
Harris, Roxy, 191
Hart, Matthew, 173, 180, 252n12,
　　253n18
Hassan, Waïl, 148
Hebrew, 38, 39, 50, 225n17, 225n19,
　　226n29, 227n33; and Kafka, 33,
　　49, 50, 55, 223n10, 226n28; in
　　Zaimoğlu, 191–93, 204
Herder, Johann Gottfried, 6–7,
　　217n22, 217n23
heteroglossia, 24, 154, 222n63
heterolingual address, 124–25, 140
Hirsch, Marianne, 4
Hoffman, Eva, 205
Hoffmann, Rainer, 232n23, 235n40,
　　238n54
Hofmannsthal, Hugo von, 69–70,
　　75, 223n5,
Hohendahl, Peter Uwe: 234n34,
　　237n48, 255n42; on Adorno
　　and Jews, 86, 233n32, 234n33;
　　on Adorno's language, 79–80,
　　232n25, 255n41
Hu, Adelheid, 215n6, 241–42n19
Hutton, Christopher, 231–32n20

Israel, Nico, 233n29, 233n33,
　　238n55
Italian, 112, 223n10

Jahn, Friedrich, 73–74, 84, 231n12
Jakobson, Roman, 117
Jameson, Fredric, 234n36
Japan, 114–15, 122–23, 139, 240n9,
　　242n19
Japanese, 114–15, 239n2
jargon, 66, 226n26, 227n30; in
　　Adorno's usage, 92, 94, 103,
　　235n42; as alternate name for
　　Yiddish, 50–51, 227–28n37,
　　228n38; as specialized language,
　　50. See also Kafka

Jay, Martin, 198, 233n30
Johnson, Barbara, 11, 127
Judson, Pieter, 216n16, 222n3,
　　223n4

Kachru, Braj, 255n33
Kafka, Franz: "Der Bau," 59; and
　　Czech, 61, 223–24n10, 224n11;
　　and French, 13, 35, 55–59, 65–
　　66, 204, 223n10; on "Jargon,"
　　52–57, 59–61, 65; letters to
　　Max Brod, 60–64; letters to
　　Milena Jesenská, 224n11,
　　229n52; and "monolingualism
　　of the Other," 26, 59; and
　　mother, 45–48; personal
　　multilingualism of, 223–
　　24n10; and Prague German,
　　33, 223n8; and uncanny, 35,
　　49, 53–57, 59, 65–66, 228n42;
　　and Yiddish, 33, 35, 43–50,
　　56–60, 225n22, 228n44; and
　　Yiddish theater, 43–46, 48–49,
　　225–26n23. See also linguistic
　　family romance
Kanak Attak, 253n17, 258n4
Kellman, Steven, 214n3, 216n14,
　　218n30, 219–20n43
Kelsky, Karen, 122–24, 141,
　　242n24, 242n25
Kermani, Navid, 167–68
Kittler, Friedrich, 11–12, 218n35,
　　218n36
Klemperer, Victor, 231n19
Konuk, Kader, 154, 221n53, 245n2,
　　246n9, 248n27, 250n40
Kramsch, Claire, 215n11, 219n39
Kraus, Karl, 69, 75, 231n15
Krauß, Andrea, 241n13
Kremnitz, Georg, 216–17n19,
　　240n5
Kristeva, Julia, 11, 193, 197
Kurdish, 19, 211, 245n4
Kuruyazıcı, Nilüfer, 146, 160

LaCapra, Dominick, 140, 249n36
Lacatus, Corina, 180, 220n44
Lamping, Dieter, 39
language: definitions of, 7, 213–
　　14n2, 217n20, 217n21, 222n63;

standardization, 12, 72, 114,
148, 151, 152, 154
languages. *See* Afrikaans; Arabic;
Czech; Dutch; English; French;
German; Greek; Hebrew;
Italian; Japanese; Jargon;
Kurdish; Latin; Russian;
Soninke; Swedish; Tajiki;
Turkish; Yiddish
Lasker-Schüler, Else, 134, 167
Latin, 10, 72, 82,91, 112, 147,
223n10, 235n39; and Latinate
German words, 68, 106,
232n23, 236n46; script, 149–51
Laudenberg, Beate, 241n15,
242–43n26
Lefevere, André, 10, 214n4
Leibniz, Gottfried Wilhelm, 72
Lennon, Brian, 217n24; on
Özdamar, 220n48, 245n3; on
trade publishing, 17, 215n11
Levin, Thomas, 70, 230n8, 231n16,
235n43
linguascape: German/Turkish,
144, 168, 209, 211; and
globalization, 109–10, 170–71,
180, 186; in Tawada, 112, 132;
in Zaimoğlu, 178–79, 191, 192,
199
linguistic family romance, 10–14,
203–4; in Adorno 71, 100–101;
in Kafka, 46, 63–64, 65–66; in
Özdamar, 152–54; in Tawada
128–30; in Zaimoğlu, 174,
181–82, 199
linguistic purism: against
postmigrants, 171; and Adorno,
78, 94; in contemporary
Germany, 239n65; history
of, 72–76; of Kafka, 61; of
Mendelssohn, 50, 227n33;
spread of, 68–69; in Turkey
151; and Zaimoğlu 178. *See also*
Thomas
Linke, Uli, 194, 258n1
Liska, Vivian, 45, 228n43
literal translation, 144, 147–49;
in Özdamar, 143–44, 146–
47, 159–60, 168, 249n33,
249–50n36, 250n38; versus

plurilingualism, 220n48, 245n3;
in postcolonial writing, 247n12;
in Tawada, 243n29, 246n5; and
trauma, 161, 163–64, 168; in
Turkish language policy, 151,
247n18; in Zaimoğlu, 183. *See
also* translation
Littler, Margaret, 248n23,
248–49n27

Mandel, Ruth, 209, 221n55,
245–46n4
Mani, Venkat, 221n53, 221n54,
221n55, 253n19, 254n26
Martin, Biddy, 219n37
Matsunaga, Miho, 242–43n26,
243n28
McGowan, Moray, 185
Mendelssohn, Moses, 32, 50,
227n33
Mennel, Barbara, 186, 256n42
Menrath, Stefanie, 190–91, 255n35,
256n39
Migration. *See* Europe;
multilingualism; postcolonial;
Turkish-German
Minnaard, Liesbeth, 220n44
monolingualism. *See*
monolingualization;
monolingual paradigm
monolingualization, 2–3, 10, 64–65,
72–73, 148, 149, 207; and
Adorno, 78, 93–94; of Japan,
114
monolingual paradigm, 4; definition
of, 2, 214–15n5; and Europe,
2–6, 10, 216n16; and German
thinkers, 6–10; and mother
tongue, 8–14, 68; and nation,
3, 31–32, 73–74, 114, 149–52,
170, 215n8; and schooling, 3,
30–31, 41, 114, 208–9, 219n40.
See also mother tongue;
postmonolingual condition
mother tongue: feminist takes on,
11, 218n31; and fetishism, 22;
history of, 10–12; as translation
from Latin, 10, 146–47. *See also*
monolingual paradigm
Müller, Regula, 154

multilingualism, 214n3, 217n16;
definitions of, 213–14n2;
disavowal of, 9, 22, 218n29;
in the European Union, 3,
217n21; and exile, 113–14,
240n8, 166–67; in film, 3, 200,
211, 215n10; and globalization,
2–4, 23–25, 106, 109–10,
114, 132–33, 169; Jewish,
17–19, 37–38, 50–52, 227n33;
medieval, 6, 214n5, 216–17n19,
251n5; and migration, 3, 19, 28,
109–10, 168, 170–71, 211; and
modernism, 15, 26, 239n62,
252n12, and subjectivity, 205.
See also Austro-Hungarian
empire; bilingualism; bilingual
writing; code-switching; Japan;
Turkey; *Wordsearch*

Nabokov, Vladimir, 27, 113, 119,
239n1, 240n7, 242n20
Natzmer Cooper, Gabriele von,
226n27
Nekula, Marek, 223–24n10
Neubert, Isolde, 154
Ngugi wa Thiong'o, 113, 247n12
Nicholsen, Shierry Weber, 230n5,
230n8, 232n34, 232n25,
236n44
Niekerk, Carl, 217n23
Noguchi, Mary Goebel and Sandra
Fotos, 114–15, 240n10

Okara, Gabriel, 28, 148, 247n12
Ören, Aras, 221n53
Özdamar, Emine Sevgi: *Die Brücke
vom Goldenen Horn*, 145,
153, 248n20, 249n28, 249n30;
Hayat bir kervansaray, 160;
*Kendi kendinin terzisi bir
kambur*, 146, 246n8; *Das
Leben ist eine Karawanserei*,
145, 147, 152–54; mothers in,
152–55, 157, 159–60, 248n20,
248n21, 249n30, 249n32;
Mutterzunge, 28, 143–44,
147, 149–50, 153, 154–68,
247n14; and postcolonial
parallels, 28, 149; *Seltsame*

Sterne starren zur Erde, 146,
156, 166–67, 251n40; status
in Germany, 246n6, 246n7;
and trauma, 161–68. *See also*
linguistic family romance; literal
translation; Turkey; Turkish;
Turkish-German

Pareigis, Christina, 226n27
Pavlenko, Aneta, 214–15n5, 219n39,
241n18
Pfaff, Carol, 252n11
Pinès, M[eyer Isser], 57–58,
227–28n37, 228n44, 229n47,
229n49
Plass, Ulrich, 233n28, 234n36
plurilingualism, 17, 214n2, 220n48,
245n3
Polenz, Peter von, 74, 75, 230n4,
231n18
polyglot, 113, 213–14n2
polylingualism, 33–34, 214n2
postcolonial, 16, 187, 216n16,
220n45; migrations, 109;
writing, 15, 28, 113, 148–49,
181,
postmigrant: definition of, 170–71,
251n2; and language, 171, 173–
74, 200–201
postmonolingual condition: as
analytic lens, 14, 16–21, 25–26,
42; definition of, 4–5
Preece, Julian, 224n13

Rajec, Elizabeth, 224n11
Raulff, Ulrich, 233n29
Richter, Gerhard, 239n64
Rindler Schjerve, Rosita and Eva
Vetter, 222n1
Robert, Marthe, 219n37
Rothberg, Michael, 235n38
Russian, 113, 240n7, 243n27

Saitô, Yumiko, 239–240n2
Sakai, Naoki, 124–25, 140, 242n25
Sander, Karin. See *Wordsearch*
Sanders, Mark, 138
Schiewe, Jürgen, 255n38
Schleiermacher, Friedrich, 7, 8–10,
12, 37, 112, 218n29

Schmidt, Gary, 254n26
Schulte, Rainer and John Biguenet,
    217n24
Şenocak, Zafer, 167, 221n53,
    256–57n47
Seyhan, Azade: 251n4; on
    literal translation, 146,
    245n2, 249n33, 249n34; on
    multilingualism in literature,
    20–21, 215n12; on Özdamar,
    154, 247n16, 246n10, 247n16,
    248n21, 251n43
Shklovsky, Victor, 234n36. See also
    defamiliarization
Sieg, Katrin, 253n19
Siegert, Bernhard, 56, 228n43
Slaymaker, Douglas, 240n4
Şölçün, Sargut, 146, 154
Sollors, Werner, 213–14n2,
    219–20n43
Sommer, Doris: and Bilingual
    Aesthetics, 12; on Derrida,
    220n46; distinction of elite and
    migrant bilingualism, 258n5; on
    Wittgenstein, 14
Soninke, 22
Spector, Scott: on Deleuze and
    Guattari, 223n9; on language
    situation in Prague, 32, 222n3,
    223n5; on Prague writers,
    223n6, 223n7
Spitzer, Leo, 69, 75, 233–34n27
Steiner, George: and "Hollow
    Miracle" 89, 103; as a
    multilingual, 121, 242n23; on
    translation 217n25, 217n26
Strutz, Johann and Peter Zima,
    216n15
Suchoff, David, 33
Suga, Keijirō, 256n21
Swedish, 113, 171, 180, 220n44,
    240n8
synthetic vernacular, 173, 176,
    179–80, 252n12, 253n18. See
    also Hart

Tachibana, Reiko, 241n10, 241n11
Tajiki, 21
Tawada, Yoko: "Absturz und
    Wiedergeburt," 123; Das

Bad, 123–24; and Beckett, 27,
    120–21; and Benjamin, 167;
    bilingual publication practice
    of, 27–28, 110–11, 239–
    240n2; "Bioskoop der Nacht,"
    135–41, 245n39; and Celan,
    167, 244n35; as expatriate,
    28, 120–21; and homonyms/
    homophones, 133–35, 137–38,
    141, 244n34; and Japanese
    women's internationalism,
    122–24, 141–42; and Lasker-
    Schüler 134; "Das Leipzig
    des Lichts und der Gelatine,"
    244n36; "Metamorphosen
    der Personennamen," 245n40;
    and monolingulism, 28,
    111, 115–21; and Nabokov,
    27, 119; Das nackte Auge,
    124, 245n40; "Schreiben im
    Netz der Sprachen," 132–
    35; "Sieben Geschichten der
    sieben Mütter," 129–130;
    Till, 116–19, 120, 121, 122,
    134; Überseezungen, 135–36;
    "Von der Muttersprache zur
    Sprachmutter," 125–32. See also
    linguistic family romance
Thomas, George, 68, 75, 230n3
Townson, Michael, 88, 231n19
translation, 8–9, 24, 56; of Adorno,
    70, 236n46, 238n58; in Kafka,
    56–59, 60–61; of Özdamar,
    249n36; studies of, 217n24; in
    Tawada, 117, 119, 124, 240n3,
    244n37, 247n14; and trauma,
    164; writing for, 124, 221n53;
    in Zaimoğlu, 177, 183. See also
    literal translation
translingual, 214n2, 216n14
transnational, 246–47n10; cultural
    forms, 15, 20, 23, 124, 173,
    179–80, 186, 189–90, 215n10;
    mobility, 122–23, 132, 141–42,
    198–99
Trost, Pavel, 223n8
Tschinag, Galsan, 210–11
Turkey, 150–52, 216n17, 221n52;
    politics in, 156–58, 211,
    248n21, 248n26

Turkish, 19, 109, 134, 150–52, 166–68, 221n53, 222n56; attitude towards in Germany, 29, 144–45, 184, 208–9, 258n6. *See also* Özdamar, Zaimoğlu

Turkish-German, 19, 145, 186, 254n25, 256n42; literature, 19–21, 185, 221n53, 221n54, 246n10, 255n28; migration, 144, 245–46n4; youth language, 199–201, 253n11, 253n16. *See also* guest worker

vernacular: versus Latin, 11, 147; in Özdamar, 153–54; in Zaimoğlu, 173, 174, 178, 179–80, 196. *See also* synthetic vernacular; vernacular literature

vernacular literature, 180, 185, 255n31

Viehöver, Vera, 246n7

Wagner, Richard: antisemitic take on language of, 36–39, 224n14, 224–25n16, 231n13; echoes of in Kafka, 62, 224n15; and monolingual paradigm, 9–10, 41

Wallraff, Günter, 253n19

Weber, Samuel, 236n46, 238n58

Wei, Li, 216n3, 241n18

Weinreich, Max, 227n32, 227n36

Weinrich, Harald, 130

Wierschke, Annette, 146

Wittbrodt, Andreas, 240n8

Word of foreign derivation. *See* *Fremdwort*

Wordsearch (artwork by Karin Sander), 2, 3, 207, 222n2, 256n45; description of, 1, 213n1, 22n60; discussion of, 21–25

Yiddish, 50–51, 226n25, 227n32. *See also* jargon; Kafka

Zabus, Chantal, 148–49, 254n24

Zaimoğlu, Feridun: and abjection, 172, 175, 193–99, 256n41, 257n51; *Abschaum*, 175, 251–52n6, 252n13, 254n26; and English, 15–16, 186–91, 199; and guest worker literature, 185; and hip-hop, 29, 187–91; Jewish references in, 191–93, 204, 257n49; *Kanak Sprak*, 15, 20, 29, 172–201; *Kopf und Kragen*, 255n37; *Koppstoff*, 251–252n6, 252n13, 255n31; *Leinwand*, 256n41; *Liebesmale, scharlachrot*, 257n49, 257n51; and masculinity, 172, 183–86, 191, 192, 196, 199, 252n8, 257n51; and *Popliteratur*, 256n37; and Turkish, 29, 173, 176, 182–86, 191,193, 199, 252n11, 253n13; *Zwölf Gramm Glück*, 251–52n6. *See also* linguistic family romance; postmigrant

Zaptçıoğlu, Dilek, 167